THE

VIEW

FROM

NOWHERE

Also by Jim Atkinson

Evidence of Love: A True Story
of Passion and Death in the Suburbs
(with John Bloom)

THE VIEW FROM NOWHERE

The only bar guide you'll ever want— or need

Jim Atkinson

PERENNIAL LIBRARY

Harper & Row, Publishers, New York
Cambridge, Philadelphia, San Francisco, Washington
London, Mexico City, São Paulo, Singapore, Sydney

With respect and affection for every barfly I ever hoisted one with—and those I haven't, for that matter—but with special affection and respect for the late Joe Miller (founder of Joe Miller's bar, Dallas), the best damned saloon keeper there ever was.

THE VIEW FROM NOWHERE. Copyright © 1987 by Jim Atkinson. All rights reserved. Printed in the United States of America. No part of this book may be used or reproduced in any manner whatsoever without written permission except in the case of brief quotations embodied in critical articles and reviews. For information address Harper & Row, Publishers, Inc., 10 East 53rd Street, New York, N.Y. 10022. Published simultaneously in Canada by Fitzhenry & Whiteside Ltd., Toronto.

FIRST EDITION

Designer: Sidney Feinberg

Copyeditor: Katherine G. Ness

Library of Congress Cataloging-in-Publication Data

Atkinson, Jim, 1949–
  The view from nowhere.

  Includes index.
1. Hotels, taverns, etc.—United States—
Guide-books. I. Title.
TX950.56.A85 1987   647'.9473   86-46041
ISBN 0-06-096058-2 (pbk.)

---

87 88 89 90 91 MPC 10 9 8 7 6 5 4 3 2 1

Contents

A Note on Technique, and Acknowledgments

Most of what follows is true, and there's even some true stuff that's not in here because I forgot it. Anyway, no half-assed journal is this: I drank and mused and interfaced and listened in every one of the joints referred to in here and some others too, which I also forgot.

Since the object here was not merely to go to bars that serve booze, but to explore and celebrate *real* bars, I couldn't possibly accept even a cent of royalties without thanking my trusted tipsters and guides who helped me in various venues in various ways. The free drinks I bought should have been enough, but I'm not going to take any chances on hurt feelings. So here they are: the best bunch of Ruppies (Recently Unemployed Persons—the only type of individual, I found, who could be *any* help with such a project) there ever was.

Special thanks to Gregory Curtis, editor of *Texas Monthly,* and Dominique Browning, now of *Newsweek,* for first encouraging me to write about this subject in the pages of *Texas Monthly.* And to my agent Vicki Eisenberg for encouraging me to write about it in book form. And to Harper & Row's Larry Ashmead and Margaret Wimberger for allowing me to do just that.

And to Ruppies Roger Albright, Bob Allen, Peter Applebome, Carole Ann Bassett, David Bauer, Jim Bauer, Jim Crumley, Carol

Davis, Karen Ellsworth, Curt Gentry, Clay Hall, John Hall, Chappy Hardy, Ralph Higginbotham, Allan Katz, Nicholas Lehmann, Renee Loth, Bob Mann, Eric Nadel, Nancy Nichols, Joe Nocera, Junius Rochester, Lloyd Sachs, Tim Schmidt, Tom Stephenson, Alex Thien, John Tideman, George Willborn, Mike Windsor, Al Wolf and Diane Zell. Also to Richard Erdoes, author of the stimulating *1000 Remarkable Facts About Booze*, which I found invaluable.

General thanks to all my drinking buddies who patiently listened to me Hold Forth about this, and particularly to my Dallas bartenders, Louis Canelakes and Steve Harris.

THE

VIEW

FROM

NOWHERE

AUTHOR'S NOTE: This is a book about bars, which means, among other things, that it's a book about civilized behavior, which, among other things, does not involve getting drunk and definitely does not involve getting behind the wheel of a car when you're drunk. Take it from me and the rest of my Bar Bar buddies: When in doubt, call a cab, hit up a friend for a lift, cool it and have a cup of coffee.

Bar Bar Theology 101: Introduction

Bartender to customer: *Gotta call. You here?*
Customer to bartender: *Depends. Can I get back to you?*
Bartender to customer: *Yeah, if I'm here.*

Uh huh, rough work if you can get it and all that, right? Your mama. If you're one of the approximately 11,987 people I ran into along the way who just couldn't believe I was doing what I said I was, then take that piña colada and stick it where the elves don't play. Mandatory liver scans—part of the contract here—aren't exactly my idea of a picnic, and besides, if you think this was so easy, you try asking that big old fellow at Hammer City in Milwaukee for a *receipt.* Guy looked at me like I'd just asked for proof of his liability insurance.

So if you're a Doubting Thomas, take a hike. You probably drink at Bennigan's or Houlihan's or O'Houli-whatever-the-hell-it-is anyway. While you're at it, enjoy your fried potato skins with guacamole and a fresh fruit garnish. And hey, if you want to crank up some Lionel Richie on the jukebox, remember it's on me. Maybe your date would like a delicious Keoki coffee. Just remember the immortal words of the late great Joe Miller, the best damned saloon owner in Dallas, or anywhere (so dubbed because he was *my* saloon owner) when confronted with a request for a similarly insidious libation. "What the fug do you think this is?" he croaked, looking a little like that guy at Hammer City. "A fuggin' Häagen Dazs?"

I'm getting ahead of myself, but that should serve as the, uh, topic sentence here, said topic sentence being another requirement in the contract. At least I only have to have one of those. The subject at hand is not mere drinking establishments, or taverns or pubs or lounges; and we are certainly not talking about anything that employs the word "bistro." We are not talking about places named Sean O'Shaughnessy's when no such person exists. Nor are we going to deal with places where people go and do things like dance. No ferns; no froufrou. No bartenders named Jason; no blackboard happy-hour specials.

No, we're not talking about places that are lit up like the *PM Magazine* set either. Food? It's begrudgingly recognized, but only if it's something on the order of the raw meat and rice I almost ate at the Swinging Door in Milwaukee. No fried zucchini, no taco salad, no shrimp in any form. Pasta only if it's made by a real Italian and doesn't have veggies on it.

We are talking here about real bars, bars and nothing else, institutions that exist as a sanctuary for those of us who just didn't want to be anyplace in particular at the moment. They are what I call Bar Bars, and if that doesn't immediately ring a bell, too bad. I'm not about to explain it all right away, not while you're at that instant of "purchase impact." If you want to know just what a Bar Bar is, you're going to have to buy the damn book and read it. I can, however, provide you with a little of your basic etiology.

Etiology, as they say, is where you find it, and in the case of the sort of bar we're talking about here, my personal benchmark involves my old friend Fred. Fred was one of my mentors when I was a cub reporter at the *Dallas Times Herald* back in '71 and he remains possibly the neatest Old Fart I've ever known, which is saying something.

Fred (of course it's not his real name) had particular management skills, among which was his habit of taking us whippersnappers out each and every payday and getting us smashed. We were paid weekly, so this became a well-oiled exercise that usually commenced about 2:30, after the front page had been replated for the last time and the only conceivable reason to hang around was to see if someone famous was going to get shot, or some such—in which case we really didn't want to be there anyway.

We had numerous haunts, some, I believe, involving bare-chested young women; but our favorite hangout was a forlorn little cinder-block affair just a stone's throw from the newsroom, which went by the moniker "The Green Glass Tavern." Fred loved the bar—a cozy, mildewy little beer joint that served free sandwiches and didn't have a waitress who didn't know just how to use the word "hon." But its appellation had always been a source of torment to the old fellow, largely because it is extremely difficult to say when you're drunk, which in Fred's case was a lot.

So it was that on a raw winter evening sometime in 1971, history was made. Fred had just put the finishing touches on an especially ferocious bit of Holding Forth (more on this later) involving some nameless hit man who had been after him ever since he'd written a series of controversial stories, topicless, of course, some time back. Among other things, the hit man in question was Fred's catchall rationalization for all manner of behavior, including the fact that he spent four out of seven nights, on average, sleeping in the backseat of his car.

No one can be dead certain who first coined the term Bar Bar, but Fred was definitely its keeper and historian. "See," he slurred one night, a breadcrumb flopping from his lip. "It's the Bar Bar beause . . . it's a . . . *bar* bar. That's what it is. That's all it is. Also, it's easier to say than that Green Grass shit."

A respectful silence fell over the table. Of course! *The Bar Bar.* It made immediate, crystalline, streamlined sense. Sure, the name of the place was the Green Glass Tavern, but the most prominent bit of neon on the exterior—the only thing you ever really saw or remembered—was the deco-ish treatment of the simple word BAR. The *Bar* Bar. And it had a certain resonance: It was one of those rare phrases that said exactly what it meant with no need for further amplification. It had the punch, the chutzpah, the inexplicable *grace* of a word like, well, onomatopoeia.

From thence, in my mind anyway (and since I'm writing this thing, that's going to have to do), an entire genre of drinking establishments was created. Well, less actually created than finally given its due, properly imprimatured at last. And while the next fifteen years spent exploring this peculiar species taught me that Bar Bars must be a lot of things, the crucial operative ethos has always been as simple and streamlined as the name itself: A Bar Bar is the only place left on earth where you can go and be Nowhere.

If you don't think this is serious culture, just go ahead and take the book back and grab a banana daiquiri. Consider the pressures of being *somewhere*, and then ponder the social importance of being able to be *nowhere*. Okay, now consider it again. Okay, *again*. See what I mean? I knew you would. Don't ever again sarcastically utter the phrase "He's nowhere." That's where you *want* to be.

Where exactly is Nowhere? Good question. As previously stated, it has to do with darkness, with absence of distractions like food and women and remotely serious talk. But its essence is a kind of transcendent egalitarianism. Inhabitants of Bar Bars don't care what you look like, and certainly don't care if you've screwed up just about everything you've laid your hands on that particular day. In the eyes of the Mother Church, you're okay just for *showing up*. Try and think of anyplace else where that's true: It sure ain't true of the office, and I don't know about you, but it ain't true of my house either.

Hence the one sure way you know you're in a Bar Bar is if you hear any one of the several variations of the following cant:

"Hey Joe, you gotta call. You here?"

Optional responses include: "No," "Maybe," "Yeah, I guess," and my personal favorite, "Is it male or female?"

This particular ritual knows no geographic or socioeconomic boundaries: I observed it at play in a bar in Santa Monica (caller was female and he *was* there), and I noted it at Koz's Mini-Bowl and Beer in South Milwaukee. I overheard it in Seattle. And at Kelley's in Kansas City (by the way, *anything* named Kelley's is a surefire Bar Bar), I heard the following variation on the theme:

"Jake, you here?"

"No, but I plan to be later."

That's thinking ahead, though when I checked in later, Jake still wasn't there.

At times, of course, this whole business of Being Nowhere can get, shall we say, a little out of hand. Consider what happened to poor Al, a regular at Gino and Carlo's in the North Beach area of San Francisco. The way I heard it—and in just the space of four hours or so, I heard it four different times, another sign that you're in a Bar Bar—it all started as just another Brand-X binge, progressed into the realm of bender, quickly turned into a Transcontinental Drunk (wherein the participant shows up at 5, takes a stool, straps on the old seat belt, and stays for the duration), and then just gradually worked its way into something else. From thence the versions tended to vary, but the bottom line was that Al had been at the bar bar for *five days,* making this a kind of drinking version of a Space Shuttle mission. No kidding. Just slept in the basement, arose rested and relaxed the next morning, and took his stool again. Al wasn't on the Transcontinental; he was in fucking orbit. When you get into *days,* that's some serious Going Nowhere, and the fact that Al was now only calling the wife once a day, instead of once an hour, suggested that maybe he was serious about staying there.

I conversed with Al only briefly—and at that, none too successfully. As you might imagine, coherence was not a big priority in his life anymore. But judging from the blissful gaze on Al's face, I knew he'd found a new one. Al had found Nowhere Nirvana, right there amidst the smoke and quiet banter of a little gin joint in North Beach. It made me reconsider the theology of the Bar Bar: It's not the only place you can be Nowhere. There's one other place: church.

Wonder what Fred would think today if he knew he hadn't just labeled a category of drinking establishments, but created a theology. I'd call and find out if I could, but I don't know where Fred is, and even if I did, he probably wouldn't be there. *Atkinson's First Rule of the Bar Bar:* If somebody knows where you are, you're not in a Bar Bar.

The Transcontinental Drunk, part 1:
The Apple

With my guiding principle firmly in hand, I had to face the sticky matter of methodology. I took two initial steps here: I bought a copy of Rand McNally's road atlas and I consorted with every sharer of the faith I could think of.

This turned out to be bad strategy in a couple of ways. The atlas, for its part, only served to intimidate me. Big country we live in, in case you've forgotten. Lotsa cities, lotsa bars. Lotsa Bar Bars. So I did the only thing any right-thinking journalist would do. I said fuck it, I'm gonna follow my nose and see where-all I can get before the advance money runs out and the yellow jaundice has crept up above my elbows.

As for my beloved fellow members of the congregation, I can only say this: Thanks a heap. Historically, Bar Bars have not been much associated with knowledge retention anyway, and about six calls deep, I was staring at a legal pad that contained the following information: The list included about 50 bars. That's the good news. Among those 50, 31 could be pinpointed as to region, 23 as to city, 8 as to street or area of town. Twenty-five actually had names. None carried the guarantee that it still existed, or ever was there in the first place. Investigative journalism is tough to begin with, but try investigating Nowhere sometime.

At a point there emerged a strange kind of networking. It

involved the following sorts of people. Journalists, of course; attorneys, insurance brokers, folks in the graphic arts. Artists and would-be artists. Bums. Rich guys. And primarily—in force, not numbers—Old Farts. Time and much perseverance began to produce something remotely resembling fact, though I certainly wouldn't capitalize the word. But it wasn't until I began to plan my first foray to the Big Apple that I discovered the true secret to Bar Bar networking: what I came to call Ruppies—the Recently Unemployed with, uh, no visible means of support.

The fellow in question here was my friend Dave Bauer, who until recently hadn't been a Ruppy but a perfectly respectable employed-type person. But he'd tired of his job, yearned to write that novel that had been lurking about in the posterior lobe all those years, and besides all that, he had a girlfriend with a good job. Bingo: I don't think I could have found a better research assistant if I'd run an ad in the classifieds.

"Look, I don't want to impose," I told him. "Just, you know, if you can check around and get me a few tips since, you know, you understand my concept here."

"No problem," Dave said cheerily. "Which days do you need me?"

You get the drift. And I have to say, Dave was worth every cent of the $567 worth of drinks I bought him. You might have started with the Chamber of Commerce or the local restaurant association or something like that. But for this kind of labor, give me a Ruppy any day. Heck, I've still got some Ruppies out there pounding the pavement and calling in new discoveries—and they're paying for their *own* drinks.

My next chore was to devise some form of rating system for these joints, in the unlikely event that someone who reads this might actually follow one of my recommendations. First off, by definition pretty much every bar in here is okay; we are merely talking about relative degrees of Nowhere. Hence Atkinson's Nowhere Coefficient, an abstruse and not entirely soberly devised model employing a varying number of factors. The general universe of factors includes:

1. *What You Feel Like When You Get There:* first impression, etc.
2. *Yuppity Doo Da:* the joint's name, and the relative absence of ferns, brass, Tiffany, etc.
3. *Oh Say Can You See?:* relative candlepower or lack thereof in the place.
4. *Crapola:* the quality of what you *can* see on walls, floor, ceiling.
5. *Holding Forth:* quality of bar talk, including bartender.
6. *What You Feel Like After Three Drinks:* just checking in, including quality of drink, distraction, etc.
7. *Just a Little Something to Wash My Drink Down With:* food.
8. *Old Fart Factor:* relative presence of single most important Bar Bar inhabitant.
9. *What You Feel Like When You Leave:* You *know.*
10. *You Go Figure:* presence of at least one endearing eccentricity or bit of arcana.

Each bar was rated in each category on a scale of 1 (worst) to 5 (sublime). Those were then totaled and the total was divided by 10, producing the Bar's Nowhere Coefficient. You believe that shit? Good. I got some more for you. I myself began to wonder how in the hell a decent drinking person would make a distinction between, say, a 3 and a 4 for Yuppity Doo Da. Good question. The general answer is that I was completely arbitrary, capricious, biased, irresponsible, and possibly wrong. There you have it: the New, New Journalism. Not only is it my impression, it might even be wrong. Bet you never heard Ted Koppel admit that. Besides, how are you going to check?

I do owe you, however, a bit of, uh, explication on those categories. Explication is kinda like etiology, so I'm glad to do it. (It's like a topic sentence: You only have to do it once.) Here we go:

1. *What You Feel Like When You Get There:* Oh, you know, is there anyone here who remotely looks like Ted Danson, for example?
2. *Yuppity Doo Da:* Is there more than one person here who

looks like Ted Danson? And besides, is there any *particular* reason why this place looks like the inside of an ersatz steam bath? Just asking.

3. *Oh Say Can You See?* Only Dick Clark looks better in natural light.

4. *Crapola:* Lemme use an example here. Place called Little Hipp's in San Antonio, where I partially grew up. Beer Bar. Floor: peanut shells and cigarette butts. Walls: on one, anyway, an aquarium containing a Brazilian turtle. On ceiling, numerous beach balls in bad fishnet. See what I mean? Thought you would.

5. *Holding Forth:* Did someone claim he actually understood the 401-K Retirement Plan, *and* did he explain it—more than once?

6. *What You Feel Like After Three Drinks:* Simple. Are you going to have another? Of course you are. There is no such thing as one drink.

7. *Just Something to Wash My Drink Down With:* Hard-boiled eggs, fine. Any other kind of eggs, not fine.

8. *Old Fart Factor:* Sure he was obnoxious, partly senile, and green-gummed. But did he listen to everything you had to say?

9. *What You Feel Like When You Leave:* If you don't encounter the out-of-doors with the sensation that you've just wandered into the face of a nuclear testing range, you've wasted your time.

10. *You Go Figure:* Oh, for example, Sloan's in Hollywood has an old restored car suspended from the ceiling, plays serious hard rock, and contains a crowd so eclectic that it can only be, say, a twentieth high-school reunion party—'cept it isn't.

In addition to the Ruppy research in each venue I took a flier or two—potluck on a joint that seemed to look right. You'll learn how this worked out as time goes on, but I will say there was just no way I could have known about Uncle Charlie's South on Third Avenue in New York. I mean, it was windowless (Early Bunker is the preferred Bar Bar architecture), had one of those nifty New

York canopies over the door, and wasn't advertising drink specials or any of that other crap. Who possibly could have known the big-screen TV would not feature the Mets game, but a video of a Lily Tomlin concert?

But I'm ahead of myself again. My foray to the Apple actually started at a joint called Pete's, somewhere around Gramercy Park. The reason I started there is because that's where Dave was when I got to New York. The other reason was that if you're going to go find Nowhere, I figure New York is the only place to start. Elsewise, you're just going to find yourself some kind of strange Somewhere, and then where are you?

Well, I'm here to tell you Pete's was not only an unavoidable but a perfectly logical and somewhat auspicious starting point. Old gin joint affair. Best touches: Absolutely taciturn and insulting bartender, and claim to be "oldest bar in New-York." You get a lot of that here, and come to think of it, you get a lot of it everywhere. It's not a prerequisite for a Bar Bar, but it certainly is better than, say, Friday's, whose only claim to uniqueness involves the number of potato skin options they have on the menu. But the true key to such a claim is that it must be in some manner a fib. Call that *Atkinson's Second Rule of the Bar Bar:* If the first thing you encounter is a lie, you know you're in a Bar Bar. In the case of Pete's, turns out the actual Bar Bar *bar* where Dave and I were bellied up was the oldest in the city. That lie, plus the frequently repeated fact that O. Henry used to drink there, gives Pete's a 5 for Holding Forth. Ditto for the bartender, who unceremoniously served up a freebie after we'd finished our third round (a universally recognized custom, I would learn). All in all, Pete's wears like a great old sweatshirt; the sort of place you'd wind up going if you couldn't think of anyplace else—a good Bar Bar sign.

PETE'S (129 E. 18th St.)

What You Feel Like When You Get There: 4

Yuppity Doo Da: 5 (Not a Yup in sight.)

Oh Say Can You See? 4

Crapola: 4 (Standard nonpostmodern tavern stuff; more than half of it appeared to be freebies from a beer company, which passes muster.)

Holding Forth: 5

What You Feel Like After Three Drinks: 5

Just a Little Something to Wash My Drink Down With: 3

Old Fart Factor: 3

What You Feel Like When You Leave: 4 (Walked all the way back to my hotel, which was someplace in the 50s.)

You Go Figure: 3 (As Bar Bar eccentricities go, it wasn't special, but I found the forlorn attempt at an outdoor patio area kind of cute. Any attempt by a Bar Bar to effect a trapping of one of those *other* types of places is a nice you-go-figure.)

Nowhere Coefficient: 3.6

The Mets were still in the hunt, so it only made sense to scope a couple sports bars that night. Next to the Oldest Bar in New York, sports bars would seem to be the Apple's most prolific and long-standing genre of Bar Bar. Sports is to the Bar Bar what sex is to those other places: a single, unifying passion, a reason to be there superseded only by the need to be Nowhere. Sports is the basis of most Bar Bar Holding Forth (followed closely by taxes, marriage, automobile troubles, weather, and gossip about other regulars), and, I found, it is often the *sole* reason for the existence of a Bar Bar. Call that *Atkinson's Third Rule of the Bar Bar:* If it's 3 P.M. and the TV is tuned to Australian football on ESPN, you're in a Bar Bar.

After some assiduous editing, Dave and I whittled our itinerary down to two exemplars of different types of sports bars. The first was Runyon's, named after you-know-who, which pretty much automatically gives it a 5 in the category of Holding Forth, sub-category Legend 'n' Lore. Place was a zoo, and most impressive was the shared sense of *mission* here. We were outsiders, to be sure, but the fact that we'd come to watch the Mets and the Cards—nothing more, nothing less—was sufficient evidence of acceptability. Among other things, Runyon's is a terrific example of how little it takes to create a great Bar Bar. It's just a little shotgun affair, with a bar along one side, tables and chairs on the other, and a small restaurant in the rear. Holding Forth was hard to gauge because of the presence of the game (a time-honored custom of Holding Forth is that if you want to bitch about the changes in, say, FICA withholding, better not start until the bottom of the ninth). But I did observe on a subsequent visit no less than sports columnist Pete Axthelm making a spirited gentleman's bet with the bartender. That won't get it a 5, but it will get it a 4. By the way, Pete is among my selections for Celebrities I Wouldn't Mind Being Stuck at a Bar With. More on this later, but three others are Ed McMahon, Rodney Dangerfield, and Bob Dylan.

RUNYON'S (305 E. 50th St.)

> **What You Feel Like When You Get There:** 4 (Like all great sports bars, it has the ambiance of a living room.)
>
> **Yuppity Doo Da:** 2 (Maybe it was just the game, but I spotted one too many Lacoste shirts in the crowd at the bar.)
>
> **Oh Say Can You See?** 5
>
> **Crapola:** 4
>
> **Holding Forth:** 4
>
> **What You Feel Like After Three Drinks:** 4 (Despite the game, the bartenders kept pace—without making a show of it.)
>
> **Just a Little Something to Wash My Drink Down With:** 3 (Unless otherwise noted, this rating indicates the joint has the obligatory attached restaurant serving burgers, steaks, a couple of Italian specials, and bar food such as pretzels, peanuts, or popcorn. All of this is acceptable Bar Bar food, neither exceptionally faggy nor exceptionally good.)

Old Fart Factor: 4 (A nice collection, and particularly impressive was the fact that they had the prime seats at the bar. That sort of pecking order is always a sure sign you're in a Bar Bar.)

What You Feel Like When You Leave: 5 (I've since been back to Runyon's every chance I get.)

You Go Figure: 4 (In case you didn't know, the presence of women, especially young women, in a Bar Bar is to be viewed with suspicion. But if the young women in question are clearly regulars in their own right, and are there to be Nowhere, like everybody else, then it qualifies as a nice quirk.)

Nowhere Coefficient: 4.0

For a taste of that other kind of sports bar, we headed way downtown, to a joint called The Sports Place. I must say I viewed this foray with a good deal of skepticism. Yes, the worship of sports is, in and of itself, *almost* enough to make any bar a Bar Bar, but this emergent breed of sports bar can give one pause. Essentially, joints like The Sports Place are another inevitable result of one of the more distressing recent trends in bardom: the invasion of the Macro-Thinkers. For goodness sakes, the fucking place was about the size of a gymnasium, a kind of ersatz amphitheater, with multiple big screens and a big bullpen-type bar in the center. It too was zoo-like, though in a much less charming way than Runyon's. Hey, guys, if I'd wanted to go to the stadium, I would have.

We stayed and watched Dwight Gooden shut down the Cards, and munched a passable cheeseburger; but even the abundant passion for sports couldn't get this joint a creditable Nowhere Coefficient. You're Somewhere here, and constantly assaulted with that fact, and even the presence of a perfectly quaint You Go Figure couldn't salvage it (bunch up in one of the peanut galleries was waving big signs with "K" on them after each of Gooden's strikeouts, a custom started at Shea Stadium). Call it *Atkinson's Fourth Rule of the Bar Bar:* Whatever a Bar Bar becomes, it's got to start out as a place where you go to drink.

THE SPORTS PLACE (I'm not even going to waste your time. Nowhere Coefficient: just barely over 1.)

Macro-Think, I was soon to discover, is not the only heresy being practiced out there in bardom. You've got all kinds of "theme" joints: Ersatz Irish, Ersatz Wild West. Ersatz Old Place, wherein Joe Bob, the entrepreneur, gets some federal funding and restores some building that no one really gave a shit about in the first place. Whatever the particular ersatz, the reasoning behind such joints is the same: Sometime between the interim and the permanent financing, Joe Bob discovers that his project has no *real* reason for being, so he gets together with his buddies and makes one up.

This can lead to some pretty weird stuff, Exhibit A being a place called the Bridge Cafe, in deep downtown New York; in fact, smack under the Brooklyn Bridge. Ostensibly this was an Old Place, part of what appeared to be a general "restoration" of the wharf area. Hence there was a lot of wharf crapola on the walls. But other quite dissonant themes were at work as well. For those inclined to munchies, there were tostados and hot sauce. For those a little hungrier, there was Hungarian goulash for 35 cents a pop. No, that's not an acceptable You Go Figure, and neither was the presence of daily specials involving crab on the blackboard.

I won't waste your time with a rating here either, though it should be pointed out that at least two tried-and-true bar barflies had obviously lost their way searching for Nowhere. They'd wound up here, and while I couldn't in good conscience call the Bridge Cafe an acceptable Bar Bar, it was the scene of a particularly stirring bit of Holding Forth. The two guys were having a spirited argument about whether one fellow's shirt was double knit or not. That's a world class topic to begin with, but what really elevated the exchange was this:

"Not double knit, huh?" said the larger of the two. "Here, I'll prove it to you." With that, he extracted a Zippo lighter and tried to torch the guy's *shirt*. That's a 5 for Holding Forth anyplace, anytime, but it ain't enough to get this place much over 1 on the Nowhere Meter.

By the way, if you happen to be in this area of New York, don't try Jeremy's either. It's also an example of Dual Ersatz, a sort of combo wharf bar–beer garden, I guess, and my guess is going to have to do because I'm pretty sure the owners no longer have any idea what they really intended. Just an observation, guys, but serving beer in Styrofoam cups isn't cute and it isn't funny. Drinks were meant to be served in glasses, you assholes. Give you credit for this, though: That small table by the window that looks out at the Brooklyn Bridge may be the best single place to sip at I've seen in a long time.

But that's not enough to even begin to get it a Nowhere Coefficient. Jeremy's was definitely Somewhere, starting with the fact that I suspect no such Jeremy actually exists—an unforgivable heresy of Bar Bar naming.

But the cosmos rewards the intrepid, and I'd suspected this little project wasn't gonna be any baby's game. Later that evening, my patience was royally rewarded. Joint was called the Raccoon Lounge, and its Bar Bar ethos was so strong that it convinced me to do something I thought I'd never do: revise one of Atkinson's Rules of the Bar Bar.

From time immemorial, *Atkinson's Fifth Rule of the Bar Bar* proclaimed: Music has about as much business in a real bar as, say, a menu with fried zucchini on it. This is particularly true of that species known as live music, and I know this firsthand because part of my misspent youth was misspent playing and singing for free beer at a little joint called The Chequered Flag, right off the University of Texas campus in Austin. Gad. Sure I was searching for an identity and all that, but did I really have to put those poor souls through a nightly set that consisted of B. J. Thomas's "I'm Hooked on a Feelin'," Richie Havens' "Just Like a Woman," and the Stones' "Satisfaction"? Now that I've got the forum, I'd like to thank each and every one of you who suffered through it. If I'd been you, I'd have shot me someplace like the kneecap, which I understand is not only incapacitating but extremely painful.

Anyway, a little background noise is perfectly okay. A joint called Marfreless in Houston plays very low-key, low-volume classical stuff, for example, and the aforementioned Joe Miller used to spin some old '40s big band type things. Fine. But if music becomes a *priority*, a *raison d'être*, so to speak, then gad, we're back to my particular version of "If I Had a Hammer." You don't want to hear any more.

So when I heard the jukebox blaring and actually saw folks doing some . . . dancing . . . I was plenty skeptical of the Raccoon Lounge. But with the help of (Special Atkinson Transcontinental Drunk Award for Tallest Bartender in America), I got plenty into the Raccoon's jukebox. This produced *Atkinson's Sixth Rule of the Bar Bar:* If something makes it feel like the living area of your best friend's apartment in college, it's probably a Bar Bar.

In this case, it was this remarkably, savagely eclectic jukebox. Example: Springsteen, "Jungleland"; Turtles, "Happy Together"; Stones, "Satisfaction" (not *my* version); Smokey Robinson, "Groovin' Together." See? It went on and on, to the point where I was sifting through the jukebox listings the way I would a friend's record collection.

Extra Special Atkinson Transcontinental Award to the Tallest Bartender in America Who I Bought Shots of Stoly For.

THE RACCOON LOUNGE (59 Warren St.)

What You Feel Like When You Get There: 4 (Real glad to find it.)

Yuppity Doo Da: 3 (I thought I espied someone wearing madras.)

Oh Say Can You See? 3

Crapola: 3

Holding Forth: 5 (No, I don't particularly remember. Knucklehead.)

What You Feel Like After Three Drinks: 5 (Includes the Stoly. Uh, he bought one back.)

Just a Little Something to Wash My Drink Down With: 3

Old Fart Factor: 3 (There was *one,* and he was tapping his foot to Springsteen.)

What You Feel Like When You Leave: 5 (I felt sorry. I wanted to jump right into some more Jerry Vail.)

You Go Figure: 4 (The strawberry alarm clock on the jukebox.)

Nowhere Coefficient: 3.8

Maybe the Raccoon Lounge signaled good Bar Bar karma to come—or maybe it was the fact that I flipped to page two of my recommendations, which did not involve any input from Dave but from a couple other Ruppies—but the next day and evening, I hit the Bar Bar jackpot. I had a handful or more of frequently recommended midtown joints, some east, some west, some well known, some not; so I decided to do a little scattershooting. Scattershooting, as the name implies, is a little different from barhopping, which is generally a somewhat organized trek through several bars. When you scattershoot, you just pick one and go, and then pick another one and go. Kinda fun, especially in New York, where you can basically do it on foot.

A reasonable starting point seemed to be P. J. Clarke's at 50th and Third Avenue. I had every reason to suspect that P.J.'s would be a member of the growing clan known as the Bar Bar That Got Too Famous for Its Own Good, sometimes known as the Six Flags Over Bar Bar. The culprit here—and hey, it's not his fault, because he's a Writer Who Got Too Famous—is Dan Jenkins, to whom I owe three debts of gratitude: one, he did the same damn thing with P.J.'s as I did with Joe Miller's in Dallas and made a lot more money; two, he's known Jap Cartwright for a number of years and still admits him a friend; three, he concocted the quintessential drunkenness scale in *Semi-Tough,* his first and best novel, which without going into great detail involved a medium range (5) dubbed "fuck dinner" and a cosmic range (10) labeled "bulletproof." I forget what I was.

I was right, P.J.'s *is* too famous for its own good, but if you catch it when I did—3 P.M.—it is still an exemplary New York Bar Bar. This would be *Atkinson's Seventh Rule of the Bar Bar:* If the bar is full at 3 P.M., you're in a Bar Bar. There was a tad too much precious P.J.'s folklore and crapola on the walls, but the following things made this a solid Bar Bar: I saw a lady buy a guy a drink. I saw what appeared to be a bettor paying off his bookie. I overheard—okay, participated in—a spirited argument about who was bigger, Herschel Walker or Eric Dickerson. The key was that no one really knew, and the whole debate ended unresolved. (*Atkinson's Eighth Rule of the Bar Bar:* People may win arguments in courtrooms, but they *never* win them in Bar Bars.) And finally, this stunning bit of Holding Forth from one of the several regulars who apparently had watched the Mets here the evening before and simply stayed on through. "I feel much better than when I came in," he announced to no one in particular. "Now I feel like shit."

So much for the good news. The bad is that when the sun goes down, this place fairly heaves with about a −5 on the Yuppity Doo Da Richter Scale. It wasn't a pretty sight, Dan: The bar area was lit up like a Sandinista interrogation room and I saw two young ladies who appeared to be trying to get laid. I will say this, though: The Too Famous for Its Own Good P.J.'s cheeseburger and house fries easily slipped into Atkinson's Top 10 Just a Little Something to Wash My Drink Down With's. As for that other New York Bar That Got Too Famous for Its Own Good—the notorious Elaine's, I've got this to say: Its transcended to a Bar Bar That's Too Famous to Go To. 'Nough said.

P.J. CLARKE'S (915 Third Ave.)

> **What You Feel Like When You Get There:** 3 (Either very much at home, or like you're on the David Letterman Show, depending on the hour.)
>
> **Yuppity Doo Da:** 2 (See above.)
>
> **Oh Say Can You See?** 1
>
> **Crapola:** 2 (I'm not sure, but I think you can get a P.J.'s T-shirt.)

Holding Forth: 5

What You Feel Like After Three Drinks: 3

Just a Little Something to Wash My Drink Down With: 5

Old Fart Factor: 2

What You Feel Like When You Leave: 3 (Also depends on when.)

You Go Figure: 2 (Solid, but predictable.)

Nowhere Coefficient: 2.8

Heading westward, I dropped by a daytime businessmen's hangout called The Landmark. This turned out to be a case where the bar itself was a You Go Figure. It's essentially an Ersatz Old attempt and definitely has too many ferns and too much polished brass. I also spotted the ubiquitous blackboard with daily specials. But the neighborhood is what makes this a Bar Bar.

It sits at the corner of 46th and Eleventh Avenue, which is sort of around an area they call Hell's Kitchen, I believe. If they don't, they should. I tend to like the ghetto custom of painting murals on building facades and playground fences, but these had an undercurrent a tad too malevolent for my taste. Also, I'm pretty sure I counted seventeen young guys dressed in stuff that had zippers all over it. But the effect was to make The Landmark a complete anomaly—which almost automatically makes it a Bar Bar. It was a cozy and comforting oasis and my white-collar barmates definitely understood Holding Forth.

"You know," said one, "I got to figuring, and me and the wife would definitely be better off making *less* money. [The Breakthrough Financial Theory is a time-honored category of Holding Forth; the allusion to "the wife" puts it over the top.] No: *look* at it. You figure with taxes and funding IRAs and that whole-life policy and just *savings,* we don't need but about half what we're pulling in. Fuck it, I'm into income reduction."

Oh yeah, one other nice touch was the Oriental help. It's a little disconcerting at first—Bar Bartenders are supposed to be taciturn old Greeks or Irishmen—but after a couple pops, it became a nice additional You Go Figure.

THE LANDMARK (46th St. at Eleventh Ave.)

> **What You Feel Like When You Get There:** 5 (Phew—I never really had been able to figure out why a lot of visitors consider New York, well, *scary*. But then, I never had been to this neighborhood before either.)
>
> **Yuppity Doo Da:** 3 (On appearances only, this rating could have been worse; but a Yup who holds forth about his own culture is what I call a Tuppy, a Tolerable Young Urban Professional.)
>
> **Oh Say Can You See?** 4
>
> **Crapola:** 1 (Sorry, this joint bumped into the red on the Fern Meter.)
>
> **Holding Forth:** 4
>
> **What You Feel Like After Three Drinks:** 3
>
> **Just a Little Something to Wash My Drink Down With:** 1
>
> **Old Fart Factor:** 2
>
> **What You Feel Like When You Leave:** 5 (Braced with a couple pops, I sauntered back through that neighborhood like Chuck Bronson.)
>
> **You Go Figure:** 5
>
> **Nowhere Coefficient:** 3.2

Time for Potluck. Joint right down from my hotel at 55th and Seventh, called Mulligan's, had immediately intrigued me, and one reason it intrigued me was that I'd walked by it at about 10 that morning and the joint was respectably full. Possible contender here for Darkest Bar in America, and the crowd of regulars was as ferociously eclectic as I've seen: two blacks, three young blue-collar types, two middle-aged gays, one Old Fart, who, as is the wont of this type, served as the unofficial bar historian and liaison with the bartender for outsiders like me. "Yeah, there's been a lot of pussy had and a lot of money made in here," he announced, exhibiting the joint's quality of Holding Forth.

One other nice touch was that there was almost a fight between two of the young blue-collar types: something about the unwarranted confiscation of space at the bar while someone was in the restroom—a catalyst of at least as many Bar Bar imbroglios as, say, women. Key here is that there was *almost* a fight. Places where there actually *are* fights aren't really Bar Bars, and of course, places where the most likely conflict is a spirited debate about the merits of the house piña colada *definitely* aren't Bar Bars.

Atkinson's Ninth Rule of the Bar Bar: If a fight almost breaks out, but never really does, you're in a Bar Bar.

As usual in this subculture, the potential conflagration was self-policed, meaning the bartender was marginally involved in the refereeing, the real dirty work being handled by the regulars, including the Old Fart. This self-policing, which at times can consist of as little as a few glowers at the offending party, is also a universal canon of the Church of the Bar Bar. There is, in fact, something quite magical and unspoken about it. As George Kennedy's character in *Cool Hand Luke* was heard to say, "You gotta follow the rules," and every self-respecting member of a Bar Bar congregation just *knows* the rules. I saw it at its zenith at a joint called Mike's 17 Bar in Providence, Rhode Island. Big old Italian regular, with this gnarled face that looked a little like a cauliflower that had been spray-painted red, got into it with the bartender, at first half in jest, then progressively a bit more seriously. Finally he invoked the time-honored "Wanna step outside?"

Fun Facts

In 1934, 4,704,000 tax gallons of gin were distilled in the US; no vodka was distilled. In 1984, 12,781,000 gallons of gin were distilled, and 13,070,000 gallons of vodka. Go Figure.

---

and the bartender said, "No, but do you wanna drink here tomorrow?" Guy sat down and shut up.

MULLIGAN'S (857 Seventh Ave.)

>   **What You Feel Like When You Get There:** 5 (Top 10.)
>
>   **Yuppity Doo Da:** 5
>
>   **Oh Say Can You See?** 5 (Possible Darkest Bar in America.)
>
>   **Crapola:** 4
>
>   **Holding Forth:** 4
>
>   **What You Feel Like After Three Drinks:** 4
>
>   **Just a Little Something to Wash My Drink Down With:** 4 (Little
>   deli-type deal on wall opposite bar, the perfect positioning for
>   food counters. Food included things like stew, which is perfectly
>   acceptable.)
>
>   **Old Fart Factor:** 5
>
>   **What You Feel Like When You Leave:** 5
>
>   **You Go Figure:** 3
>
>   **Nowhere Coefficient** 4.8

I was really on a roll now, and little did I know I was soon to fall
into Bar Bar Nirvana. On the east side, from the mid-30s on up to
50th, along Second and Third avenues, there is the damnedest run
of Bar Bars I've ever seen. There are surely other clusters of this
sort in New York that I just didn't stumble upon, but this little area
will serve as a good exemplar of that seldom seen phenomenon:
the Bar Bar Enclave, wherein, it seems, one great joint just breeds
another.

You really can't miss along here, but let me offer some high-
lights. Place called Billy Munk's at 302 East 45th St., which qualifies automatically on the basis of its inscrutable name and that
seldom seen but always revered You Go Figure: no apparent

door. You tend to see more of this in places like New Orleans and Miami, where most of the Bar Bars started as liquor stores with the bar at the rear, but Billy Munk's won my heart right off because it observed *Atkinson's Tenth Rule of the Bar Bar:* If the place is hard to find and even harder to get into, you're in a Bar Bar.

Immediately fell into some delicious Holding Forth with the Old Fart next to me, who began by bemoaning the fact that he had to work on Martin Luther King's birthday. "I basically didn't like the spook anyway," he intoned. "And I still have to work on his holiday. Pisses me off, I'll tell ya, 'cause most of *his* folks pretty much have a holiday every day, know what I mean?" (Note: The Racist Tirade, as you might expect, has ebbed drastically over the past several years as an acceptable form of Holding Forth. Still, the Minor Racist Tirade, such as this one, is politely ignored.) We meandered on to the Super Bowl, to Democratic politics in general, and finally to my none-too-well-disguised Texas accent. "Guess that'll conclude the linguistics lesson for the day," he said upon leaving. That's really world class stuff when you make fun of your own Holding Forth.

THE BILLY MUNK (302 E. 45th St.)

What You Feel Like When You Get There: 4

Yuppity Doo Da: 3

Oh Say Can You See? 5

Crapola: 5 (I counted *four* different football pools behind the bar.)

Holding Forth: 5

What You Feel Like After Three Drinks: 5 (Bartender popped me with a round on the house.)

Just a Little Something to Wash My Drink Down With: 3

Old Fart Factor: 5

What You Feel Like When You Leave: 5

You Go Figure: 5 (Name, door.)

Nowhere Coefficient: 4.5

There are others in the enclave that will do you no harm at all—notably The Pen and Pencil, The John Barleycorn, and The Brew—but the bar of choice here has to be Costello's at 44th and Second. I paid this place the homage of three visits, and it is definitely among my favorite joints *anywhere*. It's a dark little closet, with a marvelous beefy bartender who was quick to explain the presence at the alley door of that other rarely seen but definitely appreciated Bar Bar artifact: the Bar Cat. Some joints have Bar Dogs and others have Bar Kids. And as previously mentioned, at least one joint, in San Antonio, has a Bar Fish.

But I'm a cat kind of guy and one reason is that it is the only animal extant that my wife will tolerate. Another reason is that cats will mess with your head and I'm all for that. Bar Cats are useful as well. Name a kid who can catch rodents, eat scraps, and also will play with, say, a peanut shell. Dogs? Forget 'em. Great thing about this Bar Cat was that she would just stand at the alleyway door, kind of like I did once, trying to get into Studio 54, waiting for absolute approval. At that she would only wander forth when food or encouragement was offered; accepting either gratefully, she would then simply return to her outpost. All Bar Bar regulars should be so respectful of the Church.

Holding Forth was world class here too. Example: "It's just total fucking goddamn fucking disregard to what the company is all about," opined one young yuppy to someone who appeared to be a ruppy. The convulsive combining of profanities is an always respected form of HF, as is Unwarranted Acceptance of Corporate Responsibility, which generally involves some poor shmuck who's just earning a wage defending a company that's probably screwing him to the wall.

But the key here was the ruppy's response: "Sounds about right."

Elsewhere there was a GPA (Great Pointless Argument) tran-
spiring that, I swear, went from the WPA to the IRA in the span
of 8 minutes and 37 seconds. "Nah, it was more like 8:40," said the
fellow next to me, who had also timed it.

"We'll continue this on a somewhat more serious note tomorrow
at lunch," said one of the participants, who was a shambling fellow
in slacks and a red alpaca sweater and qualified as a Middle Fart.
Middle Farts, as you probably figured out, are somewhat younger
than Old Farts and somewhat older than Young Farts, though it
is only a matter of chronological fact. *Atkinson's Eleventh Rule of
the Bar Bar:* All Farts, young, middle, or old, think the same.

On a return visit to Costello's, I fell into an abyss known as
Hangover Holding Forth, a particular form of bar communication
that should need no further amplification. A few particulars are
worth noting, however: First, it is a shared malady (*Atkinson's
Twelfth Rule of the Bar Bar:* Only people with hangovers can,
should, or will talk to one another.) Second, the topic had best be
some sort of self-examination. Ed, who listed himself as thirty and
a lawyer from Queens, had just quit smoking. (That's a 5 for Holding Forth, just on topic.) He also wanted to talk about it . . . a lot.
First, though, he bummed a smoke.

"The key," he said, inhaling that baby all the way down to his
nuts, "is what they call frustration tolerance. The insidious thing
about these things is that as a drug, they suit *any* purpose. You
smoke to calm down when you're nervous; you smoke to pep up
when you're lethargic. You smoke when you're depressed and you
smoke when you're happy. You smoke after you eat, after you
screw, and when you're taking a crap. We're talking pretty primordial stuff here."

Indeed, Ed, and the same should be said of your Holding Forth.
Special Atkinson Transcontinental Award to Ed at Costello's for
Best Hangover Holding Forth I've Ever Heard. (By the way, Ed,
you eased in over that wonderful Old Fart at Kelley's in Kansas
City, who, by the way, I caught at 7 *a.m.* But there was just no way,
you see, to verify that he was actually hung over, since I had some
question as to whether he'd slept at all.)

COSTELLO'S (225 East 45th St.)

> No need to elaborate here either, but for better reasons. Costello's is all 5s—yes, that would be a perfect 5 Nowhere Coefficient. (How many of these did I actually find? Read the damn book.)

It was time to head for the hinterlands, and a good way to do that is to go to Hoboken. You know, place where Sinatra grew up. Tough old wharf town, Mafia and all that. Well, it turns out Hoboken has turned into a bit of a Yuppity Doo Da hangout, which means an awful lot of bars have two-for-one happy hours and stuff like that. Two joints of note, though.

One is called Red Heads and it is notable because it's a former strip joint cum Bar Bar. You go figure. Great crap on walls, floor, and *ceiling,* most of which had to do with the stripper in question, one Joan Torino. Old lady bartender and a suitably non-upwardly-mobile group of regulars.

RED HEADS (72 Hudson St., Hoboken, N.J.)

What You Feel Like When You Get There: 4

Yuppity Doo Da: 5

Oh Say Can You See? 3

Crapola: 5

Holding Forth: 3

What You Feel Like After Three Drinks: 3

Just a Little Something to Wash My Drink Down With: 5 (None.)

Old Fart Factor: 3

What You Feel Like When You Leave: 3

You Go Figure: 5

Nowhere Coefficient: 3.9

Shannon's Old Irish Pub was notable for the presence of the damndest Bar Bar *bar* I've ever seen. Essentially it was a big horseshoe-shaped deal, but it was so wide it had the effect of a huge conference table, like the one in *Dr. Strangelove*. These were serious hardcores. Sample Holding Forth: "Yeah, I went home last night with Coke on my breath and the wife said, "Been at the bar, eh?" I was also lucky enough to catch a glimpse of the Bar Fool—every Bar Bar has one—who was, of course, taking a bunch of shit from the rest of the regulars, which is his sole function in the ecosystem.

SHANNON'S OLD IRISH PUB (First and Bloomfield Sts., Hoboken, N.J.)

 What You Feel Like When You Get There: 4

 Yuppity Doo Da: 4

 Oh Say Can You See? 4

 Crapola: 3

 Holding Forth: 5

 What You Feel Like After Three Drinks: N/A (Hey, it was late and no way I'm going to try to find the PATH train drunk.)

 Just a Little Something to Wash My Drink Down With: 5

 Old Fart Factor: 5

 What You Feel Like When You Leave: 4

 You Go Figure: 5

 Nowhere Coefficient: 3.9

The hinterlands also involved some of your Queens, and the visitor need look no further here than the Part Two Burger Bar, which sits across Queens Boulevard from Queens Borough Hall and is an exemplary Power Bar Bar where all sorts of pols and lawyers and other kinds of crooks hang out. Architecture is Early

Bunker, windowless, in the best Bar Bar tradition.

Holding Forth this day had to do with the latest New York political scandal, involving Queens Borough President Donald Manes who got so overwrought about revelation of his involvement in a scandal he tried to kill himself. Eventually succeeded too. It was all pretty complicated but the lesson here is *Atkinson's Thirteenth Rule of the Bar Bar:* If people are talking about someone else's problems and that someone else is rich or famous, and if everyone seems to be having a great time doing it, you're in a Bar Bar.

But what really made the Part Two transcendent was the presence of that rarely seen Just a Little Something to Wash My Drink Down With: the free lunch. Make that *Atkinson's Fourteenth Rule of the Bar Bar:* There *is* such a thing as a free lunch, but you have to go to a Bar Bar to get it. No kidding: just a big table with plates of bad cold cuts and sandwich bread, some mayo and mustard and a few wilted pickles . . . If you weren't that hungry, you could get pistachios out of one of those old peanut machines, and if you weren't hungry at all, which we weren't, you could just dine off the Bloody Marys.

PART TWO BURGER BAR 125-10 Queens Blvd., Kew Gardens, Queens)

> **What You Feel Like When You Get There:** 5 (That Bunker architecture really lets you hit the wall when you walk in.)
>
> **Yuppity Doo Da:** 5
>
> **Oh Say Can You See?** 5 (Are you kidding? There weren't *any* windows.)
>
> **Crapola:** 5
>
> **Holding Forth:** 3
>
> **What You Feel Like After Three Drinks:** 5 (This bartender even asked if we wanted extra horseradish in those Bloody Marys.)
>
> **Just a Little Something to Wash My Drink Down With:** 5

Old Fart Factor: 3

What You Feel Like When You Leave: 5

You Go Figure: 5

Nowhere Coefficient: 4.5

Off to Brooklyn, which is its own kind of nowhere. Had been told that a joint called Farrell's at 16th and 9th, just off Prospect Park, was the best exemplar of the Brooklyn neighborhood pub, and I knew my sources were on the money when my *cabbie* got lost trying to find it. This place was a nowhere in the middle of nowhere.

It was 1 P.M. and of course the joint was a sea of red noses. I stood next to a guy who was roughly 102 and had just bought a fan. "It's not the heat, it's the humidity . . ." Bingo: Major League Holding Forth before I'd even finished my first. Also had a nice chat with the one fellow in the place under 87, who drove a delivery truck for a bakery and didn't seem to enjoy it much. "Thing is," he said, "I could make more if I just kinda free-lance drove, but I need the insurance 'cause I'm getting married." *Atkinson's Fifteenth Rule of the Bar Bar:* If someone is talking about how they could make more money, you're in a Bar Bar.

FARRELL'S (16th at 9th, Brooklyn)

What You Feel Like When You Get There: 5

Yuppity Doo Da: 5

Oh Say Can You See? 2 (Major drawback was the joint had too many damned windows. I like to see those red noses *glow.*)

Crapola: 5 (The red noses count.)

Holding Forth: 5

What You Feel Like After Three Drinks: 5 (Bartender popped me one on the house.)

Just a Little Something to Wash My Drink Down With: 3

Old Fart Factor: 5 (!)

What You Feel Like When You Leave: 5

You Go Figure: 5 (Just as I was about to leave, another guy about 102 walked in carrying a fan.)

Nowhere Coefficient: 4.5

Where is the hinterlands? How 'bout the Village? Yikes. The only difference between the Village and Hell's Kitchen is that Hell's Kitchen's malevolence is painted. These people are some serious screwed up, and if you want to *see*, try The Lion's Head, which used to be a semi-famous beatnik-type hangout. It's just a Bar Bar now, and quite a serviceable one at that, but the key is that it's downstairs. Remember Atkinson's Rule that had to do with the difficulty of getting to nowhere? Well, here are some more particulars.

One is that a great Bar Bar is ideally something you have to walk up or down to. Stairs are a nice intervention anyway, particularly since the task at hand is getting drunk. But the basic idea is to physically get Nowhere, and that is greatly aided by a walk up or down. Another nice thing—and you can really get into it at The Lion's Head—is that when you're downstairs, but not all the *way* downstairs, and there's a window, you can look at people in a way that you can't otherwise, if you know what I mean.

Holding Forth? I knew you'd want to know. Sample: "How 'bout Churchill's children. . . . How 'bout that?" No comment.

THE LION'S HEAD (59 Christopher St.)

> **What You Feel Like When You Get There:** 4 (Downstairs, which you are.)
>
> **Yuppity Doo Da:** 5 (Even people who look like Yuppies are not Yuppies when they are in Greenwich Village.)
>
> **Oh Say Can You See?** 4 (Yeah, you really can, too well, but the key is that you can only see outside to the sidewalk.)

Crapola: 3

Holding Forth: 5 (Any invocation of Churchill gets an automatic 5.)

What You Feel Like After Three Drinks: 4

Just a Little Something to Wash My Drink Down With: 4 (They offer pizza.)

Old Fart Factor: 2

What You Feel Like When You Leave: 3

You Go Figure: 4 (Churchill's *children?*)

Nowhere Coefficient: 3.8

But no visit to the Village is complete without stopping by McSorley's, which is another Bar Bar That Got Too Famous for Its Own Good. This bar is also the Oldest Bar in New York, which, as I've mentioned, is a kind of genre here. How old is it? Dates to 1854. That's right . . . *18*. Better yet, it didn't serve women until 1985 (!). At that, it had to be sued to do so. Based on the few women I saw there, I'd call it a damned shame.

Elsewise, a more than exemplary Bar Bar That Got Too Famous for Its Own Good. No yuppity Doo Da at all, for one thing, and then there was this guy who I happened to sit next to. Here we go: "You know, I'm 6'3" and weigh 303. People can usually guess I'm a security guard nights. But very few can guess I'm a piano teacher during the day."

"I see."

"My dad always says to me, 'You're an asshole.' Well come to think of it, so is *he.*"

"Yeah."

"You know, my granddad—and he thought my dad was an asshole too—once beat the shit out of a coupla black guys. Tried to rob him. Beat 'em with one of those ice cream spoons. He just happened to have it in the car."

"Uh huh."

"This one piano student I have, wow, she can find Bernice."

"Bernice?"

"Yeah, that old white lady named Bernice . . . you know . . ." He indicated his right nostril.

"Oh yeah."

"Last time we had a lesson . . ."

Well, you get the picture—and if you don't, go ahead, take the book back. Seriously. I'll rebate you. Love to, come to think of it. Elsewise, McSorley's did okay. Nice crapola, including sign behind bar that proclaimed WE WERE HERE BEFORE YOU WERE BORN! Also, sign to restrooms simply read "Toilets," a sort of not-so-ersatz European touch. McSorley's makes its own ale, which is supposed to be a big deal, but I'm here to tell you it isn't. It's a cream-based and definitely faggy sort of stuff: *Atkinson's Sixteenth Rule of the Bar Bar:* If the stuff remotely reminds you of dessert, it's not a drink and you're not in a Bar Bar.

McSORLEY'S OLD ALE HOUSE (15 East 7th St.)

What You Feel Like When You Get There: 3 (A little too much like a tourist.)

Yuppity Doo Da: 5

Oh Say Can You See? 3

Crapola: 5

Holding Forth: 5 (Give Andy a break—he did also say, "See ya' tomorrow!")

What You Feel Like After Three Drinks: 3

Just a Little Something to Wash My Drink Down With: 2 (Food on menu looked passable, but bartender offered me a menu. Go work for Friday's. If I wanna eat, I'll let you know.)

Old Fart Factor: 3 (Young Fart Factor—Andy.)

What You Feel Like When You Leave: 3 (All was fine, but a couple of those McSorley ales and you really do understand what a bagpipe feels like, in the key of A.

You Go Figure: 4

Nowhere Coefficient: 3.6

I skipped back uptown and decided to roam a few White Collar Bar Bars. There are several nice exemplars here—the bar at the Four Seasons is a great power hangout—but when it comes to Bar Bars, you generally find that the older have gotten nothing but better. The Oak Bar at the Plaza is still the archetypal White Collar Bar Bar, and an excellent example of that dying breed known as the Hotel Bar Bar as well. It's mineshaft-dark and smoky and fairly clatters with Holding Forth. A very nice sign at a White Collar Bar Bar is the presence of at least one regular perusing the *Wall Street Journal.* This is a perfectly acceptable Bar Bar activity, and as you might expect, a fine catalyst for spontaneous Holding Forth. The place is Yupped to the hilt, to be sure, but when you hear an aside like this—"Say, you think Qaddafi: could last even one minute one-on-one with Lawrence Taylor?"—you know you're nowhere.

THE OAK BAR AT THE PLAZA HOTEL (Fifth Ave. and 59th St.)

What You Feel Like When You Get There: 3 (Underdressed, but it's dark enough to hide the jeans and the Nikes.)

Yuppity Doo Da: 2

Oh Say Can You See? 5

Crapola: 1 (Very disappointing)

Holding Forth: 4

What You Feel Like After Three Drinks: 5 (*Gadzooks,* there are a lot of contenders for the stiffest drink in the world, but the Oak Bar has got to be up there.)

Just a Little Something to Wash My Drink Down With: 4 (Peanuts.)

Old Fart Factor: 3

What You Feel Like When You Leave: 4 (Gassed, and I must say the Oak Bar also has the niftiest Bar Bar exit I've seen in a while. Just right out on 59th, staring straight at Central Park. Can't beat that.)

You Go Figure: 1

Nowhere Coefficient: 3.2

Something was still a bit missing, and since I had to leave town, I not only went for Potluck, I went for the big one. Friend had told me about a place called Muffin's on Third Avenue near 36th Street, near the *Daily News* building. Didn't know much about it but said, "You might wind up sleeping on the floor and you wouldn't want to." That's *Atkinson's Seventeenth Rule of the Bar Bar.*

What can I say? Muffin's exists, and not only that, it *breathes*—and how.

"Could I have a vodka-soda, with some lime," I said to the pretty young lady bartender who turned out to be Argentinian and plenty smartass.

"Vodka . . . soda? That's *disgusting.*"

I like an insult right off, and you can tab that *Atkinson's Eighteenth Rule of the Bar Bar.* Other good signs: Saw a middle-aged lady who looked a little like Queen Elizabeth come in, draw down a bourbon neat, and dope out her picks at the racetrack. Are you beginning to understand? Okay, here's *Atkinson's Nineteenth Rule of the Bar Bar:* If you see someone doing something they elsewise wouldn't ever do except at home, alone, you're in a Bar Bar.

I was soon, however, to discover Holding Forth Nirvana from the lips of a slight and stooped little Cuban fellow next to me, who upon noting my friendly gaze dropped this little bombshell: "Do I have a ticket to Spain? Do I have a ticket to Cuba? No, I don't go anywhere; I don't go *anywhere!*" This existential lament was greeted with lethargic grumbles from the other patrons—two businessmen, a biker, and several Hispanics who appeared only partially employed—who had obviously heard it before. Repetition is an important tenet of Holding Forth, particularly if it's Old Fart Holding Forth.

As the afternoon wore on, I eventually became the audience for this guy who said he was a noise pollution inspector for the city, which struck me as about the most absurd thing anyone could be. You're responsible for controlling *noise* in *New York?* Oh sure, perfect. And before that, I guess you're going to tell me you were a food inspector in Juarez, or better yet, maybe an election judge.

"Yeah, it's a bunch of shit, all right," he said. "I actually had a guy complain about *car horns* the other day. But there are perks. I go to all the discos anytime I want. Just flash that card and they don't give me any of that uppity wait-outside shit at all. To them, I'm the *man.*" Turns out, in fact, he was in the club business himself—well, sort of.

"Give me a call when you get back to town," he said, handing me a business card. "I gotta place up off Park and a few girls, with a bar set up, the whole deal. You can just come and drink, or whatever. It's a class operation. I have 'em checked every week." Well, he did say he was an inspector.

MUFFIN'S (37th and Third Ave.)

> **What You Feel Like When You Get There:** 4
>
> **Yuppity Doo Da:** 5
>
> **Oh Say Can You See?** 5
>
> **Crapola:** 5
>
> **What You Feel Like After Three Drinks:** 5
>
> **Holding Forth:** 5
>
> **Just a Little Something to Wash My Drink Down With:** 5 (Chili and, I believe, burritos; excellent stuff.)

Old Fart Factor: 5

What You Feel Like When You Leave: 5 (I almost missed my plane.)

You Go Figure: 5 (I didn't.)

Nowhere Coefficient: 4.9

3

Bar Bar 101A: Only Slightly Advanced Theology (on Bar Bar Names)

Customer to other customer: *You realize I've been comin' here almost ten years, and I don't even know what this place looks like?*
Other customer to customer: *You think it really matters?*

I have been drinking at the aforementioned Joe Miller's in Dallas for the same period and have frequently asked myself and others the same question. I mean, I do know that familiarity does breed a certain premature senility, like forgetting what color your wife's eyes are, for example. But in the case of your wife's eyes, at least you can take solace that you *once* knew what color they were. I can't really say that about Joe's, and that brings us to *Atkinson's Twentieth Rule of the Bar Bar:* Liquor was not intended to be consumed in the presence of light, artificial or natural. Hey, you've just gone Nowhere. Like the guy said, what do you care what it looks like?

There are, however, certain essentials of both exterior and interior motif that are preferred. My favorite mode of Bar Bar architecture, as earlier noted, involves the Bunker Look: windowless, with only a sign and a door to indicate any form of life on the interior. This is not as frequently found as one might like. New Yorkers, for example, have a thing for windows, and New Orleans' bars like to keep open doors. But said sins against the Church are perfectly acceptable if the Atkinson Candlepower Scale is observed. It gets pretty complex, but basically a bar is at acceptable

Bar Bar darkness level if the dilation-adjustment process takes one *full* drink.

A second canon is that the Bar Bar *bar* must predominate the room. It can be linear, of the saloon variety, or bullpen-like, or even circular; but it must predominate the room, like an altar. I prefer pure stand-up types, but those seem not to exist outside of the *Gunsmoke* series.

Beyond that it really *doesn't* matter, except that I like to see crapola on floors, walls, and ceiling. The preferred wall adornment is bad clocks and bad mirrors (from beer distributors) and then whatever eclectic assortment of stuff that has just accumulated. *Atkinson's Twenty-first Rule of the Bar Bar:* If the back of the bar looks like nothing has ever been thrown away, you're in a Bar Bar.

Well, actually, there is one other thing that matters: rest rooms. The preferred style here is Spartan, and while I would recommend every Bar Bar rest room be like that one at Mac's Club Deuce in Miami (the decor could best be described as Early Hepatitis), I don't like to see things too spick-and-span, and I generally am warmed by the presence of at least one nonfunctioning piece of plumbing.

Speaking of Mac's Club Deuce, what does matter supremely is the bar's name. This particular form of communication, I discovered in my travels, is something on the order of a lost art. Jesus, there are some *bad* bar names out there. Chief offender is, of course, the Fake Pub Franchise, which by my count now includes Bennigan's, Mulligan's, O'Houlihan's, O'Shaughnessy's, and O'Hara's. This is offensive for a couple good reasons, one being that you can be pretty damned sure no such guy exists and the other being that the implicit intent is to offer the visitor an opportunity to be Somewhere.

A second genre of culprit is names that invoke one of the following euphemisms for *bar:* bistro, cafe, cutlery, patio, pub (unless it was built before 1960). *Atkinson's Twenty-second Rule of the Bar Bar:* A great Bar Bar name should include:

1.   The name of the guy who runs the joint—Mike's, for example.

2. In the absence of that, either the address—Mike's, for example—or some extremely simple and direct designation. One of my former haunts in Dallas called itself *The Point Downtown*.

3. If a word other than *bar* is going to be used, the following are acceptable: *lounge, club, tavern* (only if opened before 1960), *place*, and that most exquisite of Bar Bar appellations: *room*. For Chrissakes, just call it what it *is* and if it's a Bar Bar, it's probably little more than a room.

4. Variations from these basic rules are acceptable, but only if they add a certain, shall we say, non-sequitur quality to the name. My favorite in this regard is a little joint in Kansas City called Davy Markowitz's Uptown Rambler. Go figure indeed. Second place award: The Aub Zam Zam Room in San Francisco.

5. Additionally, statements of philosophy are acceptable, but only if they stay within the theology. Favorite of this type is a now defunct joint in Dallas called simply The He's Not Here. Also a little place down in the hill country of Texas called My Joint. The perfect Bar Bar moniker? Need you ask? Something along the lines of Fred's Nowhere Room.

Whatever other purpose a Bar Bar name serves, it should respect the sound thinking of my old friend Fred. *Atkinson's Twenty-third Rule of the Bar Bar:* If you can't say it when you're beyond drink three, you're not in a Bar Bar.

The Transcontinental Drunk, part 2: Heart of Nowhere—Milwaukee

Stuff sure goes right through, didn't it?
Yup, sure goes right through ya.
                    —*Conversation in a Bar Bar Men's Room*

New York had turned out to be as good a place to start as any because of its wide array of bars spanning every conceivable ethnic and demographic description. I'd been able to sample a smorgasbord, whet my whistle, so to speak, get my, uh, bearings. But something gnawed at me still. I had an urge to immerse myself in primordial ooze, in the very womb of the Theology of the Bar Bar. So I did the only thing any right-thinking drinker would do. I went to . . . Milwaukee.

Eventually found a Rup here too. Well, not exactly, because Alex Thien is a columnist for the local paper, but in a way that's sort of the same thing. Turned out great, too, because Alex, unlike Dave, *did* have office hours and some modicum of manners, so what he did was get on his network, put together several lists, allow me to buy him a drink or two, and turn me loose.

My intention here was simple: I wasn't just looking for Nowhere. I was looking for Nowhere in the middle of Nowhere— meaning Milwaukee. One brief sociological observation, if I may: For what it's worth, pretty much every city I barhopped lived up to each and every cliché, pro and con, about it—and

Milwaukee was no exception. I'd wanted primordial ooze and that's about as good a description of what I flew in through as I can think of. Some kind of god-awful fog/mist/*yech* close to the ground and everything else, including, I found out soon enough, one's skin. Maybe that's why Milwaukee's always gotten a bum rap: You can't see it. Then again, it could be that that's why it hasn't gotten a bigger bum rap. Either way I can't tell you, because I was there three days and I never did really see whatever there was there. Never mind, though. The soupy weather and sundry other oppressions are probably what make Milwaukee a seminal Bar Bar culture. These guys *need* their bars and there can't be so very much wrong with a place where people feel like that.

The bar at the Pfister, another ancient restoration, suffered from a bit of that decorative schizophrenia you see in all such places. You know, beautifully restored dark wood-paneled walls, an immense antique back bar . . . so far, so good . . . and then, *blam*, orange vinyl bar stools and Huey Lewis on the stereo. I observed a lot of this in my travels, in hotels, restaurants, plazas, and all that other stuff we seem to want back. And I have to say, I think it's all just one more remnant (that's the politest word I could conjure up) of the Yups. They like to bring the past back so that they can patronize it.

Two things made this bar transcend its mishmash decor: the young and solemn bartender, who mixed a vodka-soda and added lime without having to be asked and later was heard to utter an immensely profound bit of Bartender Holding Forth: "There are choices and then there are choices." This involved a conversation he was having with the cocktail waitress, wherein she was trying to decide whether to move back to Montana. "Why would anyone," he said, apparently forgetting where he lived, "want to move *back* anywhere?" That's world class stuff, and so was the You Go Figure sitting next to me: string-bean of an old black guy dressed shabbily in faded blue-jean jacket, oxford-cloth shirt, but with a Cardin tie. Go figure.

BAR AT THE PFISTER HOTEL (424 E. Wisconsin)

What You Feel Like When You Get There: 1 (Serious confusion about whether to be old or new.)

Yuppity Doo Da: 4

Oh Say Can You See? 3

Crapola: 1 (Somewhere in the midst of restoration, they'd tossed out all the essentials.)

Holding Forth: 5 (Bartender Holding forth is a rarely heard variety.)

What You Feel Like After Three Drinks: 3 (Can't really tell you, but I suspect just fine.)

Just a Little Something to Wash My Drink Down With: 1 (I glanced at a menu, and it looked terribly Yupped and wimped-out.)

Old Fart Factor: 4 (Black guy got 'em there.)

What You Feel Like When You Leave: 3

You Go Figure: 4 (Black guy.)

Nowhere Coefficient: 3.1

On my way over I had noticed a little joint called The Swinging Door, and since it was past dinner time and a Monday night (football!), I decided to make it my Potluck. It had the right look, and besides, I wanted to see the 'Skins and the Giants.

Whatever self-flagellation I put myself through for choosing Uncle Charlie's South in New York I was able to soothe with this pick. Gad, what a crew: twelve to twenty regulars crammed about a mostly stand-up bar—blue collar, new collar, white collar, open collar, you name it. The Holding Forth, given the circumstances, was almost entirely devoted to Football Betting Rationale Holding Forth, a particularly entertaining variety.

Every bettor has a system, and a Bar Bar is the best place to hear 'em. You've got bet-the-underdog-only systems; bet-the-favorite-only systems. Only-bet-7-and-under spread systems. Only-bet-the-underdog-on-Monday-night-under-7-points systems. I know several bookies, and so I can fairly scientifically guarantee you that none of the systems work. But that's what makes this such an endearing form of Holding Forth: like the argument, it has no resolution. It's there for its own sake.

One young New Collar fellow was really on a roll. "See, what I do," he said, signaling to Mike the bartender to serve him another, "is I look at who each team beat the week before. Then I look at who they're playing the next week. Next I compare offensive statistics and how the teams fared against one another the year before. Then I look at home field and the weather and injury reports. Then I ask my wife which team name she likes better. I don't even look at the spread. Then I throw one cat up in the air and see if she lands on the foot with six toes. I don't even look at the spread."

While awaiting kickoff, I began to notice a particular sound I had never heard in a Bar Bar before. It was the urgent, savage *thwack* of leather on wood followed by shouts of glee or horror. It had a vaguely S-and-M quality to it, so, curious, I asked Mike what it was. "Oh that," he said. "Bar dice. We don't play darts up here and we don't play video games. We play bar dice."

Sure enough, after glancing up and down the bar, I could see clumps of regulars earnestly engaged in the rather primitive exercise of pounding a dice cup with five dice in it on the bar. I asked Mike to show me, which was my first mistake. My best recollection is that it is loosely based on poker. Each participant takes an initial smash of the cup and puts together his highest number and his "bullet," which is like a wild card. These are compared all around as per poker and a "pace" is set for subsequent smashes. That's the easy part. The rest is somewhat inscrutable, but basically through successive rolls, players are eliminated until someone finally wins.

The game is played for drinks, not money, which makes it a class-A bar game to begin with. But the key to the game is the physics of it. As I soon discovered, there is nothing quite so satisfying as bringing that cup down on the bar with a resounding smack.

I can't say I'm terribly accomplished at it: My first attempt hit off center, sending one die into a bottle of schnapps and the other four *behind* me toward a startled young couple. But bar dice, which I would see again in San Francisco, definitely conforms to *Atkinson's Twenty-fourth Rule of the Bar Bar:* Diversions from drinking and conversation are allowed if they involve sufficient simplemindedness, aggression, cheating, and changing of rules and are not engaged in outside the confines of the Bar Bar.

Some additional rules of thumb here: Darts is perfectly respectable, but it must be some form of power darts, wherein the participants just rear back and fling the suckers as hard as they can. Video games, no; miniature bowling games, fine. Pool, fine; Trivial Pursuit, no. Arm wrestling, okay. Pinball, so long as sufficient physical effort is displayed.

The game descended into a blur, largely caused by beer, schnapps, and Holding Forth; but I can tell you that I saw all fifty-six replays of Joe Theismann breaking his leg and if it's of any interest, even these ironworkers said "Oooo!!" each and every time. I can also tell you that I subsequently heard each and every broken bone story in the bar.

THE SWINGING DOOR (219 E. Michigan)

What You Feel Like When You Get There: 4

Yuppity Doo Da: 5 (As long as I'm in Milwaukee, you can just assume 5 here; there are no Yups in Milwaukee, and based on that, I take back everything nasty I ever said about the place.)

Oh Say Can You See? 4

Crapola: 5 (Shredded, spindled, and mutilated towel rack in men's room. Sign back of bar: DRINKING MAKES YOU SEE DOUBLE, BUT THINK YOU'RE SINGLE!)

Holding Forth: 5 (Betting Rationale category.)

What You Feel Like After Three Drinks: 5 (Mike was a much better bartender than bar dice instructor.)

Just a Little Something to Wash My Drink Down With: 5 (Pizza, bratwurst, and one of my favorite Bar Bar foods of all time: raw meat and rice.)

Old Fart Factor: 4

What You Feel Like When You Leave: 5 (I *walked* ten blocks through downtown Milwaukee and enjoyed it—at midnight.)

You Go Figure: 5 (Bar dice, and raw meat and rice.)

Nowhere Coefficient: 4.3

As I headed out the next day, I had to face a sobering fact: I was going to have to revise another rule. *Atkinson's Twenty-fifth Rule of the Bar Bar* has always read: The drinking of beer never led to anything civilized whatsoever. This had been based on several facts. One is that beer sounds uncivilized going down. And it certainly sounds uncivilized coming back—whatever orifice it chooses. But the main thing about beer is that it tends to create a different kind of drinker. I swear this is true: You let a man drink five martinis, then let a man drink five beers, and you just see which one wants to kick the crap out of somebody else. Beer doesn't have nearly the alcoholic content of regular booze—about one third as much, in fact—but its effects seem to work in inverse proportion to the proof factor.

I've never seen martini or whiskey drinkers want to fight, for example; or dance or sing certain types of songs—like anything by Alabama. I've also never seen a martini or whiskey drinker belch, fart, or sweat in quite the same way a beer drinker does, by the way. Some folks say that this is because beer drinkers might just be this way sober to begin with. But I like to think that it's because beer—one sip, one case—has a particularly uncivilizing effect on *anyone*.

But there is no deflecting the historical importance of beer to the Bar Bar. It has existed in some form since a few thousands B.C. In about 2300 B.C., the Chinese (typical) drank a brew called *kiu*; Sumerians had at least sixteen varieties of beer. Even Hammurabi had a taste: He used to punish Babylonian barkeepers if they watered down their stuff. (Always knew Hammurabi was my kind of Bar Bar guy. Nice work, Ham-Man.)

From thence you had ale and most of the drinking culture of Western Europe—and thence, here. Ale, beer, whatever they called it, preceded cider or rum as the potion of choice here; and it certainly beat whiskey. So there's a keg of history there, and I'm nothing if not a historical kind of guy, so, okay, I'm wrong. I still disagree, but there's just no way to separate beer from the Bar Bar. So with some reluctance, I state *Atkinson's Revised Twenty-fifth Rule of the Bar Bar:* The drinking of beer is still uncivilized, unless,.of course, it occurs someplace like Milwaukee.

One good place to observe the beer Bar Bar in action is Turner's, a hundred-year-old landmark smack in the middle of downtown. The Turners were among the many Germans who immigrated to Milwaukee (still called the German Athens) in 1848, largely because of political repression. Along with other families, they reestablished old German customs in the New World, among them singing, gymnastics, and drinking. Go figure.

Anyway, they eventually built this monstrous structure in an apparent attempt to accommodate *all* those customs, producing the damnedest Bar Bar I've ever seen: first Special Atkinson Transcontinental Award for Biggest Bar Bar in America. The dust-colored structure is two stories high and covers almost an entire city block.

Second Special Atkinson Transcontinental Award for Damnedest You Go Figure in America, for the innards of this place are not all Bar Bar: There's a big photo gallery that includes all kinds of nifty shots of old Milwaukee, and then there's a . . . gym and health spa. The bar, a cozy little room with an. elliptical stand-up bar, sits right next to it, creating perhaps the

---

Fun Facts

As of 1984, the state with the highest percentage of dry population was Kentucky: 37.5 percent. Utah's percentage was 0.

---

most resounding cultural collision I've ever seen in a Bar Bar.

There we sat, me and a couple New Collar types with forearms that looked like heavy machinery, a couple White Collar types, and a few derelicts, sipping our beer and shots of schnapps, discussing the weather, and then *blam*, just like that, some yup in Adidas sweats and a gym bag strides by on his way to play racquetball. All I can say is . . . Jeepers! I've seen a lot of weird things attached to Bar Bars. The icehouses of the Southwest, for example, offer bait, guns, ammo, key-making services, you name it. And occasionally with Bars That Got Too Famous for Their Own Good, you see souvenir shops. But *gym* in a *bar?*

Never mind, Turner's is the real thing. The Holding Forth even had to do with the disintegration of real bars in the city. One old guy, with a head shaped like a tree stump, offered a couple of particularly chilling examples. "Used to be a joint across the river," he said. "Called it Fred's. *Fred's.* Perfect. Know what they call it now? Elsa's on the River. Jesus Christ. Oh yeah, then there's this place right over here downtown. Called The Mint Bar. Used to be a great journalists' hangout. It's still got regulars, but I don't think you'd want to go there. It's now a place for, uh, other kind of guys, if you know what I mean."

Turner's also featured that always welcome member of the Bar Bar ecosystem, the Bar Bar Bag Man, who sits someplace between Bar Bar Dog and Bar Bar Kid. No kidding. Guy just shuffled in with a big bag of aluminum cans, dropped it over the bar, and enjoyed his free one on the house. That's real Bar Bar stuff when you start offering drinks in trade. "Yeah, I just been in California," he announced to no one in particular, "and it's sunny out there." That's a 5 on the Atkinson Lie Meter.

TURNER TAP (4th and Highland)

> **What You Feel Like When You Get There:** 3 (Like you've just walked into a museum, or a gymnasium, which you *have.*)
>
> **Yuppity Doo Da:** 3 (In the gym, anyway.)
>
> **Oh Say Can You See?** 5

Crapola: 5 (Old photos nearby are great.)

Holding Forth: 5 (For the bag man's Bar Bar lie.)

What You Feel Like After Three Drinks: 4 (I'll say this, you forget about the gym.)

Just a Little Something to Wash My Drink Down With: 3

Old Fart Factor: 5

What You Feel Like When You Leave: 4

You Go Figure: 5 (!)

Nowhere Coefficient: 4.1

But the epicenter of Milwaukee bar culture, the true Nowhere in the middle of Nowhere, is in the tiny and rumpled neighborhood joints that speckle this city like freckles on a redhead. A reasonable MO here seemed to be to make a block or two run of several joints in South Milwaukee, the city's hardest-core working-class area. I couldn't have found a better run than South 7th.

At South 7th and Becher sits an archetype of this type of Bar Bar. It is called Koz's Mini-Bowl and Beer, and I'll say right off that it earned a spot in Atkinson's Top 10 Bar Bars in America, right up there with Costello's in New York. It's really just a little shanty of a joint, identical to the frame houses that proceed up the block. One room has the bar, a Trivial Pursuit video game, a pool table; the other has six miniature-bowling lanes, with pins and balls about the size of grapefruits. Didn't think it was possible: I'd just found a better Bar Bar Game than bar dice. Talk about aggression venting, *phew*. Those suckers can make some *noise* and also give one the sheer primal sensation of having destroyed something.

Bartender was a friendly young New Collar type who'd inherited the joint. Said it had been there since 1956 and that the mini-bowling was something of an institution in the neighborhood. The bar was empty when I arrived, but that didn't make any difference, because being the only guy in the bar is a revered Bar Bar tradition.

We talked some economy, but that couldn't possibly interrupt the other noise. That would be the television, and it was *daytime* television. A young black fellow and a Hispanic father and son had since joined us and so there was a decent group to witness . . . Bar Bar Daytime TV Watching. It's a custom all right, serious and actually somewhat sober.

It had started with some morning *Perry Mason* and then had proceeded to *Family Feud*. What a great Bar Bar TV game! The subject at hand was five former Miss Americas, competing—all in good fun of course! Daytime TV may best be understood in Bar Bar terms as Holding Forth, 'cept you don't have to do it yourself.

The tits-and-ass jokes fairly exploded. The bartender's uncle arrived, and on sighting contestant number three mused, "I wonder what her SAT scores were?" In the meantime, the bartender had figured out I was from Dallas and he was curious about the Sunbelt. You get a lot of that up here: Sumbitches think it's a foreign country or some such. I allowed as how it wasn't such a bad place, except that we'd only had liquor by the drink—and hence any semblance of real bars—since 1972. I explained that that was because of the Baptists.

"Yeah, we almost got pari-mutuel betting this last time, but the bastards killed that, too," I added, completing the sociology lesson.

"Why don't you just shoot the fuckers?" he asked, serious as could be, and I have to admit the notion had a certain raw elegance to it.

The consumption at hand was that Milwaukee staple, a beer and a shot of schnapps. Price varies, but at Koz's the whole shooting match costs a dollar, which basically means you can get plenty gassed for a fiver. However, this particular form of imbibing, I would learn, is not without its drawbacks. There are several variations of beer-and-a-shot drinking: In my home state, it's that insidious libation known as tequila with a beer; in the Southeast, it's bourbon up with a beer. In any event, the concoction is not called a boilermaker for no reason at all.

When you drink like this, essentially you're adding a depth charge. There's nothing so very much wrong with that, except that schnapps in particular has a sort of time-release-capsule-type effect, wherein you're just buzzing along fine for an hour or so and then *whammo,* the cumulative proof that you've consumed suddenly kicks in and renders you immediately and irretrievably *drunk* In this event, do what I do: call a cab.

Family Feud had given way to *Wheel of Fortune* or some such, and I decided to lurch onward. The bartender was fuming about the absence of much of his regular clientele and as a finishing touch to the soliloquy, he uttered what would turn out to be the single best line of Holding Forth I heard *anywhere.*

"Where *is* everybody? Person who invented *that* oughta be shot."

"What?"

"Workin' in the daytime."

(Your special Atkinson Transcontinental Award plaque is in the mail.)

KOZ'S MINI-BOWL AND BEER (South 7th and Becher Sts.)

What You Feel Like When You Get There: 5

Yuppity Doo Da: 5

Oh Say Can You See? 5

Crapola: 5 (Best touch: a gimme cap with "OLD FART" emblazoned on it.)

Holding Forth: 5

What You Feel Like After Three Drinks: 5 (Just fine. But half an hour later? I made a quick stop at the House of Pancakes.)

Just a Little Something to Wash My Drink Down With: 5 (Beef jerky.)

Old Fart Factor: 5

What You Feel Like When You Leave: 5

You Go Figure: 5 (Mini-bowl.)

Nowhere Coefficient: 5

I headed a little farther south to a joint called Big Ray's Tap, which gets a 5 for the name right off. I like the use of that word "tap" and if I ever own a bar, I'm going to stick it in there someplace. (Big Jim's Nowhere Tap Room. Not bad, eh? Any of you investment-banker types out there interested?)

A couple things about Ray's: potential Darkest Bar in America Award; definite Best Crapola Award. Big Ray, a Huggy Bear of a guy with a graying beard, is one of those proprietors who subscribes to the Bar Bar as Department Store philosophy. A careful perusal of the stuff littering his back bar revealed that Big Ray had transcended mere crapola: What he had was real *crap.*

You had a ghetto blaster or two, some watches, all manner of Christmas decor crapola, along with, of course, beef sticks and chips. Most all the stuff was for sale, though the ghetto blaster was a prize in some sort of raffle Ray was running. Ditto the lady's Rolex. "I almost was going to buy my grandson a ghetto blaster," said the Old Lady Fart next to me, "but I decided just to give him a hundred dollars. I don't know what he wants and I don't think he does either." Very nice: The Kid Lament is time-honored Holding Forth.

She continued: "You go to college?" I said I had. She gave me another once-over. "Well, you gotta job?" I said I did. "Well, nice talking to you." And she left. You go figure.

A couple other Old Farts came in, and did Big Ray have a deal for them. He rummaged through another heap of crap at the far end of the bar and produced a handful of calendars with Hallmark-card-level nature photos on them. "I'm giving these to the regulars this year," Ray said proudly. "If somebody wants to buy one, though, I'm gonna charge $200. Whaddya think? You could just cut these pictures out and frame 'em."

Tube Watch: *Never Ending Story* on HBO. Go figure indeed.

BIG RAY'S TAP (2879 N. Weil)

What You Feel Like When You Get There: 5

Yuppity Doo Da: 5

Oh Say Can You See? 5

Crapola: 5 (!)

Holding Forth: 4

What You Feel Like After Three Drinks: 5 (I think this is when Ray tends to make the majority of his sales. Just a guess.)

Just a Little Something to Wash My Drink Down With: 4

Old Fart Factor: 5

What You Feel Like When You Leave: 5 (Brave enough to drop by Hammer City, for one.)

You Go Figure: 5

Nowhere Coefficient: 4.8

No I'm not going to recommend Hammer City, but I can plug my next stop, Axel's, near the University of Wisconsin campus. These guys had lifted Bar Bar Daytime TV Watching to high art. There were about twenty Young, Middle, and Old Farts watching *Divorce Court,* a rite, I would learn, that is daily and quite serious. "Yep, damn near every day," said the Middle Fart next to me. "It's fun and you can learn stuff too."

The case in question involved a triangle including Diane, Chester, and Trixie. Chester had been carrying on with Trixie and Diane was fed up. She was also chapped about all the guns he kept around the house. There ensued a lot of legal stuff, but basically the folks at the bar were putting their money on one proposition: Is Diane going to stick Chester for $41,000 a month? There was some serious betting too. When the verdict was rendered—and in fact, Chester did get stuck—one guy said, "Fuck." Another said: "I'm gonna call Red." He did, and here's what he said: "Yeah, we're watchin' *Court.* Come on over." Go figure.

AXEL'S (2859 N. Oakland)

> **What You Feel Like When You Get There:** 5
>
> **Yuppity Doo Da:** 5
>
> **Oh Say Can You See?** 4
>
> **Crapola:** 3
>
> **Holding Forth:** 5 (Based on TV wisecracks.)
>
> **What You Feel Like After Three Drinks:** 4
>
> **Just a Little Something to Wash My Drink Down With:** 3
>
> **Old Fart Factor:** 5
>
> **What You Feel Like When You Leave:** 4
>
> **You Go Figure:** 5 ($100 on Chester?)
>
> **Nowhere Coefficient:** 4.3

Had a little din-din and then took a Potluck: This particular kind of Potluck will recur: the Motel Bar Potluck. Howard Johnson's, downtown Milwaukee. Had to go for it.

The Motel Bar Bar is a breed that needs a little explanation. Just a little. See, there are places that basically have *no* bars, let alone Bar Bars, at all. This means that you revert to *Atkinson's Twenty-sixth Rule of the Bar Bar:* In the absence of anyplace else to get a drink, any locus that serves liquor is a Bar Bar—including Bennigan's.

This kind of thing is true especially in, say, Amarillo, and maybe in Birmingham too. I figured it could be true in Milwaukee, and so that's why I took a flyer on the Howard Johnson's in downtown Milwaukee. You buy it? Good. Because I'm here to say it wasn't worth the price of the walk over.

Gad. You forget how bad motel bars can be until you do something stupid like go to one of them. Umh. Reagan and Gorbachev on the tube, two lady bartendresses who looked like a tag team.

One said: "I got accosted by this black fellow who wanted you-know-what the other night" [a big 5 on the Atkinson Bar Bar Lie Meter]. I took a cab. It was worth it to spend $48 on a cab. I swear."

No rating. The soon-to-be proprietor of Big Jim's Nowhere Tap Room isn't going to insult your intelligence. Sorry I even brought it up, as a matter of fact.

It was time to face the music. It was time to go to Hooligan's Super Bar. Little did I know—actually, I *did*—how literally I would face the music.

Here's the way this joint was presented to me by my trusted Ruppy. "Kinda, you know, ferny, but it's definitely where the young action is." Uh oh: I've learned from tough experience that when someone else says "kinda ferny," that means the Atkinson Fern Meter is gonna jump into the red and never come back.

Hooligan's (I absolutely refuse to use the term "super bar") sits in a neighborhood that you can tell used to be populated by several fine old taverns. Most of them have gone the way of the buffalo or, like Hooligan's, have been Benniganned into submission. You face the music all right: It blasts you right in the face when you swing the door open, as does the flash of the two big screens featuring MTV. No ferns, but I did sense the unmistakable presence of fried potato skins and nachos. The latter would be acceptable if we were in my home state—but in Milwaukee?

But as testament to the true Bar Bar ethos of Milwaukee, the Holding Forth, even in this Six Flags Over bar, was creditable. Indeed, I got an earful of the view from Nowhere.

Guy next to me just turned and said, "Hi, my name's Mark. I'm twenty-six. Pretty fuckin' good, huh?" And we were off. Mark had a bad beard (a Milwaukee must, it seems), scraggly hair, and in the course of fifteen minutes claimed to be an artist, a carpenter, and a musician. He was also a Milwaukee native, which made him a candidate for stuffing and mounting. He seemed a little confused about why he was still here.

"Why don't you just leave?"

"I can't," he said. "I wouldn't. It's just that all I want is to do my job and have my family, make ends meet and be left alone. It's all these strangers movin' in that are fuckin' up the town. Buy me a drink?" Here, here.

Tom, on the other side, was what I call a Would-Be Yup. He drove a restored '68 Vette, in that best Yuppity tradition, and wanted to talk some car. I'm not sure where-all it went, but I do know that we agreed that American cars are superior because they sound better. Tom introduced a great new Bar Bar game, though, a kind of impromptu Trivial Pursuit. Normal Trivial Pursuit is unacceptable because too many Yuppies play it, period. But this was made up and involved self-revelation, so it qualifies. Sample: "What's the favorite car you ever owned?" "What's the favorite rock concert you've ever been to?" It's a solid concept because the response invariably sparks further Holding Forth involving lament, bitching, and lying.

HOOLIGAN'S SUPER BAR (2017 E. North Ave.)

What You Feel Like When You Get There: 1

Yuppity Doo Da: 2

Oh Say Can You See? 3

Crapola: 1

Holding Forth: 5

What You Feel Like After Three Drinks: 3

Just a Little Something to Wash My Drink Down With: 1

Old Fart Factor: 3 (No oldies, but good Young Farts.)

What You Feel Like When You Leave: 3

You Go Figure: 3 (Nachos?)

Nowhere Coefficient: 2.5

Atkinson's Travel Tip #1

From time to time, as a special service to my readers, I'll be passing along basic travel information in the event you'd like to try this sort of thing yourself. This first installment has to do with the complex matter of pacing, i.e., if you've gotta hit ten bars in the space of eighteen hours, how do you stay remotely ambulatory?

The answer in a lot of cases is that you don't. But the following suggestions should help:

1. Don't drink tequila before 3 P.M.
2. Try to insert a junk-food break every fourth bar. A Big Mac or some such is fine, but my favorite is one of those humongo breakfasts at House of Pancakes.
3. If you can get the bartender one-on-one, just order soda with a squeeze of lime. The regulars won't catch the heresy.
4. Don't drink tequila again until after 6 P.M.
5. Try to do at least half your sleeping in the bed.
6. Don't call the wife when you get in after a hard evening's work.
7. Don't call the wife, period.
8. A shave and a fresh shirt every couple of days will do wonders.
9. Don't drink tequila again until after 9 P.M.

5

The Transcontinental Drunk, part 3: Chicago

Male customer to female customer: *You come here often?*
Female customer to male customer: "*I think so, or maybe it's some-place that looks just like it.*

I t is almost impossible to describe what's happened to the Bar Bar scene in the Windy City, but a good word to start with would be "rape." There are still seminal exemplars of the Mother Church here, but there is also a lot of Creeping Benniganism.

A good place to see this—and it ain't pretty—is on Rush and Division streets downtown. These were once proud Bar Bar enclaves, and some of the past remains, but in large part they have been pillaged and plundered by the Yuppities.

Case in point would be Butch MacGuire's, perhaps Chicago's most famous bar. Gad, what a shock. This place had been hyped to the hilt to me by just about every Ruppy I know who was familiar with Chicago. But I'm here to tell ya it ain't the real thing. Ferns. Brass. Old railroad ties. Menu. Bartenders with remnants of Clearasil on their faces. Horny young women. Horny young men. Huey Lewis and the News on the stereo. I thought I'd been magically transported back to the Sunbelt. Nowhere Coefficient: 1. 'Nough said.

Across the street sits The Lodge, and though it has been Yuppitied a bit as well, it is a serviceable Bar Bar in several ways. It's adequately dark according to the Atkinson Candlepower Scale and is a pretty straightforward kind of shotgun setup. Also, there's a miniature bowling game (not to be confused with mini-bowling). I also had an immediate and endearing conversation with a young fellow who happened to agree with me that a great bar has to have shit on the walls, shit on the floor, and shit on the ceiling. Bingo: 5.

One other nice thing was spontaneous dancing. Ordinarily this does not wash. I follow the credo of Joe Miller, which says "No fucking singing or dancing." Or something like that. But this was different. This dancing in the aisles was so spontaneous and spastic and *bad* that it could be appreciated as a kind of juvenile form of Holding Forth. *Atkinson's Twenty-seventh Rule of the Bar Bar:* Dancing or singing is acceptable so long as it's initiated by a woman, which it usually is.

THE LODGE (21 W. Division)

> **What You Feel Like When You Get There:** 2
>
> **Yuppity Doo Da:** 3
>
> **Oh Say Can You See?** 4
>
> **Crapola:** 2
>
> **Holding Forth:** 4
>
> **What You Feel Like After Three Drinks:** 3
>
> **Just a Little Something to Wash My Drink Down With:** 5 (No apparent food.)
>
> **Old Fart Factor:** 2
>
> **What You Feel Like When You Leave:** 3
>
> **You Go Figure:** 3
>
> **Nowhere Coefficient:** 3.1

It was definitely Bar Bar time, and the next afternoon we found it. I say "we" because my companions for part of this leg were two guys in insurance in Dallas who just happened to be in Chicago on business. I like these guys anyway, but I would drink with insurance people no matter what. Next to journalists and criminal defense attorneys, insurance guys are the best drinking buddies I know. This is because they don't give a shit about what they do, they don't understand what they do, and they feel vaguely guilty about what they do.

It's great to get drunk with insurance guys because it's then that they try to explain it. Gad. "I got a quote of ten cents on an apartment deal the other day, and I said, 'Shit,'" commented George. Thank you, George. I'll say this, though: Insurance guys get closer to explaining insurance when they're drunk than when they're sober. Call that *Atkinson's Twenty-eighth Rule of the Bar Bar.*

Our destination was the infamous Billy Goat, an apparent Bar Bar That Got Too Famous for Its Own Good which presently resides in the basement of the *Chicago Tribune* building. I'll give it a 5 right off for being Bar Bar in Building, a solid British tradition that somehow hasn't caught on here. No muss, no fuss. Had a bad morning? Just take the elevator down to the *bar.* Fantastic.

I'll say this, too: This Bar Bar may have gotten too famous for its own good, but it's holding up better than most. Etiology? I got some, but this is absolutely the very last time, okay?

The story is that one Bill Sianis, a Greek immigrant, established this joint in 1934 with $5. That's not the reason for the name, though. Some years later, a billy goat fell off a truck and wandered into the joint and the regulars adopted it—and so, hence, the name. (Sounds a little half-baked to me too, but what do you expect, it's etiology.)

Anyway, from thence this joint became a favored hangout of pro athletes, and of course journalists. One of the latter is Mike Royko, and one way to know that is that among the 3,456 photos on the walls here, 3,452 are of Mike Royko. That's okay, though; the crapola effect is very nice. Competing with the photos of Mike are numerous ostensibly inscrutable anti–Calvert liquor signs. Okay, *once* more. Seems a Calvert salesman some time back made a jerk of himself at the joint and it hasn't sold the brand since. That's as much as I know, and my guess is it's as much as you want to know too.

Aside from the delicious sensation of being in a basement, the Billy Goat offers perhaps America's best Just a Little Something to Wash My Drink Down With. In the center of the room is a square soda-fountain-type counter which serves up burgers, grilled cheese, souvlaki . . . just about any kind of acceptable Bar Bar food you can name. It's all short-order, which is nice, and you can just get it and eat it standing, take it to a table, or take it back to the bar. I like that: Bar Bars have as close cousins the neighborhood soda-fountain drugstore, and to combine the two in this unpretentious way is not merely ingenious, it's *art*.

THE BILLY GOAT BAR AND GRILL (in the basement of the Chicago Tribune Bldg.)

What You Feel Like When You Get There: 4

Yuppity Doo Da: 5

Oh Say Can You See? 3

Crapola: 5 (Nice insult signs like IF YOU DON'T LIKE THE WAY I SERVE, THE PRICES I CHARGE, OR THE WAY I RUN THIS INSTITUTION—THEN BUY ME OUT!

Holding Forth: 3

What You Feel Like After Three Drinks: 3

Just a Little Something to Wash My Drink Down With: 5

Old Fart Factor: 4

What You Feel Like When You Leave: 4

You Go Figure: 5 (Bar in Building)

Nowhere Coeeficient: 4.1

Things continued to perk up later that evening as well. I was in search of a seminal example of the old Irish neighborhood pub, and thanks to some Ruppy, we found it. Joint called O'Rourke's, just north of downtown, and we are talking a very probably Darkest Bar Bar in America nomination here.

Inside of ten minutes, I'd struck up a bit of Holding Forth with a retired cabdriver who had a nose roughly the shape and color of an eggplant. This fellow was engaged in that particular form of Holding Forth known as One of These Days I'm Going to Blow This Dive Holding Forth. You hear me: This is where the guy says he never did want to live here anyway and so he's just thinking about goin' to Montana, thank you. Or as this guy put it, "Chicago's a boring place, finally. I'm gonna move someplace smaller." The key to this, of course, is it's an out-and-out lie, calculated to spur argument from fellow Holders Forth. Because in the next breath, the old fellow added, "But I dunno, this is still a great fuckin' city. . . ." Bar Bars are cauldrons of existentialism, and nowhere can it be seen more clearly than in this sort of Holding Forth.

As the evening wore on, one of my drinking buddies began to fade, and now seems to be as good a time as any to discuss this particular physiological phenomenon of the Bar Bar and what, if anything, can be done about it. The Fade is a vicious, spiteful, completely amoral creature who, just when you least expect it, jumps up on the back of your neck, manacles your tongue to your ankles, your eyelids to your chin, and proceeds to allow you to make a complete lurching, slurring fool of yourself for however long it is you choose to stay at the Bar Bar. I found Stephen King's recently republished short story *The Mist* pretty damned horrifying, but I'll tell you, Steve, those things out there in the soup that ate all those people up can't hold a candle to The Fade. You can't see The Fade coming *at all*, and once he's invaded, no form of exorcism has been proved fail-safe for running the demon off.

Clinically speaking, The Fade results from the untimely intersection of several forces: too much booze, maybe one too many shooters, an earlier decision to fuck dinner, Holding Forth exhaustion, smoke inhalation, and a series of none-too-successful calls to the wife. Years of experience have taught me that preventive medicine is unacceptable here: What right-thinking Bar Bar wants a bunch of regulars standing around furtively sipping, glancing over their shoulders every few minutes, looking for some early warning of the onslaught of The Fade? Besides, The Fade doesn't work that way. He is a creature of guerilla training, and—Vietnam should have taught us this—the only way to beat those kinds of bastards is to fight 'em.

In this case, my other friend and I had noticed the symptoms just too damn late. As earlier noted, The Fade has to do with the diminution of certain crucial faculties, the first being the ability to hold your head up better than, say, an eight-month-old infant. Fades differ, but generally it goes eyelids, head, tongue, feet. At any rate, my friend was already well into Tongue Trouble before we noticed the possession.

We went through the options and tried to prioritize. Food? It's always a tempting possibility and, depending on certain mysterious biochemical factors, *can* work. The problem is, there are never any guarantees, especially with a Fade of the Tertiary Phase. Worse, the intervention of solid matter can backfire on you—literally, if you know what I mean. Look, you've long since said fuck dinner; your stomach knows that, and it's not going to be any happier about the decision now than it was then. In fact, it's probably in a kind of vengeful mood; so whether it stays down or not, food's probably not going to dispatch The Fade, because everyone knows that at a certain point, The Fade and the stomach are co-conspirators.

One other option that just won't do is the Crap Out. I've heard a lot of talk in bars about how the best way to fight The Fade is to go with the flow, find someplace like the backseat of your car and just Crap Out until The Fade gets bored and wings off into the night to find another victim. But there is a capitulation here that I find unsavory, especially for future reference. For everyone also knows that The Fade has a memory like a bartender, and like any bully, he'll be back to see those who showed some fear. Besides, the Crap Out involves Re-Entry, which in turn, of course, involves a hangover of some proportion. *Atkinsons Twenty-ninth Rule of the Bar Bar:* Drinking with a hangover is acceptable in the morning, or even the next night, but not *that* night.

A third option has had limited success, and it was the one we selected for my friend. This is called the RA method, RA standing for Rediscover Ambulation. This method works especially well in cold climates, and since the Chicago wind was brisk as ever outside and there was even a hint of snow in the air, we decided to give it a shot. I must admit I had a personal, as well as a scientific, stake in this: This was my project, my idea, and I figured that in this day and time, I might be liable at the hands of some ambulance chaser for whatever long-term disabilities my friend might incur. (Dateline: Chicago. A 40-year-old white male was found semiparalyzed and incoherent in a Chicago gutter early this morning. Authorities were withholding comment, but sources at the emergency room said he was suffering from Terminal Fade.)

Rediscovering Ambulation, as the name implies, involves retraining the patient to walk like a normal human being. This is not at all easy, and generally requires the patience of a therapist for spinal cord injury victims. That and a good dose of fresh air are mandatory. Then, employing a simple positive-reinforcement mode, you first pace the subject up the sidewalk or across the parking lot, aided. Once he seems a little more on his feet, you let him go ahead solo—but within limits. At each juncture, you make certain to stroke him for his achievements: "See, buddy, you're *walking!*" This may give him a false sense of security, but part of The Fade is psychosomatic as well, and my theory is to fight the little shit on every front.

But the best way to fight The Fade, as previously noted, is to get right down in the gutter with him and duke it out. That's right: Have another drink, preferably something really obnoxious, like Stoly on the rocks. Let the little guy know who's boss, that he may have you on the ropes but there's just no way you're going down for the count. Have another. You'll soon find him in a state of uncertainty. You've Gonzo-warfared him in just the same way he did you in the first place. For the Bar Barfly has something The Fade doesn't: a hereafter, a firm faith in the existence of a life beyond The Fade. Patience, courage, resistance to temptation (the Crap Out) will be rewarded; and even as The Fade has crept out into the night in search of fresh prey, the righteous and believing will find themselves suddenly and miraculously bulletproof. *Atkinson's Thirtieth Rule of the Bar Bar:* Beware The Fade, but do not fear him. For when all is said and done, The Fade can't have another drink. You can.

The demon successfully conquered, we had one more at O'Rourke's—long enough, it turned out, for my cabbie friend to utter this last bit of wisdom. I offered to buy him a drink, in that time-honored and mysterious rite that fellow Bar Barflies have. This is a canon of the Universal Church and to turn it down is considered blasphemy of the highest order. But that's just what he did. "Nah. No thanks. People are always trying to buy me drinks. Frankly, I'm tired of it." In time, I saw the wisdom of this apparent heresy: Yes, it is acceptable, even mandatory, for *regulars* at a Bar Bar. But a stranger? Maybe he had a point.

O'ROURKE'S (319 W. North Ave.)

What You Feel Like When You Get There: 5

Yuppity Doo Da: 5

Oh Say Can You See? 5 (Possible Darkest Bar in America.)

Crapola: 5 (Outstanding graffiti in men's room: "When the weird get going, the weird go pro . . .")

Holding Forth: 4

What You Feel Like After Three Drinks: 5+ (When you fight off The Fade, it's always a 5+.)

Just a Little Something to Wash My Drink Down With: 4

Old Fart Factor: 4

What You Feel Like When You Leave: 5 (It was snowing by now and we had a snowball fight in honor of beating The Fade.)

You Go Figure: 4

Nowhere Coefficient: 4.6

Did a little scattershooting the next day, with some mixed results. Remington's is up around the Division Street fern forest, and so we should have known. No rating, and a real good set of reasons: Presence of daily-special blackboard with the words "lentil soup" on it; bathroom euphemisms COWBOYS, COW-GIRLS. There are some times when you actually *want* The Fade to show up.

Two others, one very new, one very old, of some oddball note. Ricardo's, a journalists' hangout, is just about everything you don't like to see in a Bar Bar. It's new, it's vaguely postmodern, it's got a full-scale restaurant with stuff like entrées and appetizers. But the sensation of drinking at this long, snaking bar, surrounded by bad Goya imitations, is, if not delightful, pleasant. Keys are the Oh Say Can You See? factor, which is a clean 5, and the properly taciturn help behind the bar. And you could see several Bar Bar-flies trying to fight through all the hype and doo da of the place. Like the Old Fart next to me, who upon ordering another one commented, "I don't care. I'm through for the day anyway." That's a 5 on the Atkinson Lie Meter.

RICCARDO'S (437 N. Rush)

What You Feel Like When You Get There: 2

Yuppity Doo Da: 2

Oh Say Can You See? 5+

Crapola: 2

Holding Forth: 3

What You Feel Like After Three Drinks: 3 (Place warms to you, and you to it.)

Just a Little Something to Wash My Drink Down With: 1

Old Fart Factor: 3

What You Feel Like When You Leave: 2.5

You Go Figure: 3 (Goya imitations.)

Nowhere Coefficient: 2.6

The final scattershot got a mixed review as well, but for different reasons. Berghoff's, an ancient German beer hall, may be the most stunning Six Flags Over Bar Bar I've ever seen. In one seemingly endless shotgun room, you've got the bar—a similarly endless stand-up affair that's a little too restored for its own good—and you've got Berghoff's souvenir mugs, T-shirts, God knows whatnot, all easily perusable under the grocery-store-level lighting. In another room, similarly cavernous, is the restaurant, which serves an endless menu of German fare. It's a great old joint turned into mostly hype of the variety I find nauseating, but it deserves at least a mixed review for two reasons.

One is that any bar—even an overly restored one—that maintains the pure stand-up tradition gets a break on What You Feel Like After Three Drinks. The other is that German food is outstanding as Just a Little Something to Wash My Drink Down With. After humongous plates of Wiener schnitzel and potato salad and 100-megaton black bread, my buddy and I were more than ready for the evening roll. This joint has potential, and the sad thing is, I think it realized it long ago and now it's all been soaked up in that fresh varnish on the walls.

BERGHOFF'S (Adams at Dearborn)

What You Feel Like When You Get There: 2

Yuppity Doo Da: 3

Oh Say Can You See? 1

Crapola: 1 (Too much of it was for sale.)

Holding Forth: 3

What You Feel Like After Three Drinks: 3

Just a Little Something to Wash My Drink Down With: 5+

Old Fart Factor: 3 (They could be espied in amongst the Yups.)

What You Feel Like When You Leave: 2

You Go Figure: 1 (Everything about this place was predictable.)

Nowhere Coefficient: 2.4

It was time to get out of the city, to go find some Chicago funk and soul, and there's no better place to do that than the Wrigley Field area, a gloriously eclectic region which has thus far withstood the onslaught of the Yups. I hoped, among other things, to find a black Bar Bar here, because if I didn't, then I'd have to go to South Chicago, and they just aren't paying enough advance money for that, period.

A local Ruppy friend (well, he did have a job, but it was as a music critic, which is like being unemployed) showed me around, and his choices were succinct and seminal. For a perfectly astounding mix of Yuppities and New Collars, not to mention one of the best Sports Bar Bars in America, a must is Murphy's Bleachers, a little joint right by Wrigley Field that has the ambiance of a modular home. It's too light, too loud, and a little too heavy on For Sale crapola. But what the hell, you do know about *Atkinson's Thirty-first Rule of the Bar Bar,* don't you? It says I can change my mind about any of my rating rules any time I want, and for absolutely no good reason.

I grew attached to this joint, because of its sheer energy and the fact that the announcer Harry Caray drinks here after ball games, as do as many bleacher rowdies as can fit in. Just a Little Something to Wash My Drink Down With included serviceable burgers and dogs, and the Holding Forth was non-stop Sports Baiting. Sports Baiting is where one guy decides to get the other's goat by bringing up a perfectly ridiculous sports premise. Example: "I don't care what you say, they don't make 'em like Jim Taylor anymore!"

"Yeah, but Jim Taylor was slow, and he was white."

"That's what I mean. He was white."

That'll generally do it, and as you might imagine, Sports Baiting usually will lead to your Almost But Not Quite Fight. By the way, the Almost But Not Quite Fight count at Murphy's was 6.7, which will earn the joint an Atkinson Special Transcontinental Award plaque.

MURPHY'S BLEACHERS (right behind Wrigley Field)

What You Feel Like When You Get There: 4

Yuppity Doo Da: 3 (But these Yups were Cub fans, which helps a heap.)

Oh Say Can You See? 1

Crapola: 3

Holding Forth: 4

What You Feel Like After Three Drinks: 3

Just a Little Something to Wash My Drink Down With: 4

Old Fart Factor: 2 (A little weak here, but the fact that Harry Caray drinks here gets it an extra point. By the way, you can include Harry in my celebrities I Wouldn't Mind Getting Trashed With.)

What You Feel Like When You Leave: 3

You Go Figure: 3

Nowhere Coefficient: 3.2

The old Almost But Not Quite Fight factor was at play as well at our final stop that night, The Green Mill. Let's get the You Go Figure out of the way right off, 'cause it's crucial: The Green Mill is a Black Muslim Bar Bar, or at least that's what it appeared to be. Yep: guys in turbans and stuff, sitting around knocking 'em back and chewin' the fat. Joint also provided cause for further revision of Atkinson's rule about music: The Green Mill had acceptable live music. No kidding. Tubby black guy who did Fats

Domino sort of stuff, also a kind of You Go Figure.

As for the Almost But Not Quite Fight, it involved this stringy young black fellow who'd long since fallen into his cups and who was bitching about treatment from a white cop, and something about pork. Uh oh. My buddies and I were suddenly looking over our shoulders a lot, and it wasn't for The Fade. But never mind: Big bartender with a purple turban showed him the door and then returned to perform a little Bartender Sabotage on me. I was drinking scotch and soda and was about three quarters done with the last one. Instead of pulling a new glass and mixing me a fresh one, he just tipped the bottle and filled the whole damn glass with scotch, adding, "Better take it easy on that one." Thanks a heap, whatever-your-name-was. Finished that and I was staring straight at Potential Fade.

No problem, though: When we left it was snowing even harder, so we had another snowball fight, a sure cure.

THE GREEN MILL (4802 N. Broadway)

What You Feel Like When You Get There: 3

Yuppity Doo Da: 5 (No, I think not.)

Oh Say Can You See? 5

Crapola: 4

Holding Forth: 3

What You Feel Like After Three Drinks: 5

Just a Little Something to Wash My Drink Down With: 5

Old Fart Factor: 5 (Black Old Farts are the best. Period.)

What You Feel Like When You Leave: 5

You Go Figure: 5 (The whole damn place.)

Nowhere Coefficient: 4.5

Fun Facts*

Before 1900, "goin' to get a brewski" was known as "rushing the growler."

*Erdoes (see Acknowledgments).

Bar Bar 201: Somewhat Fairly More Advanced Theology (on Holding Forth)

Customer to other customer: *"See, I been workin' on this deal for ten years, off and on, and if I can just pull together the seed money, that baby'll take off and shoot right through the power curve, and then it's off-to-the-races time. Katy bar the door. I'm talking ultimate market segmentation here, kind of reverse market share, you know? Accounting would be accrual, so there'd be no way to get caught in any sort of reverse-market riptide. I'll guarantee you one goddamn thing: I know it ain't no baby's game out there, but this sucker has legs. See what I mean?"*

Other customer: *"Uh huh. Exactly."*

If you've been reading this carefully (and yes, I *do* care), you've probably noticed that Holding Forth, the critical cant of any Bar Bar, is a particular form of conversation that does not exist outside of Nowhere. In its primal form, Holding Forth is a verbal stew of more or less equal parts bitch, brag, lament, confession, and just plain mindless bullshit. It is completely pointless and engaged in for its own sake. It is expressly forbidden for it to make sense or to have any semblance of resolution. Holding Forth is small talk raised to the transcendent.

The ritual of Holding Forth does, however, have its rules. A primary one is *Atkinson's Thirty-second Rule of the Bar Bar:* If a fellow Bar Barfly indicates he wants to Hold Forth, it is the duty of any other regular to listen and act like he understands. There are no exceptions to this rule and there is a mysterious—no, *mysti-*

cal—payback system to it. It doesn't have to be said: You just know when it's your turn to listen rather than talk; and you know that sooner or later, you'll get your turn on the soapbox with the regular in question. Bar Bars operate on a remarkable balance-of-nature scheme: There are few spoken or posted rules (the ones that are, like "No Gambling," are generally complete bullshit), and yet a good Bar Bar is one of the most perfectly civilized places I can think of.

Holding Forth is the glue of the civilization, and hence it has become its very own language. As another special service to my readers:

● *Atkinson's Newly Abridged Glossary* ● *of Bar Bar Holding Forth*

I'll guaran-damn-tee you one damn thing: a staple expletive of any decent piece of Holding Forth. Used either to announce impending Holding Forth or to close off a soliloquy. Variations such as substituting "goddamn" for "damn" are acceptable. Employed especially by Old Farts, who generally punctuate it physically with a firm thrust of the right hand, which generally bears a burning cigarette with an untapped ash approximately 6 inches long, which magically never drops from the cigarette.

The whole shitteree: noun generally used to describe some colossal failure, as in "Boy, last night I blew the whole shitteree with the wife."

Old lady: the aforementioned wife.

Doctor: frequently invoked euphemism for bartender.

Nurse: ditto for bar waitress.

Got drunk out last night: generally used as an intro for Hangover Holding Forth, wherein the Holder Forth brags about how trashed he got the night before.

Left some brain cells here last night: same as above.

Got invisible last night: same as above.

He's on the dialysis machine: presently acceptable substitute for "He's on the wagon."

I'll have one more: indication that Bar Barfly intends to get extremely drunk.

In his cups: drunk.

Sit down before somebody sees ya: Bartender Holding Forth, generally directed at customer he hasn't given any shit to lately.

Eighty-sixed: barred from the bar for a probationary period because of some transgression of Bar Bar etiquette, such as throwing up outside the confines of the men's room.

Protein: food.

Splitting the sheets: derived from archaic "four sheets to the wind," wherein Bar Barfly got drunk at two different bars the night before.

Fasten seat belts: announcement of impending Transcontinental Drunk.

You have *types* of Holding Forth as well. Extra special service to my readers:

● *Atkinson's Field Guide to Species* ● *of Holding Forth*

Old Fart Holding Forth: the original kind, like Levi's. It's about Eisenhower, it's about Truman, it's about Roosevelt. It's about plumbing and the shit you're supposed to put on roses in the spring. It's about how Tony Dorsett doesn't have the damned right to ask that much money, and it's also about grandchildren. It's about FICA payments, it's about Lee Iaccoca, it's about storm windows.

It's about grandma, it's about grandpa, it's about grandma and grandpa's (1) disease, (2) will, (3) will. It's about growing old, not being too terribly graceful about it, and enjoying it all the while. *Atkinson's Thirty-third Rule of the Bar Bar,* stated with deep love for every Old Fart I've ever talked to: Old Farts *can* tell you a lot, if you'll just shut up and listen, which you generally have to do anyway.

There is as well *Ethnic Holding Forth,* for which I have one and only one exemplar. His name is Hawk; he is a garage attendant in Dallas. He is also my favorite person in the world to listen to. Man, can this Old Fart rap. Listen: "Damn *right!* Fact! Lesson of life, is meaning of life . . . essence of life. Lord, on my soul, how many chickens I stole! Take a BC and come back strong! Cause essence of life, being there of life. With thy rod and thy staff, go an' populate! Inveterate! Machinate! Everybody pick on me, but that's okay, 'cause, you go through *life,* invent life . . ." Hawk, love ya, you knucklehead.

You've also got the aforementioned *Sports Baiting Holding Forth; I Never Did Want to Live Here Holding Forth; Lemme Tell You 'Bout My Sprained Wrist Holding Forth; Old Lady Holding Forth.* You've got *My Kid's an Adolescent Holding Forth; Did You Read in the Paper Holding Forth. Alger Hiss Got Screwed Holding Forth. Horny Holding Forth.*

Uh oh. There you have it. Yep, it was bound to come up sooner or later, so let's just make this sooner. Not much to add, really: Horny Holding Forth is pretty self-explanatory, but it does involve *Atkinson's Thirty-fourth Rule of the Bar Bar:* The hustling of women is strictly prohibited in a Bar Bar. But talking about hustling women is encouraged.

Indeed, there are as many kinds of Holding Forth as there are kinds of Bar Barflies. But my personal favorite is the *Breakthrough Entrepreneurial Theory Holding Forth.* This is because this particular form of Holding Forth springs from a central, primordial fact of the Bar Bar Ethos: Inhabitants of the Bar Bar are, by definition, contra-mainstream in almost every way imaginable. They are eccentrics, loners, rebels, underdogs. Hence they have a strong tendency to believe they are getting screwed by just about everybody and everything, in particular taxing authorities and the free enterprise system.

Further hence, the average Bar Barfly is primally preoccupied with ways to beat the system. This can take a lot of forms, but a personal favorite is the scheme me and some drinking buddies at one of my Dallas haunts, The Bullington Point, concocted a year or so ago. This is what is known as Over Time Holding Forth, meaning that we'd bullshit about the same thing over and over for, say, a year. The Breakthrough Entrepreneurial Theory was developed by a banker friend. "It's really very simple," he said one afternoon. "Ever since you were a kid, you were taught to make a profit—personally, in business, whatever. That's okay until April 15 every year, when you generally go: Why in the fuck did I make all this money? Right?

"So my deal is to concentrate on loss, not profit. Stocks, real estate, whatever, I'm out to capture that capital loss like *early* in the year, so that when April rolls around, I don't owe the sumbitches nothing. Even got a motto: Don't lose that loss!"

As you might imagine, we had a dandy time running that one into the ground over the next several months. (*Atkinson's Thirty-fifth Rule of the Bar Bar:* Any observation, joke, argument, or anecdote that can be repeated will be.)

The key with the Breakthrough Entrepreneurial Theory, as well as other types of Holding Forth, is that it's got to be a tad harebrained, obtuse, and abstruse-kinky. For example, sports is fine, but something along the lines of just how the government computes your FICA payments is much better. It is also nice if the Holder Forth has no idea what he's talking about. Bad day at the office? That's okay, too, but *good* day at the office is much preferable, because it's always a complete lie. *Atkinson's Thirty-sixth Rule of the Bar Bar:* If more than one person is telling the truth or making sense at the same time, you aren't in a Bar Bar.

Ask Dr. Bar Bar

Also as a special service to my readers, I will from time to time answer pressing questions about Bar Bar life that have cropped up in the course of my travels.

Dear Dr. Bar Bar:

I was in a bar recently and paid cash for my drink. When the bartender returned my change, I stuck it back in my pocket just like I always do. But from then on, he treated me like a cancer patient. What did I do wrong?

Sincerely,

I'M REALLY NOT A NERD BUT I SURE FELT LIKE ONE

Dear I'M REALLY NOT A NERD BUT I SURE FELT LIKE ONE:

Wrong, wine-cooler-breath. You are a nerd. Every upstanding Bar Barfly knows that returned change must be left on the bar, for two very simple reasons. One, it indicates that you're going to buy another drink, which will generally warm the heart of any bartender. Two, it displays the appropriate faith in the Mother Church. You can even leave it there and go to the john. People lie and cheat in Bar Bars, but they never steal—and that applies even to the lowliest dive.

The Transcontinental Drunk, part 4:
Kansas City

Customer to no one in particular: *Well, hell, who gives a shit, right?*

A solid modus operandi had developed. My best Bar Bar hauntings had been of the scattershooting variety. I decided to do the whole damn project that way. I'll scattershoot the whole thing. See what happens. Anyway, that's why I wound up in Kansas City next.

Also, I had a serious Ruppy here. Actually, Tom Stephenson is a RRuppy, meaning a Rich and Recently Unemployed Person. Tom was in the bar business in Dallas, had bought up some land, somehow got a deal to sell all of it at a completely obnoxious price. Bingo: Rich and Recently Unemployed.

He knows his bars, though, and he definitely knows Kansas City, where he's from. His mom even lives there still. Name's Big Janet. She knows her Bar Bars too.

We headed out the first night without Big Janet, which was, by the way, a big mistake. Our first stop was Davy Markowitz's Uptown Rambler. No more necessary. Name's an automatic fivoroony. So's Davy.

Culturally, Kansas City may best be understood as a head-on collision between solid, bedrock middle-American values and Irish Catholic immigrant ethos—a nasty wreck if there ever was one. The place is crazy, is what it is, but it may be the best hidden jewel of a Bar Bar town I ran across (Providence is up there too).

Davy might be seen as standing in the middle of the aforementioned cultural collision, since Davy is Jewish. "Ah, the Jews always did screw the Micks," my friend Tom said as we bellied up at Davy's. Davy is a wizened wisp of a man who presides over his little joint with unceremonious paternalism. I was told the joint used to be a classic of the Kansas City Corrupt Political Bar genre and that at one time, the pols would gather in Davy's back room to hammer out how they were going to steal the next election.

That doesn't happen much anymore, but that's about all that would appear to have changed about this joint. It gets a 5 for Bar Bar Mustiness. Excellent crapola behind bar and a very nice You Go Figure: Davy doesn't play music; he plays all news/talk radio.

The evening we dropped by, a regular was lamenting the gradual attrition of the old gang. "There used to be twelve of us," he said, raising a wobbly finger toward a large round table in one corner. "Now there are only three." Tom had worked here as a kid and was anxious to get the regulars to tell me some of the great legend and lore of the joint. This exercise went generally like it always does: Nobody could remember shit. You know: "Yeah, all kindsa shit's happened in here. Davy, 'member that time . . . what was his name? You 'member."

"No, that was what's-his-face, wudn't it?"

"Maybe so, you 'member he . . . how it go now, I wanto get this right."

And so it went. I can't say that my minor attempt to develop some hard information worked all that well either. I was struck by the absolute poetry of the name of Davy's joint—it wins an Atkinson Transcontinental Award for Best Bar Bar Name in the nation—and so I asked the old fellow its derivation.

"That, oh yeah. See, we used to be located further uptown, and we just called it Davy's Uptown. But when we moved here, we weren't uptown anymore, so I added Rambler." Oh.

DAVY MARKOWITZ'S UPTOWN RAMBLER (3402 Main)

What You Feel Like When You Get There: 5+ (For name alone.)

Yuppity Doo Da: 5

Oh Say Can You See? 5

Crapola: 4

Holding Forth: 4

What You Feel Like After Three Drinks: 5 (That all news/talk radio in the background has a delicious effect.)

Just a Little Something to Wash My Drink Down With: 5

Old Fart Factor: 5 (Just for Davy.)

What You Feel Like When You Leave: 5

You Go Figure: 5

Nowhere Coefficient: 4.7

Headed on over to a place called Romanelli's, which is actually a tony little Italian restaurant and fairly screamed with Yuppity Doo Da. The bar was too bright and was presided over by the single worst kind of bartender in all of bardom: a Pretty Young Girl Who Knows It.

Despite all this negative vibration, the joint kind of grew on me. One real good reason was the Old Fart sitting next to me. This guy had refined Introspective Holding Forth to some kind of transcendent art that I could only marvel at. I'd barely gotten the stir stick out of my first one and he was off to the races. "Yeah, I'm seventy years old and all by myself. But, who gives a shit, right?" That's world class stuff, particularly when it was the furthest thing from being solicited.

"I haven't seen a woman in ten years, but who gives a shit, right? The pension's all set, and I'm goin' to Hawaii next week. Who gives a shit. I don't."

ROMANELLI'S (7116 Wornall Rd.)

What You Feel Like When You Get There: 2

Yuppity Doo Da: 2

Oh Say Can You See? 1

Crapola: 1

Holding Forth: 5

What You Feel Like After Three Drinks: 3

Just a Little Something to Wash My Drink Down With: 2

Old Fart Factor: 5

What You Feel Like When You Leave: 3

You Go Figure: 2

Nowhere Coefficient: 2.6

What could possibly be wrong with a place called Corner Cocktails? Not much, really. Solid New Collar joint with the obligatory pool tables, shuffleboard games, and cadre of mean-spirited Contra-Yuppies in mackinaws and gimme caps. Two of them were known as the Lobotomy Brothers, and based on the tone of the bartender's voice when he said it, I don't think it was all that much of a joke.

Two other things of note: One was the presence of that emergent Bar Barfly, the thirty-five-year-old overweight divorcee who will be glad to tell you life didn't really work out the way she had envisioned it, if you'll only ask. We didn't, but she told us anyway. "It's just that all the *sensitive* guys are taken. You know? I don't know, who gives a shit, right?" I was tempted to tell her to drop by Romanelli's the next evening, but got sidetracked overhearing the bartender eighty-sixing the Lobotomy Brothers. Something about an unpaid back tab.

CORNER COCKTAILS (downtown Kansas City)

What You Feel Like When You Get There: 3

Yuppity Doo Da: 5 (Contra-Yups.)

Oh Say Can You See? 4

Crapola: 3 (Serviceable sports-type crap.)

Holding Forth: 4 (Sex was on a lot of folks' minds, apparently. Guys on the other side of the lady were engaged in Contra Holding Forth, wherein one participant attempts to get the other to talk about something real Holding Forthy, like the fact that his wife's cheating on him, and the other guy refuses.)

What You Feel Like After Three Drinks: 3

Just a Little Something to Wash My Drink Down With: 3

Old Fart Factor: 2

What You Feel Like When You Leave: 3

You Go Figure: 4 (The Lobotomy Brothers?)

Nowhere Coefficient: 3.4

Well, no more nominations necessary. I found the Darkest Bar in America, and it is known as Milton's Tap Room; that'll be a fiver for the name as well. How dark was it? Put it this way: At a point, Tom was in the process of paying for another round and dropped a wad of about $70 on the floor. It was so dark *that* . . . none of us could find it. Just been swallowed up. After a few minutes of rummaging about on our hands and knees, Tom announced evenly, "Oh, fuck it." Any bar that can swallow money is *dark*.

But Milton's had its problems. One of them was that it allowed live jazz later in the evening and no, this didn't give me cause to grant an exemption to Atkinson's rule regarding *that*. Some kind of nasty, jangling fusion, which as you may know, is where the musicians decide they can't play the regular shit right so they combine some stuff. Apparently Milton had always fancied himself quite the cabaret owner, for behind the make-shift bandstand was a sign that read LAND OF 100 ENTERTAIN-ERS.

"That really wouldn't be so troubling," observed Tom, "except this joint's been around for at least sixty."

MILTON'S TAP ROOM (3241 Main St.)

> **What You Feel Like When You Get There:** 4
>
> **Yuppity Doo Da:** 4
>
> **Oh Say Can You See?** 5+
>
> **Crapola:** 5 (The sign alone gets a 5.)
>
> **Holding Forth:** 1 (Sorry, Holding Forth doesn't go with loud, bad jazz.)
>
> **What You Feel Like After Three Drinks:** 3
>
> **Just a Little Something to Wash My Drink Down With:** 5
>
> **Old Fart Factor:** 3
>
> **What You Feel Like When You Leave:** 3
>
> **You Go Figure:** 4 (Where *did* Tom's money go?)
>
> **Nowhere Coefficient:** 3.5

We Potlucked the last stop of the night, and while I can't say it was much of a Bar Bar, it was a solid cultural experience. Place called the Pink Garter Strip-o-Rama—that's right, a good old-fashioned strip joint. One thing can be said right off: The Pink Garter may be the only strip joint I've ever been in where they didn't hustle drinks. No kidding. We must have sat there for twenty minutes before some languid-eyed lady decided to take our order. Then she got it wrong.

Ah, but Major Art was just over the horizon. The Pink Garter was one of those joints where the girls pick out their favorite tune on the jukebox to do their number to. This was about the time the *We Are the World* mania was sweeping the nation so . . . *guess what?*

I swear I'm not making it up. Big black lady with thighs about the size of Fridge Perry's, just dancing up a storm to Lionel and Michael and The Boss and the rest of those do-gooders. Go figure indeed. Tom was right: It was definitely serious art, serious art being the melding of two types of pornography—in this case, the dancer and the song. Tell you what, too: That woman could clear a room. We weren't even up to Michael's "When you're down and out" riff and there was a line at the door—heading out.

From time to time, you've probably wondered just how serious I was about this. *Rough work but somebody had to do it indeed.* The following should dispel any qualms you may have about my willingness to give this project 110 percent—which, by the way, is precisely the percentage of my advance that I spent on the damn thing. (Wrote it off, too: Don't lose that loss!)

The following morning, I arose at 6 A.M. to participate in the damnedest drinking ritual with which I have ever been associated; and that would include some stuff I did in college that I couldn't even bear to put in print. The bar in question was Kelley's, which claims to be the oldest in Kansas City; and if it isn't that, it certainly is the funkiest. The ritual was the Morning Shift, that bunch of graveyard-shift workers and plain old hard cores who watch the sun *come up* through a glass darkly.

Sure enough, the joint was jumping when I arrived about 6:45: twenty or so regulars, including a rowdy bunch of New Collar types playing grab-ass over in one corner. But my interest was in the bunch at the bar, a collection of half a dozen of the finest Old Farts I've ever seen. I had coffee, thank you, but the guy next to me was banging down Wild Turkey 101, *up*—that's no ice, no nuthin. He said he was a truck driver and was used to weird hours. I decided to ask him a burning question, one that had been on my mind since arriving: "Uh, what do you do, you know, when you *leave* here?"

He slugged on the Turkey and replied, "Well today, I'm gonna work on my truck."

"Nothing, complex, I gather."

"Nah, just some electrical stuff." Yikes.

We had a dandy round of Holding Forth thereafter. Turned out he was a cat lover. "Yeah, I got this stray I've kinda adopted. Little all-white thing. Named him Shitbird. Hey, he comes to it just like he would to any other name, so I figured, who gives a shit. 'Course,

Atkinson's Travel Tip #2

At hand in this installment is the matter of travel arrangements
for your Transcontinental Drunk. A few tips from one who may
not be older or wiser, but who is certainly the only idiot you
know of who's ever done this.

1.   Try to find a travel agent who is also a bookie—like mine.
     Aside from being able to commingle accounts, these folks
     know how to cheat anybody they suspect is richer than
     they—which would include airlines, hotel chains, and rent-
     a-car companies.
2.   Don't even countenance a flight before the hour of noon.
3.   Don't tell the cabdriver why you're in town on business.
     Through firsthand experience, I can tell you that cabdrivers
     sit at the opposite end of the axis from Ruppies when it
     comes to Bar Bar tips.
4.   Stay in a hotel that offers the following amenities: down-
     town or near-downtown location; plenty of cabs; decent
     lobby bar for warm-up and warm-down; Do Not Disturb
     signs; 24-hour room service; check-cashing privileges.
5.   Wangle multiple check-cashing privileges.

it doesn't impress a lady much when you bring her home and the first thing you say is 'Here, Shitbird.'"

At this point we were joined by Mr. Shakes. Mr. Shakes is more or less a universal Bar Bar character, but this was about as serious a case of alcohol palsy as I've ever seen. Guy drank Jim Beam and he was, in that grand Bar Bar tradition, definitely a look-ma-no-hands kind of drinker. Yep: just lowered that mouth to the straw, took a big slurp, and uprighted again. Mr. Shakes wasn't in a real good mood either.

"I'm gonna go on over here," he said, retreating to a table and losing about half his drink during the trek. "I'm gonna sort some things out. You know, I don't really like people that much."

Later he returned to the bar, seemingly refreshed from his inward journey. "You know," he said, triumphantly lifting the glass to his lips. "I owe my life to Jim Beam." You can sit at my bar anytime, buddy.

I can't possibly describe the surreality of watching the sun rise from a *bar*. It's like the sensation of walking backwards or sleeping during the daytime. Or like when you skip a meal. Everything's upside down, backwards, out of whack. The whole world's a tuxedo and you're a pair of brown shoes. At a point, you don't want to leave, ever, because somehow you're afraid life out there won't ever make sense again—and in a way it doesn't. If nothing else, that's a good reason to keep Bar Bars around. They're a good place to remind yourself that life wasn't intended to make sense, and at that, wasn't intended to be fair either.

The morning dragged on and soon enough the regular bartender arrived, and it didn't take long for him to earn a special Atkinson Transcontinental Award for Best Insulting Bartender in America. Observing Mr. Shakes, he commented, "That sumbitch has been in here more hours than *I* have this week."

He'd had a bit of a rough night himself, it seems, and he proceeded to perform the damnedest hangover drinking ritual I've ever seen. Mixed himself a big, nasty screwdriver; then without comment or fanfare, strapped a bar towel about his neck and hoisted the drink up to his mouth, pulley-style. "You oughtta try it, Charley," he said to Mr. Shakes. "Cuts down on spillage."

Elsewhere Kelley's made a solid bid for Atkinson's Top 10 as well. A particularly nice touch was Repeat Crapola, which is where you can observe dozens of different renderings of the same thing on the back bar wall. It can be the bartender or owner, a famous visitor to the bar, whatever. In this case, the object of immortalization was the Kelley's edifice itself, which was displayed about the walls in cartoon form, in architect's rendering form, in photos from every conceivable angle. And amidst the self-serving crapola was another gem: a rumpled old black and white photo of an extremely drunk and unidentified regular from the past.

My final discovery about this place definitely eased it into Atkinson's Top 10. Kelley's does have food, but it is the damndest and most endearing Just a Little Something to Wash My Drink Down With I ran across. (1) It's Mexican food, which is a 5 for You Go Figure alone. (2) It's Mexican food as could only be interpreted by an Irish pub: Menu includes stuff like cactus salad, which they don't even have down my way. (3) The restaurant portion at the rear is not actually owned or run by Kelley's. The way I heard it—and this is one of those things that just has to be true, even if it isn't (Yes, that would be *Atkinson's Thirty-seventh Rule of the Bar Bar*)—the ownership at Kelley's found the idea of food-in-bar so distasteful they decided to *lease* part of their unused space to a restaurateur. Now *that* is some serious theology.

KELLEY'S (500 Westport Rd.)

> **What You Feel Like When You Get There:** 5 (6:45 A.M. in a Bar Bar.)
>
> **Yuppity Doo Da:** 5
>
> **Oh Say Can You See?** 5 (Especially impressive was that somehow, even after the sun was up, it didn't intrude.)
>
> **Crapola:** 5
>
> **Holding Forth:** 5+

What You Feel Like After Three Drinks: 5 (Special credit to insulting bartender.)

Old Fart Factor: 5+ (Any place that includes a Mr. Shakes is a 5; the rest was gravy.)

Just a Little Something to Wash My Drink Down With: 5+

What You Feel Like When You Leave: 5 (Very, very disoriented.)

You Go Figure: 5

Nowhere Coefficient: 5 (!!!)

I rounded out my trip to KC that night with an odd but fitting little scattershoot that involved solely Anti-Bar Bars. It made a perverse kind of sense, having spent that very morning immersed in the real thing. Anti-Bar Barhopping is not advisable as a steady diet, but as an occasional aberration, it actually has some religious value: No better way to remember where Nowhere is than by going to some Somewheres.

My hotel was across the street from Alameda Plaza, which claims to be the oldest shopping center in Kansas City, but it certainly doesn't reflect that in its bars—one being the ubiquitous Houlihan's, the genetically deficient offspring of the inbreeding of Friday's and Bennigan's. The resulting mutant is an even crazier mix of colliding ersaatzes than some of those joints I stumbled upon in New York.

Reviewing the menu, the decor, the dress of the help, I was able to decipher the following attempted subliminal messages from Houlihan's Inc.: Irish pub, New York steak house, French bistro, Los Angeles dance bar, Boston hotel lobby tea room. And that's just what I could decipher through my post-Kelley's, post-nap haze. Landsakes, you guys, I know that since their inception fern bars have always been about being Somewhere—and Somewhere Else at that. But you're throwing a whole *bunch* of Somewheres at these poor patrons, and the only reason I can think of is that you want their circuits to be overloaded when they get the tab.

I moved on to another mutant, Graffon's, and discovered some-

thing else about these joints. It is perversely fitting that the Benni-
gans and Houlihans and Mulligans of the world begin and end with
the fern. For in their way, they are as foreboding and enveloping
as a Costa Rican fern forest. You are entering strange and ominous
territory when you walk in, and no matter how careful you are to
stay on your toes, sooner or later the strength of the undergrowth
will pull you under. Example? Okay. I maneuvered my way
through the bramble of lip gloss and tartan plaid and finally caught
a bartender's attention. (By the way: *Atkinson's Thirty-eighth
Rule of the Bar Bar:* Any joint with more than one bartender
working at the same time is not a Bar Bar.) I ordered a vodka and
soda. I know I said it loudly and succinctly because Huey Lewis
and the News had been turned up to mega-decibel.

Bartender returned and flopped down a . . . Kahlua and soda.
Yikes! Gadzooks! I'd ordered a regular drink, I really had, guys. But
the force field of the fern bar, the cosmic power, had just whisked
the request off to some black hole and served me a froufrou! It was
terrifying, humiliating. I knew better than to reorder. The demon
who controls this universe, the Darth Vader of bardom, would
have once again rendered that bartender deaf and dumb. He
wanted me to have that Kahlua and soda and somehow I knew
that I would not be able to leave unless I drank it. I did, and
returned to my hotel room ruefully remembering *Atkinson's
Thirty-ninth Rule of the Bar Bar:* Beware the fern bar. It can be
a sobering experience.

Bar Bar 301: More Advanced Theology (on Bar Bar Characters)

Customer: *I'm telling you, Reagan was the illegitimate son of Mary Pickford . . .*
Other customer: *No he wasn't. He was adopted.*

If you've ever been in a Bar Bar, *anywhere,* you've met either or both of these guys. Every decent Bar Bar is grounded in a core cast of universal characters. Regular crowds in Bar Bars vary in size and scope, come and go to a certain extent. But every Bar Bar has these guys, these guys being Mr. Knowsit and his faithful sidekick, Mr. Hellyoudo.

Mr. Knowsit and Mr. Hellyoudo are generally Middle Farts, and their pedagogical and argumentative impulses have little to do with vocation. Teachers have been known to inhabit Bar Bars, but they rarely turn out to be Mr. Knowsits or Mr. Hellyoudos. No, Mr. Knowsits and Mr. Hellyoudos are among that growing breed of Bar Barfly—the slightly prematurely retired guy who's found a way out of a generally banal profession or craft and is now going to make the rest of us pay for the fact that he had to put up or shut up all those years. I know this well because my dad is a Mr. Knowsit.

Mr. Knowsit's academic credentials are, in fact, quite suspect: He tends to be more your self-taught kind of guy, and one who skews to the arcane at that. What do Mr. Knowsits know most about? It really can vary, but my research revealed these topics:

1. Home repair, particularly of the electrical variety.
2. The tax code.
3. Long-term investments.
4. Gardening.
5. Divorce.
6. Family lineages and other scintilla about people in the news.
7. The revised tax code.
8. The problem with———(fill in name of your local football or baseball team.)
9. DWI law.
10. Revised DWI law.

In my experience, Mr. Knowsit's extemporizations on these and other matters don't really sparkle in the absence of Mr. Hellyoudo, and this has to do with *Atkinson's Fortieth Rule of the Bar Bar:* Every lie has a counter-lie. The latter is Mr. Hellyoudo's responsibility in each and every case, because generally speaking, elsewise a Mr. Knowsit is going to be surrounded by a crowd of Mr. Ondeafears. The critical duty of Mr. Hellyoudo is not merely to dispute as obnoxiously as he possibly can, but to substitute a larger mistruth. Tough work, but somebody has to do it and I'd like to hand over a special Atkinson Transcontinental Award to that Mr. Hellyoudo at the Chart Room in New Orleans.

This Mr. Hellyoudo was a former shipping agent or some such, and his symbiotic Mr. Knowsit was a former truck driver. Uh oh. You got it: Serious The Best Way to Get There Holding Forth.

Mr. Knowsit: "You know, you take the back road to Baton Rouge and you can cut eight minutes off the Interstate. First time I did, I didn't think it was possible. But I kept usin' it, and damned if I didn't make a discovery."

Mr. Hellyoudo: "That might be true on a weekend, but I drove those roads for years, *years,* and you get out there on Wednesday morning and no way you're going to beat the Interstate."

Mr. Knowsit: "I been out there on Wednesday morning."

Mr. Hellyoudo: "Hell you have. If you were, it musta been a day when everybody in that part of the state was at a funeral."

Mr. Knowsit: "No it was just last week . . ."

Mr. Hellyoudo: "Well, that's simple. That's when they had the Interstate all torn up with construction."

No doubt you've got a Mr. Knowsit and a Mr. Hellyoudo someplace in your life, even if you don't habituate Bar Bars. Here are some others you may recognize.

● *Atkinson's Supplemental Bar Bar Field Guide* ●

Mr. Don'tknowit: For a reason that remains a mystery, this fellow is generally at the other end of the bar from Mr. Knowsit. He loves to opinionate, pontificate, relate; he is a seriously motivated Holder Forth. His only problem is that his end of the conversation contains absolutely no facts. Example: "I read in the paper the other day where that big fellow who plays for Chicago . . . what's his name? Anyway, he's gonna do this commercial with that big guy from Dallas. You know, that one with the funny nickname. Oh, what's that guy from Chicago's name?"

Dr. Dryout: Individual who is in a constant state of going on the wagon, being on the wagon, or having just got off the wagon. Of course, like everyone else in a Bar Bar he's a complete liar.

Bar Fool: Any one of a small number of particularly dull, obnoxious, or unliked Bar Bar regulars who are indulged and tolerated because like most balanced environs, Bar Bars need prey as well as predators. By the way, you can recognize the Bar Bar Fool by the simple fact that even though he might have been drinking there for a decade, he still has no clear territory at the bar—no favored stool or previously staked-out place to stand. Hence he can generally be found standing someplace silly, like smack in the middle of the room, dutifully receiving his sustenance from the help whenever they choose to serve him.

Captain 86: Bar Barfly who by current measure has been eighty-sixed or otherwise punished by the high tribunal of the Bar Bar the most times in recent memory. As you might imagine, you frequently have several Lieutenant 86s.

Mr. Knowsthehelp: I ran into a lot of these, being as how I was generally a stranger in the Bar Bars I visited. Every Bar Barfly, of course, knows the help, but this guy makes a production of it with loud and constant use of first names and intimate references.

The Scoremaster: You probably knew this guy as a "cocksman" in high school or the fraternity or the Marine Corps. Only difference with him is he never grew out of bragging about Sex That Never Happened. Always leads Holding Forth sweepstakes in Horny Holding Forth, regardless of how much he claims he's gotten.

Mr. He'salwaysthere: These types generally pass muster on your 3 P.M. bar check. That's because whatever business they're in, they do it out of the Bar Bar. I have a good friend who drinks at Joe Miller's and does quite well in real estate brokerage, and I swear, he takes all his messages, cuts most of his deals, even reviews documents at the Bar Bar. 'Course, he does some drinking there, too, which has led to some times he hasn't done so well at real estate brokerage. Like the time he took a client out to show him a prime swatch of acreage and just *never* did find it. Closed the deal too, or at least that's what he said.

Mr. He'sneverthere: Always that truest of Bar Bar devotees, this fellow, of course, is there a *lot* and he tends to get a lot of phone calls. But he's the only guy who *never,* under any circumstances, takes one.

The Man With No Job: Most inhabitants of Bar Bars have somewhat unclear means of support. Over time, even the ones you don't get to know that well emerge as retirees, lawyers, journalists, or some other kind of lout. But you can know The Man With

No Job for ten years and still hear other regulars ask, "What does he do now?"

The Old Fart: You already know a lot about him, and you're going to hear a lot more, for he is the true glue of any Bar Bar, less conspicuous than Mr. Knowsit but ultimately more important. After all, Old Farts have spent a long time searching out Nowhere, so it stands to reason that wherever they are has got to be it. (*Atkinson's Forty-first Rule of the Bar Bar,* by the way.)

The Transcontinental Drunk, part 5: New Orleans

Customer to bartender: *I guess I'll have one more . . .*
Bartender to customer: *You want the other three now, or later?*

I 've heard that conversation many more times than once, and it has to do with *Atkinson's Forty-second Rule of the Bar Bar:* There is no such thing as one drink. I have frequented about half a dozen Bar Bars in my career and I can tell you as scientific fact that I have never seen anyone have *one* drink. It's akin to a law of physics—immutable.

I bring all this up because my nose next led me south to New Orleans, and there is no better place on earth to be reminded of the aforementioned truism than in this place. Jesus, this isn't a town full of Bar Bars; this town *is* a Bar Bar. You can drink twenty-four hours a day here, on the streets and in your car. New Orleans is the Big Bar Bar in the Sky, the Cosmic Bar Bar, and that is why if there seem to be a few, uh, holes in the presentation here, it's because New Orleans afforded me my first encounter with Memory Loss.

More on that later (or is it less?). Part of what led me to the Crescent City was that by now my stream of consciousness mode of research had refined itself even further. I wasn't really just following my nose toward towns with great Bar Bar cultures; I was following tips on great Ruppies.

New Orleans is a town filled with Ruppies and I must say, I'm pretty sure I was led to the top dog. Name's Chappy Hardy and he led me on the damnedest three-day scattershoot of Bar Bars that's ever escaped my memory. The Chap-man gets an Atkinson Transcontinental Award for that; and he also gets one for Best Bar Scattershooting Transport. Drove a souped-up and redone old Checker cab. It's big, it's a bully, you can take a nap in it, keep a *lot* of beer in it. But the main thing is, you can trash it.

The afternoon I arrived Chap-man was busy doing whatever it is he pretends to do for a living, so I decided to get my feet wet just the way any tourist would: I wandered down Bourbon Street in the French Quarter to one of the two Old Absinthe Bars. This is an Oldest Bar in City type and as such, a potential Six Flags Over Bar Bar. But credit should go to the Chamber of Commerce or someone: For a tourist trap, the French Quarter of New Orleans has done a better job of avoiding the Tourist Bar Bar trap than any other city I visited.

Joint's been around since 1806, so that should tell you that the crapola is just fine. The basic motif is unique indeed. Instead of beer company clocks and sundry other stuff, Absinthe has plastered the walls with one-dollar bills signed by drunken regulars and tourists. "There's more than $10,000 up there," said the young bartendress. "I counted 'em." That's not bad as Bartender Lies go.

A kind of amusing diversion here is tourist watching. You quickly discover that most tourists don't actually *enter* joints like the Old Absinthe Bar; they just kind of turkey-neck their heads in the door and gawk. Allow me one more quick sociological observation: I had for some time wondered where people from Kansas go when they vacate. I now know at least one place they go. Gadzooks, I've never seen so many lumpy moms and pops in imitation Adidas sweats in my life. And yeah, it's true: Kansans don't appear to be having fun, even when they're on vacation.

THE OLD ABSINTHE BAR (400 Bourbon St.)

What You Feel Like When You Get There: 3

Yuppity Doo Da: 5

Oh Say Can You See? 4

Crapola: 5

Holding Forth: 3 (I was the only one in the bar for a while, but the bartendress was a serviceable conversation partner.)

What You Feel Like After Three Drinks: 3

Just a Little Something to Wash My Drink Down With: 5 (A lot of New Orleans bars eschew food altogether, which is nice. Those that do serve food serve Cajun food, which is very acceptable stuff, so you're going to see a lot of 5s here.)

Old Fart Factor: 4

What You Feel Like When You Leave: 3

You Go Figure: 4 (Dollar bill crapola.)

Nowhere Coefficient: 3.9

The Chap-man and I had been underway for about an hour later that evening when I realized New Orleans would demand a slight modification of my rating process. This is because New Orleanians don't really drink at just one bar or the other. Rather, they tend to drink at clusters of bars in the same neighborhood, sort of a Neighborhood as Bar Bar concept.

The cluster we ran that night included seven or so bars of almost identical exterior and interior styling. Just a low-slung, wood-frame shotgun-type structure, with a long bar, a loud jukebox, and a busy pool table. We cycled and recycled through these bars God knows how many times. Fortunately, Chappy had

---

Fun Facts

In 1935 only 90,000 gallons of distilled spirits were shipped to the United States from Puerto Rico. In 1984 the number was 20,556,000.

---

agreed to remain straight and sober for the driving.

We'd have a pop at Franky and Johnny's, then over to the Parkview, then the Parkway Inn, then Jed's, then the Maple Leaf, then back to Franky and Johnny's, then on to the F and M Patio. It all became a dizzying blur, and at one time I felt like I was in the midst of one of those Irwin Allen disaster flicks like *Earthquake*, where even though the setting is Los Angeles, the same eight characters keep running into one another all the time. It was pretty much the same crowd in each joint, Bar Cycling just like we were, a drinking custom I've really never seen before or since.

What's nice is that because of New Orleans' lax (or sophisticated if you wish) drinking laws, you can just sort of take an unfinished toddie with you to the next joint. You can take it in with you or just stand out in the street and drink, which is what we did at my personal favorite in this cluster, Benny's Bar.

Street Corner as Bar Bar is a very nice touch and reminded me of my fraternity days. Just a bunch of us guys, standing around sipping Dixie beer, talkin' some sports and making fun of the passersby. Great fun!

One thing you learn quickly with New Orleans Bar Bars is that you can't escape the presence of the outdoors. The Bunker style doesn't have much presence here: Almost all the joints have all their windows or French doors wide open, day and night; and many have patios. And a few, like Benny's, have a serviceable street corner. But the magic is that you can still find Bar Bar isolation. That street corner was its own kind of Nowhere.

One other thing you can't escape with New Orleans Bar Bars is music. Gad-o-rama. You've got live—some good, some bad. You've mainly got jukeboxes—of every conceivable stripe. Oldies jukeboxes. Yuppy jukeboxes (Huey Lewis and the News again). Yuppy Oldy jukeboxes. Blues jukeboxes; soul jukeboxes. Jazz jukeboxes. You name it. New Orleans definitely gets an Atkinson Transcontinental Award for Greatest Number and Widest Array of Jukeboxes; though if I had my druthers, I'd pitch most of 'em into Lake Pontchartrain.

Our cycling pace wound down at a joint called the F and M Patio, where I met a regular I came to call The Rapper, basically because he was full of non-stop bullshit. "I dunno what I'd do without this bar," he said. "Die maybe." He allowed that he lived upstairs—which one-ups Al at Gino and Carlo's. That's some serious regulardom when you basically have Bar Bar as residence. "Yeah, I got three new pool cues. Wanna see 'em?" Uh, no thanks, Rapper.

The Rapper was blond, slight, and somewhat misshapen in an indiscernible way. Indiscernible, at least, to everyone but Chap's doctor buddy who'd joined us. "Looks like scoliosis to me," he said matter-of-factly. "I wouldn't give him a full life." Thanks a heap, Doc. *Atkinson's Forty-third Rule of the Bar Bar:* Pretty much anybody's welcome in a Bar Bar with the exception of doctors and federal bureaucrats.

I know I promised that the sociology was over, but just one more itty-bitty observation: One other superlative that may be applied to New Orleans Bar Bars is that they are the most integrated I hung out at—*anywhere.* If that doesn't seem to make sense it's because it doesn't. The only possible explanation is not really a bad one: The New Orleans drinking ethos is so strong, so total, that it supersedes every other possible distinction people might be tempted to make amongst themselves: race, economic class, gender, you name it. Or as a good friend who grew up in New Orleans told me: "People in New Orleans are dedicated to fucking off. As long as you're fucking off, people don't care much else about you."

Because of the peculiar nature of New Orleans Bar Bars I'm going to rate most of them in clusters. This will also serve the purpose of glossing over the considerable amount of detail about particular joints that at some point just slithered off my left anterior lobe. I won't lie. I fucked off in New Orleans too.

F AND M PATIO 4841 Tchoupitoulas, **FRANKY AND JOHN-NY'S** 321 Arabella, **BENNY'S BAR** 933 Valence, **THE PARK-VIEW** 910 N. Carrolton, **THE PARKWAY INN** 5135 Canal, **JED'S** 8301 Oak, **THE MAPLE LEAF** 8316 Oak

What You Feel Like When You Get There: 3

Yuppity Doo Da: 5

Oh Say Can You See? 5

Crapola: 1 (New Orleans Bar Bars aren't into crapola, for some reason.)

Holding Forth: 3

What You Feel Like After Three Drinks: 4

Just a Little Something to Wash My Drink Down With: 5

What You Feel Like When You Leave: 4

You Go Figure: 5

Nowhere Coefficient: 3.5

A second worthwhile cluster may be found in the French Quarter, if you're careful to stay out of the way of Frank and Mabel from Wichita. It even includes the Way Too Famous for Its Own Good Pat O'Brien's: Key here is to skip the piano bar and the patio bar, unless you're one of those people who think something called a Hurricane is actually an acceptable cocktail. When you walk in, hook a hard left. There is a tiny little shotgun-type bar there where the locals hang out, and as you might imagine, it is some serious Bar Bar because of its surroundings.

I can't really in good conscience call Cosmo's in the Quarter a Bar Bar, but it's worth dropping by just to see the bartendress's tan. Absolutely sinful. *Atkinson's Forty-fourth Rule of the Bar Bar:* If you see someone who looks vaguely healthy, you're probably not in a Bar Bar.

Trujaques near the market is a nice exemplar of the New Orleans Day Bar Bar, which means it's too bright. But the experience of sipping a Bloody Mary by a French door wide open to the street is definitely something that can grow on you. Trujaques also earned an Atkinson Transcontinental Award for Best Communique on Wall just out of left field. Most decent Bar Bars have amongst their wall crapola one or two oddball solicitations or pleas for something or another. Mostly they have to do with off-the-wall political groups or abstruse self-help programs. But I have never

before or since seen one quite like the advertisement posted at
Trujaques: WE BUY DEAD CATS, it said. 23 FEB., 3 P.M. BE THERE.
All righty.

The Chart Room and the Napoleon House are more or less
identical time-honored Power Bar Bars, where what passes for the
local political structure hangs out and mulls over who they're
going to cheat out of what next. I grew especially fond of the Chart
Room, for despite the large French doors it has an excellent Oh
Say Can You See? factor, and the Weather Holding Forth I heard
there was definitely the real thing. "Yeah, you can pretty much get
all four seasons in one day in New Orleans," observed the fellow
next to me.

But the real gems in the Quarter cluster were a couple of
Potlucks I tried. One more Atkinson Transcontinental Award:
New Orleans is the best Potluck Bar Bar town I ran across. You
almost can't miss, but Harry's Place and Fritzel's were real winners. The former caught my eye based on name alone, and it
didn't disappoint. A nice touch in a lot of New Orleans Bar Bars
is a simple concrete floor, which gives the place a spartan and
utilitarian feel: You're here to drink, by God, so there shouldn't
be any need for frills like carpeting or, worse, hardwood floor-
ing.

Bartender at Harry's was an immense old fellow who inadvert-
ently coined *Atkinson's Forty-fifth Rule of the Bar Bar.* Responding to a particularly putrid joke that had been related by a regular,
he said, "You know, I've been back here for more than thirty
years, and one thing I've learned is that jokes aren't funny." He's
right. Ad libs can be funny; people are definitely funny. But jokes
never have been and never will be.

Fritzel's, as you can probably guess, is a definitely not-ersatz
German beer joint which features, among other things, real loud
and bad German music on the jukebox. Ordinarily I like German
music about as much as I like, say, mariachi music, but here on
lower Bourbon Street the effect was such a stunning You Go Figure that I kind of got into it.

TRUJAQUES, THE CHART ROOM, THE NAPOLEON HOUSE, HARRY'S PLACE, FRITZEL'S (all in the French Quarter)

What You Feel Like When You Get There: 4

Yuppity Doo Da: 4

Oh Say Can You See? 5

Crapola: 1

Holding Forth: 4

What You Feel Like After Three Drinks: 4

Just a Little Something to Wash My Drink Down With: 5

Old Fart Factor: 4

What You Feel Like When You Leave: 4

You Go Figure: 4

Nowhere Coefficient: 4.1

A slightly different cluster in the Quarter involves old Greek seamen's bars, and one good bit of advice here would be to visit in the daylight. The Tradewinds, the Acropolis, and the Atheneum Room are more or less indistinguishable dives, but the Holding Forth at The Tradewinds was superior. Conversation was about how this guy had gotten thrown through the window one night the week before and no, it didn't register on the Atkinson Lie Meter.

But the ultimate You Go Figure in New Orleans had nothing to do with a Bar Bar; it was at a restaurant. Long about night number three, having spent the previous seventy-two hours stuffing myself with crawfish and crab, I got an intense craving for good old-fashioned grease. I wanted a cheeseburger, *bad,* and that ain't the easiest thing to find in the French Quarter.

As if by fate, however, a good old-fashioned diner—or what

appeared to be a good old-fashioned diner—just suddenly appeared across the street. I wasted no time taking Potluck. This turned out to be a mistake, for what I had stumbled upon was an ersatz diner, which puts the Atkinson Ersatz Meter right into the red. That's New Orleans for you: The whole damn town is a Bar Bar and the whole damn town is a You Go Figure.

10

Bar Bar 401: Not Quite Totally Advanced Theology (on Bar Bar Etiquette)

Bar Bar regular to other Bar Bar regular, elsewhere: *Hey Frank, what's happening?*
Oh, Joe! I didn't recognize you in the daylight.

Maintaining one's standing in a Bar Bar is not at all an effortless task. Yes, showing up and paying your tab every now and then will generally keep you in good graces, but there is a broader range of etiquette that must be observed as well.

Bar Bars are set up on a positive reinforcement model. You follow the rules, show that you're a stand-up kind of guy, and over time the bartender extends certain privileges. For example, never throwing up will earn you something like triple-digit check-writing privileges; not hustling the help may get you a fifteen-day extension on your tab. (Tabs are generally paid every thirty days, and that particular day is not a happy one.)

Joe Miller has been deceased now for a year, but I can't say that any of his rules of the Bar Bar have wilted in the least. As with most bartenders, Joe's rules were an extension of his personality—meaning they were arbitrary and somewhat abstruse. But even if you didn't understand them, you followed them, for truly there is no worse feeling on earth than being on the outs with one's Bar Bar.

I know this firsthand because I was once eighty-sixed from Joe's for the unseemly sin of singing. Joe hated singing and had every right to, but you know how it goes: me and a couple of buddies had strapped in for a Transcontinental at a rear table and as generally happens on these voyages, we became engrossed in that academic exercise known as Try to Remember All the Lyrics. This is generally no big deal if you're dealing with something like "Satisfaction" by the Stones. But we were trying to remember all the lyrics to Marty Robbins' "El Paso."

It goes without saying, so let's not say it. Not only did this involve syntactical matter, but narrative problems as well. For example, I thought I had it down cold until one of my buddies pointed out that I had the guy in the saloon *after* somebody had shot him. "It's called cause and effect, dumbshit," he observed.

Joe tried to be patient, he really did. But at the 57-decibel level, he'd had enough. "Get the fuck outta here and for the next week do your drinking at some other McGilly." Joe said a lot of stuff like that. Whether telling a joke or issuing an admonition, he'd always set it up in plain English and then drop in some private gibberish on the punch line—so that you really didn't know what he meant.

We did, though. The problem with being eighty-sixed is deciding what to do next. I have some do's and don'ts here:

1. *Don't* go back in the next day and apologize. That's not enough time, and also it shows some weakness on your part. Say, two days.
2. Don't go in then, either.
3. When you do go back in, make sure Joe or his equivalent is not there.
5. When you do go back in, don't sing.
6. Thinking on it . . . don't go back in then, either.

You're going to have to go back sooner or later, so here's what you do when you do: Lie. Any childhood variety will do. That's right, blame it on any possible co-conspirator. "Hey, it wasn't *me* who needed to know for some goddamn reason why he fell for the wicked Felina . . ." was my first gambit. "And oh yeah, Joe, sorry." These sorts of make-amends were received with priestly grace by Joe, who, like any good parent, knew it was the thought that counted. Then he'd usually buy you one on the house.

Actually, there are two layers of Bar Bar Etiquette: the one a set of covenants between patron and bartender, the other a slightly more ethereal set of agreements between fellow regulars.

● *Atkinson's Newly Abridged Field Guide* ● *to Bar Bar Etiquette*

Patron-Bartender Relations

The following basics are required of the Bar Bar patron:

1. Show up.
2. Show up fairly often.
3. Don't play grab-ass with the female help.
4. Pay your tab every thirty days; tip minimum 20 percent.
5. If you are paying cash, pay with a twenty-dollar bill or larger and leave the change on the bar.
6. *Never* refuse a drink on the house from the bartender or manager. Yes, this would even include that particular free cocktail known as a Retrograder. More on this later in Advanced Theology, but as the name implies, this single drink, because of its timing, generally has the effect of blowing any lofty intentions you might have had of going home.
7. Laugh at the bartender's jokes.
8. If you've changed your normal cocktail of choice for some reason, announce it when you hit the door.
9. No singing or dancing.
10. No fighting.
11. No Holding Forth over 51.7 decibels.
12. Dogs and kids are accepted. Wives? It's a long story, so just wait for Advanced Theology.
13. Don't stiff the bartender's bookie.
14. Don't stiff the bartender if *he* is a bookie.
15. Required monthly expenditures vary, but as a general rule of thumb, try to spend at least as much as you do on food.
16. If you run into the bartender at another joint and you still owe him for that month, don't offer to buy him a drink.

The following, in turn, are required of the bar:

1. Thirty-day tabs.
2. Check-writing privileges.
3. Betting privileges.
4. A drink on the house every now and then—particularly on tab collection day.
5. Responsiveness to requests to reduce candlepower in room or decibel level of music, if applicable.
6. Responsiveness to request for depth charge in cocktail.
7. Secretarial services, up to and including lying to the wife should she call the bar.
8. Regular and personalized insults.
9. Automatic recall of patron's favored libation, second favored libation, wife's name, and latest notable success or failure in business.
10. Unlimited sympathy.

Far more intricate is the set of codes that has developed between Bar Bar patrons. I saw some variations in these in my travels, but remarkably few, considering the ethnic and economic range I traversed. The Holding Forth Rule of Reciprocity is, of course, universal. Failure to listen when it's your turn, or to pitch in your fair share of bullshit, is grounds for something much worse than eighty-sixing. You could become an Untouchable, an orbit that rests someplace beyond the Bar Fool. The ostracism here is subtle, but cruel, and there's really not very much the bartender can do about it. As earlier noted, Bar Bars are self-policing ecosystems, and in many ways the unspoken rules amongst regulars are more inviolate than those handed down by the bartender.

Other do's and don'ts of this genre:

1. If a fellow regular buys you one, *do* return the favor. It's a bit untoward to do it that very night, unless you're both on a Transcontinental. But it's certainly expected within the week.
2. If the Bar Fool buys you one, *don't* buy him one back.

3. Don't hustle lady regulars. This is strictly bush league. Now if it's somebody's wife or girlfriend or something, fine.

4. You lady regulars: *Do* buy fellow male regulars drinks; it'll be understood.

5. *Do* spread yourself around. Bar Bars in and of themselves are the very definition of a clique; but cliques within the clique are frowned upon. Other than the Bar Fool and sundry Untouchables, you are expected to play with the cards you have been dealt, regardless of when you arrive and who happens to be there.

6. *Don't* make fun of Mr. Knowsit. He may be obnoxious, but he's too valuable to the life flow of the Bar Bar.

7. *Do* make fun of Dr. Dryout whenever you want. You can always find another Dr. Dryout if you run him off.

8. If a fellow regular appears to be hung over, *do* bring it up. As with terminal cancer patients, honesty and forthrightness are always the best policy. Besides, really the only joy in the particular condition of the hangover is being able to talk about it.

9. It is, however, *not* de rigueur to bring up your own hangover, which would be sort of like bringing up your own terminal cancer.

10. For matters involving marital infidelity, divorce, Chapter 11 bankruptcy, herpes, and impending root canals, the reverse is true. Problems caused by forces outside the Bar Bar are strictly your own and it is up to you to put them on the floor for discussion.

11. Contrary to some belief, Bar Bars are about drinking and communing; but they are not about the considerably less civilized process of getting drunk. Leave that to the amatuers. So if a buddy is a tad too much in his cups, it is a recognized obligation to keep him out of an automobile: A cab, a drive home, coffee, food, whatever it takes. By the way, Bar Bars have long been the most responsible drinking establishments in this vein: Hey, it's a brotherhood and nobody wants a brother on probation or worse, wrapped around a guardrail someplace.

11

The Transcontinental Drunk, part 6: Fort Lauderdale/Miami

Wherever you're going, there you are.

A h, where the hell else would a young man's nose lead him in spring but to that primal rite of the season: baseball spring training. There were practical considerations here, too: I had always understood that South Florida was a weird bar culture, which made sense, since it's a weird culture in just about every other way. Dave was going anyway—as he does every spring—and a mutual friend, John, agreed to join us to serve as driver and basic sober-type guy in situations requiring that state of mind. A fourth friend, Eric, was already in Pompano Beach in his capacity as a broadcaster for the Texas Rangers. Bingo: instant boys' week out, rush week, summer camp—however far we chose to regress.

Well, John blew Atkinson's Travel Tip #2 to smithereens by securing us a 6 A.M. flight to Miami, with a stop in Atlanta, which meant by the time we got to Miami it was about noon Eastern Standard Time, but about 4 P.M. Atkinson Liver Standard Time. Translated, this means that while the rest of my body had been operating for six hours, due to a Bloody Mary in Atlanta and a few beers on the plane, my liver had been working a sort of time and a half. Liver Standard Time, of course, has both short- and long-term effects, the former being The Fade, the latter a certain premature aging common to all barflies. The math here is a little difficult to explain, but basically *Atkinson's Forty-sixth Rule of the Bar Bar* is: The average Bar Barfly's actual age may best be computed my multiplying his chronological age by four, dividing by the square root of 5.678, and then multiplying that by the proof of whatever he drinks. In lay terms, this would mean that the average beer drinker might be only five years older that his actual age. A guy who drinks Stoly martinis or Ron Rico 101 rum, however, could actually be as much as twice his real age.

After a few brews at the ballyard, we charted out a scattershoot of Fort Lauderdale bars. Let me say right here that I was pretty sure this would yield no Bar Bars. Bar Bars were meant to be a lot of places, but Fort Lauderdale is not one of them. Besides, we were approaching Easter weekend and already the area had been invaded by gawky acne-faced guys wearing stuff like "A&M Sucks!" T-shirts and acne-faced little Bimbettes who could be overheard to say things like "Do you think Boy George is really gay? He's so *cute.*"

But what the hell: Like my brief foray into the fern grotto in Kansas City, I figured a scattershoot of whatever it was Fort Lauderdale was calling a bar these days might be instructive as per the present thinking of The Enemy. Our first stop was a place called September's, and it will receive an Atkinson Transcontinental Award for being the single bar in America with absolutely *everything* wrong with it. I'll try to be brief, but it's going to be hard:

1. Valet parking.
2. Multi-level seating.
3. Drinks in stemmed glasses.
4. Loud live music.
5. A black guy in the men's room who turns on the water for you and then looks like he's going to file an EEOC suit when you leave only 50 cents.
6. Jewish princesses.
7. Gays.
8. Gays dressed like Jewish princesses.

One thing a bar like this will remind you of is how, in the long and the short of it, it really was worth it to get married and to stay that way. Eric was the only single among us. (Actually Dave's not married, but he does have that girlfriend with the good job, and for a Ruppy that's the same thing.) And while I had to admire his resolve as Eric stalked the room like a panther in heat, I have to say I was just as happy to sit at the bar and make fun of the band. Yeah, okay, so I *did* dance a little. That's okay 'cause it was with Dave.

There ensued a seemingly endless trek through similar joints, places called Roland's and Pickle's and Crockett's. They became indistinguishable, with their elliptical amphitheater structure, overpriced drinks in stemmed glasses, thundering live music, and Bimbettes. I was tempted to write this off to just that much more Yuppity Doo Da refuse, but the generalization troubled me: These weren't Yuppity Doo Da joints of the Friday's et al. phylum that had emerged from the primal sludge in the early '70s. These somehow seemed to predate that. These were singles bars of the sort that used to dot First Avenue in New York and then began to have problems with the IRS and various lending institutions when the Baby Boomers started getting married and *Time* and *Newsweek* started doing cover stories on herpes. (The epiphanic moment here would be the movie *Looking for Mr. Goodbar.*) Singles bars definitely are a progenitor of the fern bar, but not having been in one since the early '70s I was struck by the difference. There's something strangely less pretentious about this sort of joint, maybe because nowadays they are a quaint relic of the near past, relegated to strange outbacks like Fort Lauderdale. But the outing taught me a valuable lesson, something I'd suspected for some time. At any rate, for an enemy reconnaissance mission, they are eminently more enjoyable, funky, and soulful than Big Sean O'Fern's Munchie Bar and Wine Bistro.

A nice sidelight to a singles bar scattershoot—should you ever decide to try one—is that it will tend to refuel even the most adult male's scatological vocabulary as regards the opposite sex. It was at Pickle's, I believe, that we heard a dandy round of various adolescent euphemisms for the female breast. We'd run through the basics pretty fast, and it was finally Dave who won the Wheel of Fortune. Inspired by a particularly arresting set of the aforementioned near our territory at the bar, Dave said, "Yeah, well, there are breasts, there are tits. But *those* . . . those are *hogans.*" That's right up there with the term Bar Bar as a coinage that says exactly what it means without a smidgen of amplification.

We arose early the next morning, which was unfortunate but necessary, as Dave had decided to move his rollaway out onto the patio for the night, and, well, you know that South Florida weather. There was an almost immediate benefit, though: We had to do something quickly about the hangover factor and that led us directly to the Laughing Fish Tail, which was the poolside bar at the Pompano Beach Holiday Inn. Midway into the second Bloody Mary I fairly belched forth *Atkinson's Forty-seventh Rule of the Bar Bar:* In a state of hangover, *anything* is a Bar Bar. I mean, we're talking bad nautical crapola on the back bar; screeching tots and Bimbettes in the nearby pool; and very loud and very bad extra-special Easter weekend live music from Herb Bailey and the Caribbean Survivors. Get the picture? Okay, try this: Herb and clan tended to a sort of limping, clunky type of reggae, which would have been okay (since all reggae sounds limping and clunky) if they hadn't attempted numbers like Eric Clapton's "I Shot the Sheriff" and Dire Straits' "Walk of Life."
Never mind, though. Under the care of a great Old Fart bartender named Bob, we couldn't have cared less. I think Dave even made a request, the Beatles' "Michelle" if I recall. Anyway, we were plenty shipshape later that day for our trek to downtown Miami.
One thing should be said for Miami bars: You *never* know what you're getting into. This whole place is a house of mirrors anyway, a culture that is equal parts Cuban immigrant, northeastern Jewish retiree, and Tacky Tourist. It's a bigger You Go Figure than New Orleans, and its bars reflect it.
Take Tobacco Road, a downtown Bar Bar highly recommended by several Miami Ruppies. Ostensibly, this would appear to be just another little blues bar, with a long stand-up bar and a bandstand at the far end. But that's only if you stay downstairs. If you have the fortitude to negotiate the crowd past the band and up a twist-

ing and somewhat lopsided staircase, you will discover that rarest of Bar Bar phenomena: Bar Bar within Bar.

Yep, just a little upstairs loft, the only apparent decor of which was billows of cigarette smoke of various densities and shapes. Special Award of Merit for Darkest Bar in America if I hadn't already sent the plaque to Milton's Tap Room in Kansas City. I really like the idea of Bar Bar in Bar, particularly of the loft variety, because if you become a regular, it's a little like having a secret tree fort when you were a kid.

One of my former haunts, the late Point Downtown in Dallas, had a similar setup: a huge dance-hall-type room downstairs for people who wanted to eat and sundry other foreigners, and then a tiny loft up a relatively obscure set of stairs for the regulars. This is tantamount to setting up a secret chapel within the cathedral for the purest of faith: You never had to worry about ringers or amateurs up there. Hell, you didn't even have to worry when you overheard your boss saying he was going to the same joint for lunch, and that is about as serious as a Bar Bar can get.

Tobacco Road was suitably rambunctious and terribly crowded, but I'll say this: I paid for a round and left about $14 on the bar and never worried for a second, though I was positioned three-deep back. But its specialty as a Bar Bar was destined to go well beyond that. Tobacco Roads earned an Atkinson Transcontinental Award for coming the closest to making the Bar as Church concept a reality.

As the hour approached midnight, heading toward Easter morning, the crowd hushed and a spotlight probed the rear of the room. When it finally stilled on a bent old black woman, who appeared to be dressed in her first prom dress, a thunderous roar went up from the crowd. She was introduced as Sister Mary Smith McClean and I gathered she was something of a local legend.

It didn't take long to see why. As the clock passed midnight, Sister Mary began a slow processional-type walk to a small bandstand. Midway, she began a throaty a cappella rendition of "Amazing Grace." It was the only time I've ever heard a Bar Bar entirely quiet for the right reason.

For the next hour, Sister Mary street-rapped and sang hymns

and I swear I didn't see a regular leave. That's more than any bartender can say when he's telling jokes. Try that hazy memory on as the first thing you think of the next morning. *Atkinson's Forty-eighth Rule of the Bar Bar:* Anything that comes to mind the next day as a bit surreal probably did happen—in a Bar Bar.

TOBACCO ROAD (626 S. Miami)

> **What You Feel Like When You Get There:** 2 downstairs; 5 upstairs
>
> **Yuppity Doo Da:** 5
>
> **Oh Say Can You See?** 5
>
> **Crapola:** 3
>
> **Holding Forth:** 5 (For Sister Mary alone.)
>
> **What You Feel Like After Three Drinks:** 4 (In this case, like making my first confession in a couple of decades.)
>
> **Just a Little Something to Wash My Drink Down With:** 5
>
> **Old Fart Factor:** 3
>
> **What You Feel Like When You Leave:** 5
>
> **You Go Figure:** 5+
>
> **Nowhere Coefficient:** 4.0

Miami, in its way, is as big a Nowhere as Milwaukee. So it stood to reason that there were a lot more Middle of Nowheres out there someplace. Thanks to Dave's friend Al Woolf, we found them. Miami is as opaque a place as you'd ever want to not see; but that just makes its few Bar Bars that much more Nowhere.

Fox's was a small and innocuous storefront which featured an attached liquor store, as do many bars in this area. What did I tell you about you never know what you're going to find when you open a door in Miami? This joint reminded me more of my Dallas haunt, Joe Miller's, than any other Bar Bar I had been in. The

NCAA finals were on, and Dave and I had little trouble deciding where we would be for the next three hours.

First, though, we had a little encounter with that specter known as Our Adolescent Past. Fox's parking is in the rear and so we had to park next to the liquor store. As we pulled in, we were approached by a frail but pretty little sixteen-year-old girl with a broad smile that revealed about 28 megatons of metal.

"Excuse me, *sir*," she said, not realizing the pain she had just inflicted. "But me and my friends need a bottle . . . and . . . could you go in there and get it? Bacardi." God, *that* hadn't changed. I left a good portion of my mom's home cooking on several San Antonio roadsides as a result of *that* demon rum.

This was what you would call your fairly serious existential moment, for even Bar Barflies like Dave and me become hypocrites about booze as we ease into our late thirties. Actually, it's not all hypocrisy, for contrary to popular belief, Bar Barflies are among the more responsible folks around when it comes to the consumption of liquor and its effects. A frequently heard Bar Bar cant on New Year's Eve is "I'm stayin' home. The amateurs are out tonight." And it's not entirely a joke. I never saw Joe Miller let a regular leave his bar too drunk to drive. Indeed, he'd belt you into the stool and force-feed you coffee. If that didn't work, he'd call a cab. Hell, I even got a ride home one evening from Joe's bartender sidekick, Louis. *Atkinson's Forty-ninth Rule of the Bar Bar:* The principal activity of the Bar Bar is drinking; it is not getting drunk.

Anyway, we had to face it. Like most normal adolescents, we had vowed as sixteen-year-olds faced with a similar state of affairs never to turn down such a request once we had become Middle or Old Farts. But observing that sweet little thing and assuming—rightly as it turns out—that she had been dispatched by one or more young men, we did a lot of hemming and hawing.

"That's against the law," Dave said weakly. "We could get in trouble for that."

She gave us a tired smirk. "Come on. I won't get in trouble. I'm going home tonight."

Yeah, sure, Dave and I said to one another. And then we proceeded to get out of the car and get her as much Bacardi as $17 would buy.

"What did *that* mean?" I asked as we shuffled into the bar, having delivered the contraband to the kid and her friends.

"I'm not sure," said Dave, "but I think it means we're assholes."

"That's what I thought."

Ah, but Fox's was just the perfect antidote to our self-doubt and guilt. A little cubbyhole of a place, with those wonderful old red vinyl circular booths, an L-shaped bar, and a color TV set about the size of a Buick LeSabre. Sweet young lady bartender, who will forthwith get an Atkinson Transcontinental Award for Only Good Pretty Young Lady Bartender in America. How good was she? Refused to take my cash and automatically ran a tab. Automatically mixed a second in same glass (the preferred style because the ice is marinated). Music, yeah. But it was Sinatra, Percy Faith, and Pete Fountain. That'll slip past the Atkinson music bias any day.

Add this as well: Anytime you can watch the NCAA finals and simultaneously listen to an absolutely rhapsodic bit of Holding Forth from a housepainter about how he'd gotten stiffed on a $40 job that day and had decided the best medicine was to spend about $40 more getting wasted, you're in a Bar Bar *(Atkinson's Fiftieth)*. But what really made Fox's transcend, what made it a contender for the Top 10, was this stirring bit of Bar Bar Legend 'n' Lore that was passed on by just about everyone I talked to.

Seems Fox's had burned down several years back and there had been the predictable confusion about how to rebuild it. This is a tortuous exercise for both management and regulardom: How indeed do you rebuild a cathedral? Divine guidance must have spoken, for fueled by contributions from regulars, Fox's was rebuilt exactly as it had been. That tops even Sister Mary for sheer religiosity.

By the way, I won my Bar Bar bet with Dave on the game. How does a Bar Bar bet differ from the ordinary kind? Put it this way: Our finally negotiated stakes involved lunch at the Four Seasons in New York, and I know some bookies who wouldn't take that.

FOX'S (6030 S. Dixie Hwy.)

> **What You Feel Like When You Get There:** 5
>
> **Yuppity Doo Da:** 4 (A slight invasion, maybe because of the game.)
>
> **Oh Say Can You See?** 5
>
> **Crapola:** 5
>
> **Holding Forth:** 5
>
> **What You Feel Like After Three Drinks:** 5
>
> **Just a Little Something to Wash My Drink Down With:** 4 (There was a somewhat extensive menu, but the painter next to me had some nasty fried chicken, so I'll give it the benefit of the doubt.)
>
> **Old Fart Factor:** 5
>
> **What You Feel Like When You Leave:** 5
>
> **You Go Figure:** 5 (They rebuilt it *exactly* as it had been?)
>
> **Nowhere Coefficient:** 4.7

Miami is a visually assaulting place, with its pinks and purples and Cuban-influenced urban art. But Miami Beach is like an acid flash. With its restored Deco hotels and storefronts, it looks exactly like a visual riff from *Miami Vice*.

Our destination was the bar at the Carlisle Hotel, but first we had to negotiate ourselves past a fairly nasty, it appeared, domestic dispute between a middle-aged black guy and his girlfriend. He was staggering around out in the street and she was someplace upstairs in an apartment, which made some of the dialogue audible from the Carlisle. Bar Bar Voyeurism? Why not?

Unfortunately, the Carlisle elsewise was a little too preciously restored for its own good, and too damned bright on top of that. But Miami Beach is just so *weird*, it was an okay place to drink—made more so by the bartender's rebuke of this gay guy who couldn't understand why he couldn't get his Cognac in a larger snifter. *"Nothing* has any class anymore!" fumed the queen, returning to his outpost on the patio section of the bar. No full rating for the Carlisle, but you might want to give it a shot.

How could a Bar Bar earn a spot in Atkinson's Top 10 at 3 A.M. through a considerable haze? It was open, that's one reason. It was called Club Deuce, and that's another very good one. A third would be the architecture of the joint, which approximated a bomb shelter.

Inside, one is confronted with the damnedest Bar Bar bar I've seen in a while: a strange serpentine sort of deal that just wound and twisted all over the room. A jukebox and a pool table. An old lady bartender. That was it, and that was plenty.

Inhabitants here were members of the underclass I call the Bar Bar Third World, meaning folks with just enough money to get good and wasted for that particular twenty-four-hour stretch. Who *are* these guys? Well, the one I met in the men's room—Special Transcontinental Award for Funkiest Men's Room in America— was in a service industry.

"You want?" he slurred, holding up a joint about the size of a tree trunk.

"Nah, I gotta drive," I said.

"Well, anything you want, you see this face, you just ask." Sounds good to me.

But when I really knew we'd found Bar Bar Nirvana was when this terrific-looking Old Fart lurched in after a roughly ten-minute grapple with the door, sat down, ordered a beer, and promptly fell into the Missionary Position of Passing Out. This is where your neck suddenly develops a hinge and just lops completely forward, resting at a perfect 90-degree angle to your back. Nothing else is affected, just the head, and I've seen guys rest quite placidly in this position for as long as several hours.

CLUB DEUCE (222 14th, Miami Beach)

What You Feel Like When You Get There: 5 (Bomb-shelter cozy.)

Yuppity Doo Da: 5

Oh Say Can You See? 5 (Sure, if you're the small tabby who wandered in about 3:30.)

Crapola: 5

Holding Forth: 3

What You Feel Like After Three Drinks: 5

Just a Little Something to Wash My Drink Down With: 5

Old Fart Factor: 5

What You Feel Like When You Leave: 5 (Like you can make it back to Miami. Any time you can lie to yourself, you're in a Bar Bar.)

You Go Figure: 5 (The whole damn place.)

Nowhere Coefficient: 4.7

Did a pretty nice two-part scattershoot the next night in Lauderdale to close out all this madcap zaniness. One was a nice find and the other was just plain strange.

Brownies at least tried to prove wrong my theory that Lauderdale didn't have any Bar Bars. It's a low-ceilinged joint with a cement floor and no apparent door. Liquor store in the front. A nice kind of campy touch was the Designated Bar Bar Celebrity, which in this case turned out to be Paul Newman. Seems a scene or two from *Harry and Son* had been shot here for some reason, and the joint fairly bristled with *Harry and Son* crapola: T-shirts, mugs, and an altar-like presentation of the part of the set used in the filming. That sort of thing is a decent You Go Figure.

BROWNIES (1411 S. Andrews)

What You Feel Like When You Get There: 3

Yuppity Doo Da: 5

Oh Say Can You See? 4

Crapola: 5 (Self-serving crapola is generally to be frowned upon, but when a joint actually sets up a crapola *shop,* as this one had, that's a fiver.)

Holding Forth: 3

What You Feel Like After Three Drinks: 4 (Joint grows on you.)

Old Fart Factor: 4

Just a Little Something to Wash My Drink Down With: 3

What You Feel Like When You Leave: 3

You Go Figure: 5

Nowhere Coefficient: 3.9

Is there any particular reason why along about 10 P.M. the subject of hogans came up? I don't really know, but I do know that at about 10:05, we found ourselves ensconced at the bar in a joint called Solid Gold. This was even less a Bar Bar than the Pink Garter Strip-o-Rama in Kansas City, but it represents a trend out there in bardom of some note. You're beginning to see a lot of joints like Solid Gold, particularly in the Sunbelt. Call them a sort of Yuppy Titty Bar, the inevitable upscale version of the old-fashioned strip joint. The places are Las Vegas snazzy and the ladies all look like University of Georgia coeds. For a cover, you can just watch the dancer or dancers on stage; for an extra $5, one of the ladies will dance especially for you, and show you her you-know-what. It's Playboy sex, and in that way, the Solid Golds of bardom may be less an upscaling of strip joints than a downscaling of singles bars.

Either way, if you suddenly find yourself preoccuppied with hogans, you might find one of these joints an interesting diversion. It'll definitely satisfy the preoccupation. We lucked out, too, because this turned out to be something called Amateur Night, where just any young thing off the street could come in and bounce her hogans around. I'm not sure what they meant by amateur, but I'll say this: Not one of them appeared to be, uh, particularly embarrassed by the hogan exposure—not to mention the you-know-what exposure.

But the finale was a surreal stunner: Including the "amateurs," there were roughly fifty girls who had danced at one time or another during the evening. At last call, at 2 A.M., all fifty of 'em came out on stage and flounced their private parts around. Whew. "That's exactly one hundred hogans we're lookin' at," observed Dave. "I counted 'em." Miami didn't inspire many rules of the Bar Bar, but at that moment I discovered *Atkinson's Fifty-first Rule of the Bar Bar:* If you're staring straight at a hundred hogans, you're probably not in a Bar Bar, but what the hey, everybody's gotta be someplace once in a while.

Fun Facts

As of 1984, there were 165,721 bars in America. New York had the most: nearly 24,000. Alaska had the most per 1,000 population—3.21.

12

Bar Bar 501: Okay—Advanced Theology (on Bar Bar Food)

Customer to bartender: *You guys got any munchies or anything?*
Bartender: *No, but we got somethin' to eat if you want it.*

I have this recurring nightmare. I am being held hostage at Big Jed O'Fern's Munchie Bar and Wine Bistro and about six guys who look just like Richard Thomas are force-feeding me everything on the "munchie menu." It's horrifying. "You *vill* eat the fried potato skins with guacamole and then you *vill* eat the assorted veggie tray!!" With each bite, my taste buds wince and my stomach howls. Mostly, though, it is my manhood that has been violated. At last I am broken. "Enough! I'll do as you say. I'll never make another joke about Neil Diamond again. Ever! Just don't make me eat the artichoke hearts in vinaigrette."

My tormentors vary. In one version it was Tom Selleck; in another, I was forced to eat make-your-own pasta salad at the hands of David Eisenhower. And just when I thought I had exorcised the demon, here came Neil himself in the title role, and he not only made me scarf down some swordfish kabobs, he made me listen to an "In a Gadda Da Vida"–length version of "They're Coming to America." That's powerful stuff, and if you don't believe me, you should have heard me finally tell Neil that on reflection, I'd decided The Boss was a big wimp and that, yes, I did think it was time to remix "Kentucky Woman" and show him who the real boss is.

121

Atkinson's Travel Tip #3

When I return from my travels, a consistent question from those few friends who actually believe I'm doing this is: How do you remember *anything?* The answer gets into some pretty technical journalistic technique, but I'll try to reduce it to layman's language:

1. Try to take a lot of notes *before* you visit the bar. That way you don't have to worry if you wind up getting in your cups and forget everything that happened *at* the bar. The stuff you put down beforehand might be totally wrong, but you're not going to know the difference, so how is anyone else?

2. When you take notes at the bar, do it in the men's room. Otherwise you look like a narc or a health inspector or somebody from the competition.

3. If you decide to do a scattershoot of reasonable length, pick up a book of matches at each joint; at least that way you can remember *where* you went, even if you can't remember anything about the specific places.

4. Go ahead and believe anything anyone tells you about the joint. Bar Bars are based on The Lie, so there's no sense questioning anything.

5. You can tell folks what you're up to if you want, since they're not going to believe you anyway.

All those nights spent shivering in a cold REM sleep led to the formulation of *Atkinson's Fifty-second Rule of the Bar Bar:* The fried mushroom may be food, but only in the sense that Tom Selleck is an actor, Neil Diamond is a musician, and David Eisenhower is an actual person.

One more shot of etiology here, because when it comes to the broad topic of Fern Food, it is very important to understand the genealogy of The Enemy. It would be easy enough to blame all the slop that's being served in bars these days on the folks at Friday's or Bennigan's. But they didn't really invent the stuff; they're just making money off it. There were, in fact, larger social forces at work. Elementally, Fern Food may best be understood as the result of a massive unspoken conspiracy on the part of the four predominant cultural forces of the past decade or so: professional women, Yups, wimps, and gays. I'm not sure who was the first out of the box, but upon viewing lentil soup with a parsley garnish. I'm gonna lay it on our brothers of the other persuasion. Look at it this way guys: You've been blamed for a lot worse.

Whatever, the Yups, the working women, the wimps, were soon enough in lockstep, and gradually—no, it seemed more like all at once—restaurants and bars began serving *cuisine* rather than food. Women and gays, we would learn, had always eaten this stuff, but in private. Yups certainly wanted to, if only because it sounded better when you said it. The wimps don't count because they always do what the gays and the women and the Yups say to do anyway. (Bet you 100 to 1 David Eisenhower has a Huey Lewis record.)

You began to see stuff like leek soup, mushroom omelettes, Béarnaise sauce, unfried fish of various kinds, diet plates, salads as a whole meal, something called a "petite filet." For goodness sakes, even the hamburger got pillaged. Next time you have a chance, take a good hard look at the guacamole burger and then go ahead, take my wager that David Eisenhower has eaten at least 7,891 of the damned things. It's a menace, is what it is, and so that you may head out into the night armed with an intricate knowledge of The Enemy—

ATKINSON'S BAR BAR PROHIBITED SUBSTANCES
MANUAL: PART ONE—SOLID SUBSTANCES

Normal, everyday, maybe-it's-macho-and-probably-bad-for-you-but-who-cares Food Food	Yup, You-Didn't-Like-It-When-You-Were-A-Kid-So-Why-Are-You-Pretending-Now Fern Food
Cheeseburger	Cheeseburger with guacamole
French fries	Those silly curlicue-type fries
Scrambled eggs	Omelette
Baked potato	Fried potato skins
Raw meat and rice	Most anything else with rice
Hard-boiled eggs	Poached eggs
Noodles	Pasta (unless made by a real Italian guy)
Meatballs	Meatballs with stuff on them
Catfish	Sole
Steak	Veal
Grilled cheese	Pimiento cheese
Chef's salad	Any other salad
Bean with bacon soup	Lentil soup
Crawfish	Shrimp
Jalapeños (raw)	Jalapeños (fried)
Burritos	Flautas
Oysters (raw)	Oysters any other way
Buffalo wings	Chicken salad
Pretzels	Goldfish
Chicken-fried anything	Tuna anything
Nachos with beef, beans, cheese, and jalapeños	Nachos with anything else
Beef sticks	Cheese sticks
Goulash	Veggies
Any kind of sausage	Anything in vinaigrette
Ice cream	Ice cream cake
Pigs-in-a-blanket	Croissants
Goose liver	Pâté
Pistachios	Cashews
Chili	Chili that has identifiable ingredients
Tomatillo sauce	Tomato aspic

Barbecued anything	Flambéed anything
Cheddar cheese and saltines	Brie and those sissy cookie-crackers
Stuffed bell pepper	Stuffed flounder
Clam chowder	Clam chowder that has identifiable ingredients
Cabrito	Goat cheese
Artichokes	Artichoke hearts
Potato salad	Potatoes au gratin
Tater Tots	Twice-baked potatoes with those little scallions in them
Bacon	Prosciutto
Corn on the cob	Corn soup
Sweet roll	Pastry
Black-eyed peas	Snow peas
Juevos rancheros	Continental breakfast
No breakfast	Brunch

I'll tell you how insidious this is. The fernies have become so arrogant about this "cuisine" business that in many bars they've just up and turned drinks into *food.* That's some plenty serious blasphemy and if you don't believe me, consider this: In one of the fern grottos I wandered into along the way, I actually heard a young lady say she couldn't finish her veggie pizza because the two strawberry daiquiris had *filled her up. Atkinson's Fifty-third Rule of the Bar Bar:* Any society that cannot distinguish between food and drink is probably a society that is confused about other things as well—like, say, the difference between men and women.

ATKINSON'S BAR BAR PROHIBITED SUBSTANCES MANUAL:
PART TWO—LIQUIDS

Booze, Cocktail, Drink Drinks	Fern, Yup Froufrous
Scotch and water	Piña colada
American beer	Foreign beer
Martini	Strawberry daiquiri
Tequila	Tequila sunrise
Peppermint schnapps	Apple schnapps

Vodka rickey	Grapefruit juice and vodka
Old-fashioned	Whiskey sour
Black Russian	White Russian
Cuba libre	Just about anything with rum
Margarita	Frozen margarita
Bloody Mary	Virgin Mary
Bourbon up	Bourbon and Coke
Sambuca	Kamikaze
White wine with food	White wine without food
Campari and soda	Kir
Brandy	Amaretto
Anything on the rocks	Anything poured from a computerized gun
Anything double	Anything served at two-for-one happy hour
Bullshot	Wine spritzer
Icepick (vodka and iced tea)	Iced tea
B&B	Bourbon and 7-Up
Ouzo	Galliano

13

The Transcontinental Drunk, part 7: The West Coast

Customer to other customer: *What is the realm of possibility?*
Other customer: *I'm not sure.*

You hear a lot of that kind of talk in Lotusland, which is where I headed next. I'm truly surprised people still attempt to converse out there; nobody's made any sense—and nobody's been listening—since John Huston directed his first film, which had to be sometime back around the Gold Rush.

You're definitely on CST (Cocaine Standard Time) there, and that makes the Bar Bars flat weird. But as in Miami, there are a few gems to be found beneath all the snow.

My plan was, I must say, damned ambitious. I was going to scattershoot, barhop, not just a whole city, but a whole *coast.* Yep. Rent a car, do LA, and then just drink my way up the coast to Seattle. More ambitious yet was the fact that I agreed to take the wife along—sort of a working vacation, don't you know. More on that later, if I still feel like talking about it.

My LA Ruppy first directed me to Barney's Beanery in West Hollywood, a city within a city that can best be described as a minefield, if you happen to be straight. But Barney's had not only precursed the invasion, it was still kicking. Indeed, this joint will share an Atkinson Transcontinental Award with McSorley's in New York for Best Bar Bar Orneriness in the Face of Change.

Specifically, it seems when West Hollywood incorporated in

1984, it was not merely a city with a large gay population; it was a *gay city*. Gays predominated the newly elected city council and one of their first actions was to pass an ordinance prohibiting anyone from discriminating against gay folk. This, it would seem, was more or less aimed directly at Barney's, which featured a sign over the front door that stated bluntly NO FAGOTS ALLOWED. A picture of the advisory was featured in *Life* magazine and even inspired a sculpture by Dutch artist Ed Kienholz—for whatever that's worth.

At any rate, Barney finally took the sign down, but the walls here remain adorned with framed newspaper clips concerning the brouhaha, much in the way the folks at McSorley's commemorated their losing legal battle over excluding women. I like the public display of Bar Bar history, particularly if it's history that involves the Bar Bar's fight against progress or change. Make that *Atkinson's Fifty-fourth Rule of the Bar Bar:* If a joint is bragging about its backwardness, it's probably a Bar Bar.

The architecture of Barney's may best be described as a combination roadhouse/drive-in type thing. A nice You Go Figure is the roof decor, which is thousands of old newspapers. The interior is equal parts bar and diner, but the bar does not suffer from the intrusion of food.

Barney's also earned a plaque for Best Job of Making a Bad Gimmick Work. The gimmick in question was the old we-serve-eight-trillion-brands-of-beer hype, which ordinarily should be considered a Six Flags Over bar-type concept. But Barney's makes it work, if only because his selections are truly off the wall. Put it this way: I had something called a Kriek, which is this Belgian stuff that tasted like rosé mixed with Alka-Seltzer.

As for food, Barney's should get an award along with The Billy Goat in Chicago for Just a Little Something to Wash My Drink Down With. Here too, Barney seemed inclined to the mega menu: How mega? It's got a #1371 is how mega. By the way, that's a grilled cheese with bacon and tomato. Barney's got hot dogs; Barney's got chili. Club sandwiches of every possible permutation. Barbecue. Ninety-two kinds of omelettes. It's a kind of a Six Flags Over diner/deli, but any joint that serves french fries with chili on them will slip past me in the food category. That's some serious Food Food, even if it did make the wife a little sick.

BARNEY'S BEANERY (8447 Santa Monica Blvd.)

What You Feel Like When You Get There: 4 (Very glad to be off Sunset Blvd.)

Yuppity Doo Da: 5

Oh Say Can You See? 4

Crapola: 5 (News clips.)

Holding Forth: 4 (I'm not sure, but I think I overheard a guy say "Jack Nicholson couldn't act his way out of a paper bag.")

What You Feel Like After Three Drinks: 4 (Much better than you do after eating the french fries with chili.)

Just a Little Something to Wash My Drink Down With: 5+

Old Fart Factor: 3

What You Feel Like When You Leave: 4

You Go Figure: 5

Nowhere Coefficient: 4.1

Bar Bar Star Watch is an interesting deal, and a nice place to start is Dantana's on Santa Monica Boulevard. Little Italian food joint, with Bar Bar in the middle of the room, which I like a lot. Star Watch? Sure—Don Henley. Looked like shit, too.

Next there was this regular who somehow got to eat at the bar even though there was a waiting list because he had to go to some kind of awards thing. Bartender was cool, though. I asked for another and he said, "Take your time. I'll be here." Extra Transcontinental Award for Bartender Holding Forth there.

It was at Dantana's that I confronted a basic Bar Fact of Life in California: It was this:

Lady next to me: "Give me another one."

"That's the white wine with the soda back?"

"Yeah."

Okay. We need to talk about the genre of wine coolers here because they appear to be taking over the western world. That's *not* okay, by the way; but I have come to begrudgingly accept them as a kind of different law of a different jungle.

What I won't accept is taking them a step further and attempting to make them into some kind of legitimate drink by splitting them in the way one might a bourbon and soda—bourbon neat, soda back. White wine and soda back is sort of like saying pizza crust, sausage back, twist of anchovies.

This is the sort of thing that happens on Cocaine Standard Time, and by the way, another thing that happens is this: Lady next ordered an espresso with a brandy back. Go figure.

All in all, though, I'd have to include Dantana's on any LA barhopping trip. Where else are you going to see Don Henley? How else are you going to remember Don Henley?

DANTANA'S (9071 Santa Monica Blvd.)

> **What You Feel Like When You Get There:** 4 (Overdressed; you can't underdress in LA.)
>
> **Yuppity Doo Da:** 5
>
> **Oh Say Can You See?** 5
>
> **Crapola:** 3
>
> **Holding Forth:** 4 (Bartender variety.)
>
> **What You Feel Like After Three Drinks:** 3
>
> **Just a Little Something to Wash My Drink Down With:** 4 (Heavy-duty, no froufrou Italian food is always acceptable.)
>
> **Old Fart Factor:** 1
>
> **What You Feel Like When You Leave:** 3

You Go Figure: 4 (Don Henley?)

Nowhere Coefficient: 3.6

If you want to upscale your stargazing a bit, drop by Hollywood's latest palace of glitz, Le Dome on Sunset Boulevard. I didn't see any stars, but I did see what appeared to be a couple of black hookers, which was just as entertaining.

Actually, I did see several stars of the would-be variety, which, I soon figured out, is about the only kind you really see here. Hey, Jack Nicholson lives in a multimillion-dollar mansion up on Mulholland Drive overlooking the city. Why the hell is he gonna go out to a *bar* to have a drink?

Generally speaking, the would-be stars were sweet young things with impossibly perfect teeth who were all hanging on the arm of what appeared to be the same fat Old Fart. Guy gets around.

Just a Little Something to Wash My Drink Down With? Yep, and how: The bar menu was in double digits and I can't be certain, but I think I saw an entrée for $30 or so on the dinner menu. Just a question, but who and where was it that someone decided that a *meal* could cost $30? I can get a week's worth of laundry done for that, not to mention stratospherically nowhere in some Bar Bar.

LE DOME (8720 Sunset)

What You Feel Like When You Get There: 2

Yuppity Doo Da: 5 (There are no Yuppies in LA, only Wuppies—Wired Young Urban Professionals.)

Oh Say Can You See? 4

Crapola: 1

Holding Forth: 1 (Place was reasonably full, but everyone seemed to be talking in that tone reserved for Doing a Deal. It could have been movies, but I think it might have been something else.)

What You Feel Like After Three Drinks: 2 (Glad you brought a credit card.)

Just a Little Something to Wash My Drink Down With: 1

Old Fart Factor: 4

What You Feel Like When You Leave: 2

You Go Figure: 2

Nowhere Coefficient: 2.0

To find remnants of the Theology, I found, you need to get away from the new Hollywood. One easy way to do that is to go to the old Hollywood. You can try the Polo Lounge—in fact it's a must if you've never been—but my favorite from the Errol Flynn days is a funky gymnasium-size joint on Hollywood Boulevard.

Musso and Frank's claims to be the Oldest Bar in LA and it earned an Atkinson Transcontinental Award right off for Best Old Neon Bar Sign I've ever seen. Inside, one huge room is set aside for dining, the other for drinking. The bar itself is impossibly long and elegant in a rustic way, and the crowd is no-nonsense.

The restaurant is a little imposing for my taste, but it saves itself with those nifty old wooden booths with hat racks. The Just a Little Something to Wash My Drink Down With will pass muster as well: a lot of heavy German fare, steaks, and egg dishes.

It ain't Nirvana, but the joint did have *some* sense of character and history, in a city that doesn't seem to care to have a great deal of either. Oh yeah: Another Transcontinental Award for Best Street Bums. I don't know if it's the weather or what, but when these folks decide to tune in and drop out, they really go in a big way.

MUSSO AND FRANK'S (6667 Hollywood Blvd.)

What You Feel Like When You Get There: 5 (It's really the best place to get a true feeling of the old Hollywood.)

Yuppity Doo Da: 5

Oh Say Can You See? 4

Crapola: 5 (That neon bar sign does it.)

Holding Forth: 3

What You Feel Like After Three Drinks: 3

Just a Little Something to Wash My Drink Down With: 4

Old Fart Factor: 3

What You Feel Like When You Leave: 5

You Go Figure: 3

Nowhere Coefficient: 4.0

We have another winner here by the name of Sloan's, on Melrose. The award is for Most You Go Figures in a Single Bar Bar. Jeez, this little and ostensibly unremarkable neighborhood joint is a real fun house. For the full effect, let me just list what-all I observed, roughly in order:

1. Above the back bar, a huge old organ with a sign announcing, THIS OPERATING STEAM ORGAN WAS TAKEN FROM THE RAMP OF THE OLD BIJOU THEATRE IN PLATTSBURG, NEW YORK."
2. Suspended from the ceiling, a rebuilt Model T or some such. No explanation.
3. Strewn about the room in varying states of stupor, the strangest crowd of Young Urban Somethings I've ever seen. They were all in their mid-thirties, but there was no particular racial skew and the dress was New Collar. The few sets of forearms and hands I saw did not suggest manual labor. Too old to be students. Too tough-talking and get-down to be Yuppies. Aha: a Bar Bar filled with *Ruppies?* Could be.

Elsewhere, Sloan's qualified for a couple of other awards. One was the Best Bar Bar Nerd I saw in my travels. You know about the Bar Bar Nerd: He's just like the Bar Bar Fool except he's not a customer—he's help. This is the sort of fellow who might arise on a Sunday morning and go on down to the bar just to tidy up a bit more, or maybe just to *be there*. He's the Jesuit monk of the faith, a guy who would punch out anybody who dared suggest anything negative about the bar.

This particular Bar Bar Nerd was an audio freak and had he spent some time on the tape collection. It was all reel to reel, which should tell you how serious he was, and the cataloging system could put the Library of Congress to shame. In addition, he seemed to enjoy playing deejay. The Ruppies had long since taken to spontaneous fits of dancing and the Bar Bar Nerd kept a watchful eye on the crowd, noting the ebb and flow of dancing activity and adjusting his tunes likewise.

But the pièce de résistance of this particular joint came from the damnedest source. The door of any Bar Bar is an important piece of equipment: As earlier noted, the harder it is to find and to open, the better. A personal favorite is the door to a joint in Houston called Marfreless. It's on the side, for one thing, and it is anything but the archetypal swinging variety: It's just a big heavy metal deal with a knob, like the door to the utility room in an office.

Sloan's door involved the back one, and the gimmick was perfectly ingenious—never seen it before or since. A little more theological explanation is necessary first: *Atkinson's Fifty-fifth Rule of the Bar Bar* states flatly that you can leave any time you want, but you better not do so unannounced. This is designed primarily to test the mettle of someone who might be considering just having *one* and then slipping out the back door. No way: You gotta face the music, and if the bartender or some regular decides to hit you with a Retrograder, you have no choice but to once again place the bar before your marriage or your job.

Sloan's ensured this by rigging up a loud and obnoxious bell on the back door, which would go off every time somebody tried to slip out into the alley. In this way, regulars were able to keep score on who's wimping out and who's not. A side benefit is that if the regular in question subsequently returns, it's a safe bet he might be packing some prohibited substance.

SLOAN'S (8623 Melrose)

   What You Feel Like When You Get There: 5

   Yuppity Doo Da: 5 (Ruppity Doo Da maybe; but not Yuppity.)

   Oh Say Can You See? 3 (Only category this joint fell down in.)

   Crapola: 5+ (Car, organ.)

   Holding Forth: 4 (Spontaneous dancing counts.)

   What You Feel Like After Three Drinks: 5

   Just a Little Something to Wash My Drink Down With: 5 (No food in sight.)

   Old Fart Factor: 2

   What You Feel Like When You Leave: 5

   You Go Figure: 5+

   Nowhere Coefficient: 4.4

Can Bar Bar Nirvana be found in the Cocaine Standard Time zone? Sure, if you go to the pier at Santa Monica and belly up at the tiny bar at Chez Jay's. If you didn't already mark off a 5+ for name, you haven't been reading this book very carefully.

This little '50s Pier Bar Bar was very strong on personalized crapola of the sort that made it seem a bit like one of those bad museums they have in little towns in Colorado and all over the place in Santa Fe. It's a tough choice, but I'll go ahead and give Chez Jay's an award for Best Bar Bar Crapola.

The stuff in question involved owner Jay, who was a World War II vet and had made it a pet project of his to unearth two WW II P-38s that are allegedly buried under some ice in Greenland. Go figure. Anyway, that would explain the two model P-38s suspended on the back bar, the numerous pictures of Greenland, and perhaps the mounted fish, which allegedly was caught by Gen. George F. Patton. "Yeah, Jay's quite a patriot," said the regular next to me. Bingo: That's a 5+ on Legend 'n' Lore Holding Forth.

Jay's patriotism, however, does not explain the Christmas lights that are suspended above the booths across from the bar. Figure.

CHEZ JAY'S (1657 Ocean Blvd., Santa Monica)

> **What You Feel Like When You Get There:** 5+ (Name.)
>
> **Yuppity Doo Da:** 5
>
> **Oh Say Can You See?** 4
>
> **Crapola:** 5+
>
> **Holding Forth:** 5
>
> **What You Feel Like After Three Drinks:** 4
>
> **Just a Little Something to Wash My Drink Down With:** 3
>
> **Old Fart Factor:** 4
>
> **What You Feel Like When You Leave:** 5
>
> **You Go Figure:** 5
>
> **Nowhere Coefficient:** 4.5

Where else to wind up a scattershot of LA than world-famous Venice Beach, home of the post-beach-bum, post-hippie, we-still-don't-have-jobs-but-now-we're-into-body-building culture? I can't give you a rating on the West Beach Cafe because in typically abstruse LA fashion, management closes it between lunch and dinner. But I will say that in some weird way, Venice Beach itself is a kind of Bar Bar. It's definitely too light, and the Holding Forth is inscrutable. You don't see many Old Farts, and you don't feel much better when you leave than when you got there. But it's Nowhere.

We headed up the coast on Highway 1 and discovered a rather quaint diversion for your California road trip: It's called Count the Winnebagos. Pretty fun, too, especially when you start breaking

Ask Dr. Bar Bar

Dear Dr. Bar Bar:

I was out of town on business recently and found myself stuck at a Bennigan's and they were serving two drinks for the price of one at happy hour. When I said I just wanted one drink and I'd pay the full price anyway, they said they couldn't do that. Any suggestions?

Signed,
JUST WENT ON BACK TO THE HOTEL ROOM

Dear JUST WENT ON BACK TO THE HOTEL ROOM:

My profoundest sympathies. I got stuck at a Bennigan's once too, in Wichita Falls, I believe it was. The key here is to pull an end run on 'em. You can get one drink if you ask for a double. *They desperately want to give you that booze cheap, for some reason, so don't screw up their management/marketing theories. Just tell the guy to give you two drinks in one glass. Hell, that's a normal drink at most real bars anyway.*

them down into categories of Winnebagos. First update: as of our next stop, Carmel, 57 and counting.

This was not really a vacation portion of the trip, as you might be thinking. I had serious reconnaissance work here that had to do with that presently most publicized of Bars That Got Too Famous for Their Own Good, the Hogsbreath Inn, owned by noted statesman and part-time actor Clint Eastwood. This had a Transcontinental Award going in as the Bar Bar I've Already Heard Way Too Much About, and after a visit or so, I can safely tell you I wished I'd left it at that.

It's a Six Flags Over bar, with a small indoor saloon area, a dining room, and a large, meandering patio. Holding Forth will receive an award as well, for Most People Who Claim to Know the Owner.

It all gets a little old, and as for Just a Little Something to Wash My Drink Down With, let me put it this way: There's something called an Eiger Sanction Burger on the menu. No, that's not a You Go Figure. Lemme make your day, Clint. Your movies tend to have a pretty good Nowhere Coefficient, but your bar is one of the biggest Somewheres I've ever overpaid for a drink at. No rating.

But if you can pick through the minefield of alpaca sweaters, double-knit pants suits, and freshly purchased designer jogging shoes that is downtown Carmel, you can find some outposts of the Faith. Jack London's and The Red Lion are both serviceable pubs, but you really need only visit Sade's right there on Ocean Avenue to get spiritual sustenance.

Oldest Bar in Carmel—since 1919—and I knew when the bartender struck up a conversation about the wind that I'd found home. Interior design is beyond Early Bunker, into Early Dungeon. Door is a nice touch: one of those doors that's cut in half, like they used to have all over the place somewhere like England, I believe.

Young lady Ruppy next to me spent about ten minutes engaged in what can only be called Lotusland Holding Forth. Seems she'd become fixated on whether she preferred a red straw or a blue in her gin and tonic.

Better hurry, though, because the bartender told me the joint had just been bought by a group from Houston, a very bad sign, and that they were considering redoing the interior, a worse sign. Uh oh: I have a feeling that if you owned a greenhouse in Carmel and you doubled your order for Boston ferns this month, you might just make a bundle pretty soon.

SADE'S (Ocean Ave. between Monte Verde and Lincoln)

What You Feel Like When You Get There: 5

Yuppity Doo Da: 5

Oh Say Can You See? 4

Crapola: 2 (A weakness, to be sure. But the bartender assured us there *used* to be a lot of great stuff. Seems the regulars began ripping it off once they heard it was going to be remodeled.)

Holding Forth: 5

What You Feel Like After Three Drinks: 5

Just a Little Something to Wash My Drink Down With: 5

Old Fart Factor: 2

What You Feel Like When You Leave: 4

You Go Figure: 3

Nowhere Coefficient: 4.0

Before heading to San Francisco, we slipped down the coast to the Big Sur for the day and dropped by a joint called Nepenthe, which is sort of what you might call an EST Bar Bar. This joint was built by the followers of some weird drop-out faith several years ago, and while the restaurant-and-curio-shop and the presence of Mom and Pop from Kansas are a bit unsettling, you can still discuss just about any kind of existentialism you want at the bar. That won't get it a rating, but I have to admit, sitting there discussing Sartre, gazing at the blue Pacific, ain't half bad.

Winnebago update: As of San Francisco, 93 and counting.

Just about every bar in San Francisco is a Bar Bar, and to prove it, let me tell you about Stars, one of the more frequently mentioned joints these days. To the casual observer, Stars would appear to have just about everything wrong with it that a bar could. It's light, it's postmodern glitzy, it serves Nouvelle Cuisine, the latest permutation put out by the Yup-Fern Food lobby.

The bar rests smack in the middle of the dining room, a concept you're beginning to see a lot of these days. It works surprisingly well, I suppose because bar patrons are forced to work at ignoring the food.

What makes this joint surpass its considerable Yuppity Doo Da factor is a fine old bartender named Shamus and the regular quaffing of a relatively new and very wicked shooter: pepper vodka. This stuff can get you Nowhere in a hurry, and that may explain why Stars will get a Transcontinental Award for Best Job of Overcoming Yuppity Doo Da.

STARS (150 Redwood Alley)

> **What You Feel Like When You Get There: 2**
>
> **Yuppity Doo Da: 1** (Sorry, but that menu just couldn't be totally overcome by the pepper vodka.)
>
> **Oh Say Can You See?** 1
>
> **Crapola: 2**
>
> **Holding Forth: 3**
>
> **What You Feel Like After Three Drinks: 5** (Bartender and pepper vodka.)
>
> **Just a Little Something to Wash My Drink Down With: 1**
>
> **Old Fart Factor: 3**
>
> **What You Feel Like When You Leave: 3**

You Go Figure: 3 (Pepper vodka?)

Nowhere Coefficient: 2.4

But the best joints in San Francisco are still to be found in the North Beach area. In fact, let me give this near-downtown neighborhood a Transcontinental Award for Best Maintenance of a *Real* Downtown Area I've ever seen. As I've mentioned before, this gentrification bit has really gotten out of hand, to where every city has a sort of Six Flags Over downtown area, wherein urban street life is "created" by restoring a bunch of buildings that (a) nobody gives a damn about to begin with or (b) ought to be left just the way they are.

North Beach has pretty much stuck with the latter. What renovation or new construction you see has clearly happened organically, of its own accord, instead of as the result of federal grants and tax incentives. The result is a pleasant mix of old and new and the sense that you are in a real place. The *Hungry I* is still there on Broadway, plus a bunch of old '50s strip joints, a new boutique or two, an old Italian restaurant. Downtown revitalization? Yeah, San Fran's got the trick: You leave the damned stuff alone.

You can hardly miss in North Beach. Enrico's and Vesuvio's are solid, no-nonsense shotgun bars, with ethnic underpinnings and all manner of remnants of the Beat era. But my favorites in this general area were Gino and Carlo's and Spec's.

Gino and Carlo's is a writer/journalist hangout that at first blush appears to have as much right about it as Stars had wrong. Dark. Small. And Gino and Carlo are what I like to call a Tag Team Bartender—Gino's the young smart-ass one, Carlo's the old smart-ass one.

We got to talking about Bar Bar etiquette and one reason was the very much aforementioned Al: Remember him? Guy that was at the Bar Bar for five days? Yep. Well, that wasn't lead-in hyperbole. It actually happened, as best I can remember.

I wondered if Al would be barred for his sins, but then I remembered that his wife didn't run the bar. Gino and Carlo did. "No prob," said Gino. "I've eighty-sixed people, plenty of times. Cussin' too much. That sort of thing. But Al? Heck, he's payin' as he goes."

GINO AND CARLO'S (548 Green)

> **What You Feel Like When You Get There:** 5
>
> **Yuppity Doo Da:** 5
>
> **Oh Say Can You See?** 5
>
> **Crapola:** 5
>
> **Holding Forth:** 5
>
> **What You Feel Like After Three Drinks:** 5
>
> **Just a Little Something to Wash My Drink Down With:** 5
>
> **Old Fart Factor:** 5 (Al: Young Fart Factor.)
>
> **What You Feel Like When You Leave:** 5
>
> **You Go Figure:** 5
>
> **Nowhere Coefficient:** 5

As for Spec's, this will suffice: I had to stand at the bar for about seventeen minutes before the bartender recognized that I wanted a drink. That's not only okay, that's *great!* Ultimate insult, deserved. Hey, it's not my bar. I understand.

Atkinson Transcontinental Award for Best Warmed-Over '60s Ambiance, too—a fact helped immeasurably by the presence of nearby City Lights bookstore.

SPEC'S (12 Adler)

> **What You Feel Like When You Get There:** 5 (Properly ignored as an obvious outsider.)
>
> **Yuppity Doo Da:** 5
>
> **Oh Say Can You See?** 4

Crapola: 5 (Lots of cryptic moral pleas and exhortations to save this or that.)

Holding Forth: 3

What You Feel Like After Three Drinks: 5

Just a Little Something to Wash My Drink Down With: 4

What You Feel Like When You Leave: 5

You Go Figure: 3

Nowhere Coefficient: 3.9

Fun Facts*

In nineteenth-century America, both condemned and executioner were provided pre-gallows sustenance at government expense. (Who says we were never civilized?)

I'm going to prove the ultimate usefulness of this national bar-hop with the following. If you're in San Francisco and you're a frequenter of Bar Bars, you may be tempted, or instructed, to visit the by-now-internationally-famous Buena Vista on the Wharf. Home of the world-famous Irish coffee. Poets' hangout, and all that.

Fine. But it's turned into one humongous Six Flags Over Bar Bar. Time much better spent would be to hop a cab out to Haight-Ashbury and to visit a joint that is anything but a Six Flags Over Bar Bar.

The Aub Zam Zam Room (Okay, class: What does it mean when the *name* is a You Go Figure?) is so inconspicuously placed that you almost miss it—a very good sign. But it's worth the trouble, because it is an Atkinson Top 10 in America, though I doubt the

*Erdoes (see Acknowledgments).

dozen or so regulars particularly give a damn—an even better sign.

Rather than get discursive about it, let me just list the superlatives I discovered in a scant hour-and-a-half visit:

1. Darkest Bar in America Honorable Mention: beyond Early Bunker and Early Dungeon, on to Early Grotto.
2. Absolutely *no* place to sit other than the semicircular bar, which occupies the middle of the room. By the way, though "room" is a preferred designation for Bar Bars, this is the only bar I was in that took it quite so literally. The Aub Zam Zam is just a room—nothing more, nothing less.
3. The best martini—a house specialty—I've ever put down my gullet. Price: $1.50. Bingo: Atkinson Transcontinental Award for Best Non-Happy-Hour Deal in America.
4. Owner/bartender Bruno Mooshei who also gets an award for Best Surly Bartender in America. Example? Okay. When I commented that the martinis were damned good, he said, "Yeah. I know." He's also been known to say things like:

    "If people don't like it here . . . they can go drink in a fern bar down the street."
5. A dandy group of regulars who acted for all the world like supplicants in some rarefied sect of The Faith. The Holding Forth was hushed, and at that, there wasn't much of it. They had come for their daily meditation, to take their Communion, and it was as seriously regarded as I've ever seen anywhere. Put it this way: When a young fellow began to hail Bruno by saying, "Hey, bartender," a lady regular clutched his forearm and whispered, "No. He doesn't like to be called that."

THE AUB ZAM ZAM ROOM (near the intersection of Haight & Ashbury)

What You Feel Like When You Get There: 5

Yuppity Doo Da: 5

Oh Say Can You See? 5

Crapola: 5

Holding Forth: 5

What You Feel Like After Three Drinks: 5

Just a Little Something to Wash My Drink Down With: 5

Old Fart Factor: 5

What You Feel Like When You Leave: 5

You Go Figure: 5

Nowhere Coefficient: 5

Back into the rental car. (By the way, is there any reason all rental cars are Zephyrs or some other oddity that no one actually *owns?*) And off to Mendocino, which was intended as a vacation stop; but damned if I didn't find another Atkinson Top Bar Bar. More on that in a sec. First, the Winnebago Update: as of Mendocino, 132 and counting.

The Bar Bar in question is a little hole in the wall called Dick's Place on Mendocino's main drag. Of initial import here is the fact that Dick's is part of the Mendocino Hotel, one of those froufrou restoration "inns" that charge you an arm and a leg to walk up and down creaky stairs and reacquaint yourself with the plumbing of old. But Dick's had somehow escaped the fresh paint job and so what you had was a genuine roadhouse sort of deal from at least the Depression, if not before.

Old Fart half-blind bartender during the day; big mountain-man type at night. Giants on the *radio.* Talk about your nice touches: sports on the radio. Just a Little Something to Wash My Drink Down With? Yep: try chili dogs. Perfecto.

Nice crapola too: old mildewed pictures of Mendocino as it used to be. Also, this kind of Holding Forth: "You know, if one more tourist sticks his head in here, I'm gonna shoot him." Also, regular at the bar brought his own sack lunch and just ate it.

But the real trip at Dick's involves a slight revision of Atkinson's rule regarding candlepower and windows and the like. It would be this: The consumption of liquor was not meant to take place in the presence of light, artificial or natural, except if the light happens to be reflected off the Pacific Ocean.

DICK'S PLACE (45080 Main St.)

> **What You Feel Like When You Get There:** 4
>
> **Yuppity Doo Da:** 5
>
> **Oh Say Can You See?** 3
>
> **Crapola:** 4
>
> **Holding Forth:** 4
>
> **What You Feel Like After Three Drinks:** 5
>
> **Just a Little Something to Wash My Drink Down With:** 5
>
> **Old Fart Factor:** 5
>
> **What You Feel Like When You Leave:** 5
>
> **You Go Figure:** 4
>
> **Nowhere Coefficient:** 4.5

I had never really thought about being in Portland, and so I had no idea what its bars might be like. I tended to picture a lot of guys who look like Bill Walton, sitting around sloshing back cherry-flavored beer and munching on granola sticks, talking about someone like George McGovern.

That's about what you get, in fact, at The Goose Hollow Inn. Oops, before I get into that too far, Winnebago Update: as of Portland, 189 and counting.

There weren't any granola bars on the menu and the folks here did seem to be drinking just regular brew; but everyone did pretty much look like Bill Walton, including the women. But the Goose Hollow has sufficient You Go Figures and a particular warmth to it that make it qualify.

You Go Figures? Okay, let's start with the name. Seems this area of West Portland is known as Goose Hollow and the reason for that is that people used to raise geese here—up 'til not too long ago, I gathered. Second, the Goose Hollow gets an Atkinson Transcontinental Award for Best Kind of Bar Bar Owner to have. This joint is owned by the *mayor*. Name's Bud Clark and he also looks like Bill Walton, or at least his pictures do. I didn't get to meet him because he was in Japan or some such. Too bad, too, because I wanted to ask him about stuff like, oh, health inspections, for example.

Anyway, the key to this place is that despite its absolute desecration of the Atkinson Candlepower Scale, it has a curious and unique Bar Bar ambiance. The regulars, rather than clustering about the small bar, just kind of sit in ungainly clumps around the room. At that, they sit wherever and however they wish—on the bar stools and chairs, on the Formica-topped tables, on the floor. This body language gave the place the feel of the TV room at a fraternity house, and there's nothing wrong with that.

I'm not sure what kind of mayor Bud is—the papers reported that he was in a bit of a pickle about his former police chief, a lady—but he'll definitely pass muster as a barkeep.

THE GOOSE HOLLOW INN (1927 S.W. Jefferson)

What You Feel Like When You Get There: 3

Yuppity Doo Da: 3 (A sense of it, but people who look like Bill Walton can only be so Yuppy.)

Oh Say Can You See? 1

Crapola: 4 (How many pictures of the mayor were there?)

Holding Forth: 3 (What little I heard had to do with Portland politics, which has to mean something; but I wasn't sure what.)

What You Feel Like After Three Drinks: 3

Just a Little Something to Wash My Drink Down With: 4

Old Fart Factor: 3

What You Feel Like When You Leave: 3

You Go Figure: 5

Nowhere Coefficient: 4.1

Portland, of course, has its Oldest Bar in City. It's called the White Eagle Tavern, and talk about You Go Figures. By day, this wonderful old saloon remains what it's been since 1905: a gathering place for Ruppies, Old Farts, Blue and New Collars, and the sundry ethnics who inhabit this marvelously mixed East Portland neighborhood. By night, it becomes a . . . live music bar.

That's okay, though, because I went during the day. Sample Holding Forth from nearby Old Farts: "I just wanna say . . . Are you listening? . . . I just wanna say . . . No, listen . . . " I lost track of the guy's punch line, but I think it had something to do with God Bless You.

The White Eagle was introducing something new on the menu, which is ordinarily a very bad sign these days. But this'll do: burritos. So will the efficient lady bartender, who had given me directions to the place by phone. "Yeah, it's real hard to find, but that's okay," she said. Come on, class: That's a 5 and you know it.

You Go Figure? Yeah, there's sort of one. It's not in the bar, but up the street. Indeed, this couple-block area that leads into the old Union Pacific railyard is the damnedest urban polyglot I've ever seen: railyards; electrical works factories; seedy bum apartments; and then smack in the middle of it, next to the White Eagle, a Yuppity Doo Da joint called the Belly Deli. Whatever.

THE WHITE EAGLE TAVERN (836 N. Russell Ave.)

What You Feel Like When You Get There: 4

Yuppity Doo Da: 5

Oh Say Can You See? 5

Crapola: 3

> **Holding Forth:** 5
>
> **What You Feel Like After Three Drinks:** 4
>
> **Just a Little Something to Wash My Drink Down With:** 5
>
> **Old Fart Factor:** 5
>
> **What You Feel Like When You Leave:** 5
>
> **You Go Figure:** 4
>
> **Nowhere Coefficient:** 4.5

I hadn't partaken of a Potluck in some time, and cruising back down Grand Avenue toward the bridge, I discovered I was smack in the middle of a Bar Bar Enclave. Some of the joints, like Digger O'Dell's, fairly screamed Ersatz Something, but the Grand-Stark Tavern didn't.

This is going to be a Perfect Five, so let me be as brief as possible. (First, though, an Atkinson Transcontinental for Best Potluck Find.) Okay: Right away you notice an ecologically perfect set of Bar Bar regulars. There's a Mr. Knowsit, who was talking about Reagan; a Mr. Hellyoudo, who was responding. There was even a Bar Fool, who was dispatched by the Old Lady Fart bartender to pick up some paper towels at the market across the street.

The crapola was exemplary as well, including a sign reading HANGOVERS INSTALLED AND SERVICED and a rumpled paper sack on the back bar bearing the legend JACK'S TABS. Just a Little Something to Wash My Drink Down With? Try potato wheels and dill cakes. That's world class Food Food, when you get into made-up stuff. Beer only, a drawback, but it was Rainier and Hamm's, a couple of golden oldies you're not likely to find at Bennigan's.

Hours? Yeah, they open at 9; not sure when they close.

THE GRAND-STARK TAVERN (438 S.E. Grand)

> **What You Feel Like When You Get There:** 5
>
> **Yuppity Doo Da:** 5

Oh Say Can You See? 5

Crapola: 5+

Holding Forth: 5

What You Feel Like After Three Drinks: 5

Just a Little Something to Wash My Drink Down With: 5

Old Fart Factor: 5

What You Feel Like When You Leave: 5

You Go Figure: 5

Nowhere Coefficient: 5+

What could possibly be wrong with a joint called the Rock Creek Tavern? Nestled in the rolling and pastoral farmland west of town, hard as bejeezus to get to, highly recommended by everyone.

Well, nothing, as for looks. Nice old roadhouse-type deal just stuck on some farm road. Inside, dark and woody. But closer inspection began to reveal some serious dual Ersatzes, or more properly, Colliding Intentions.

Let's start with *piña coladas on special*. Nope, that won't qualify as a You Go Figure, and neither will the presence of what was clearly a bandstand. I guess if I lived out here I'd come here, which makes it a Bar Bar through the back door. But whoever put those piña coladas on that blackboard ought to be damned to an eternal hell along the lines of being locked in a Pullman car, coast to coast, with Mac Davis—and he has his guitar.

ROCK CREEK TAVERN (You Go Find It)

What You Feel Like When You Get There: 4

Yuppity Doo Da: 3

Oh Say Can You See? 5

Crapola: 3

Holding Forth: 3

Just a Little Something to Wash My Drink Down With: 4

What You Feel Like After Three Drinks: 2

Old Fart Factor: 3

What You Feel Like When You Leave: 3

You Go Figure: 2

Nowhere Coefficient: 3.2

There are hidden delights in Portland's inner city, however. One is another place that claims to be the Oldest Bar in Portland, joint called Huber's. Huber's fairly leaped in my initial estimation when I discovered it's just a room tucked away in the old Pioneer Building downtown. Bar Bar in Building is such a rare and civilized tradition here that it alone can make up for a lot of deficiencies.

The deficiency in question here—and it really was the only one—was that Huber's turned out to be a bit of a Six Flags Over Coffee Drink. Why they insisted on this gimmick I don't know— coffee drinks are anathema to Bar Bars, for obvious reasons—but it clearly had become such a well-oiled gimmick that the bartenders actually had an ongoing competition over who could pour 'em with the greatest flourish. You had flaming this and ice cream that; guys pouring B&B behind the back, brandy under the leg; kind of a slam dunk contest of coffee drinks.

That's okay as well, because this joint was very dark, very small, and you had the feeling you could disappear here if you wanted to.

HUBER'S (320 S.W. Stark)

What You Feel Like When You Get There: 4

Yuppity Doo Da: 3

Oh Say Can You See? 5

Crapola: 2

Holding Forth: 4

What You Feel Like After Three Drinks: 3

Just a Little Something to Wash My Drink Down With: 2

Old Fart Factor: 2

What You Feel Like When You Leave: 3

You Go Figure: 3

Nowhere Coefficient: 3.1

A last note about Portland—which by the way is a great, weird city—is about Chinatown. Should have figured it: West Coast. Orientals go someplace else besides San Francisco and LA. Wherever they go, Orientals start restaurants.

They will start bars as well, and one among many to try in Portland's Chinatown is Rickshaw Charlie's. If this joint doesn't smack you square between the eyes as something straight out of a Charlie Chan movie, something's terribly wrong with you.

For some reason the Winnebagos crapped out between Portland and Seattle: 201 was the final tally. But the bars in this hidden jewel of a city were more than adequate. I say hidden jewel because I hadn't been to Seattle since I was a child and I had forgotten it's basically San Francisco with a good deal less big-city bullshit. By the way, this has nothing to do with anything, but, as scenic as this place is, it has a helluva lot of bums, particularly of the teenage variety. You might think this is because the city has a dearth of social services for the homeless, but my guides told me it's quite the opposite: It's because the city has *too many* bum services, which is something I would like to hear George McGovern explain. On second thought, no, I wouldn't.

Your best barhopping here is going to be in the Broadway district, which is just about the funkiest place I've seen in a long time.

Punkers, hookers, bums—you name it. It's sort of a Times Square, except everybody's dressed like they're in a music video.

A nice all-purpose Bar Bar here is the Deluxe, a kind of New Collar neighborhood joint whose only problem was that they wouldn't let you sit in a booth unless you were going to order food. Wrong, fried-zuchini-breath.

One oddity you notice about Seattle Bar Bars is the absence of two staples of Holding Forth: sports and weather. The former may owe to the fact that, hey, what you gonna say about the *Mariners* or the *Seahawks* or the *Sonics?* The latter is probably a case of more or less the same thing: What you gonna say when it rains *every* day?

What do they Hold Forth about? Sample: "I was sailing the other day and I swear, I saw a whale that was at least as big as that one in that Orca movie, or whatever the shit it was."

"That wasn't a whale in that movie, it was a shark. . . . " The subject matter may vary, but you can always find a Mr. Knowsit and a Mr. Hellyoudo.

THE DELUXE I (625 Broadway)

What You Feel Like When You Get There: 3

Yuppity Doo Da: 2

Oh Say Can You See? 3

Crapola: 2

Holding Forth: 4 (Fish stories?)

What You Feel Like After Three Drinks: 3

Just a Little Something to Wash My Drink Down With: 1 (I don't care what was on the menu; any joint that won't let you just drink at a booth or table is flirting dangerously with restaurantdom.)

Old Fart Factor: 2

What You Feel Like When You Leave: 3

You Go Figure: 3

Nowhere Coefficient: 2.6

Nearby is the Ritz, which I was told was a gay joint, and if so, it's a Transcontinental Award winner as Best Gay Bar Bar I found in my travels. Yep: no disco pickup joint here. Just a nice, civilized, woody little Bar Bar, where young to middle-aged gays gather and tell fish stories. Goes to show you the strength of the Church: I was here a couple of hours and didn't perceive anything different about this place from any other Bar Bar.

THE RITZ (429 E. 15th)

What You Feel Like When You Get There: 3

Yuppity Doo Da: 5

Oh Say Can You See? 3

Crapola: 2 (It was a little *too* neat and shiny, but you know . . .)

Holding Forth: 3

What You Feel Like After Three Drinks: 3

Just a Little Something to Wash My Drink Down With: 1 (Problem is presence of you-know-what food.)

Old Fart Factor: 1 (Are you kidding?)

What You Feel Like When You Leave: 3

You Go Figure: 5 (A *gay* Bar Bar?)

Nowhere Coefficient: 2.8

My favorite Bar Bar downtown—and maybe anywhere in Seattle—was a joint called Vito's, a hangout for pols, ex-professional jocks, and sundry other reprobates with time and money.

A very nice indication right off is the sign at the doorway which announces NON-SMOKING SECTION IS NOT AVAILABLE, and an even better one is the Old Fart Bartender who was at least 121. Very nice Oh Say Can You See? factor too, and some of the Holding Forth went like this: "Maybe they should just *combine* the fucking Mariners and Sonics and Seahawks and field one of those Australian football teams." Well, every rule has its exception, and besides, this is a book about bars, so why would you assume any of this is actually true?

VITO'S (927 9th)

What You Feel Like When You Get There: 4

Yuppity Doo Da: 4

Oh Say Can You See? 5

Crapola: 3

Holding Forth: 4

What You Feel Like After Three Drinks: 3

Just a Little Something to Wash My Drink Down With: 3

Old Fart Factor: 4

What You Feel Like When You Leave: 4

You Go Figure: 3

Nowhere Coefficient: 4.3

An excellent Potluck shot was the Tradewinds, which is not really a Bar Bar but is a plenty funky, get-down music joint, with wonderful bad Hawaiian crapola. I won't give it a rating, but you should give it a visit next time you happen to be, uh, barhopping in Seattle.

There are numerous little cafe/bistro-type deals down around the Market area: Il Bistro and Cafe Pagual, to name two. They are generally a bit too much bistro'd up—wine-of-the-day special and that sort of garbage. But they can be serviceable Bar Bars, mainly because they're hard to find.

My favorite of this genre was Emmett Watson's, and somehow I knew I'd like this place before I went in. Here's why: One of my Seattle Ruppy guides said she really couldn't tell when the best time to go to the joint would be because the owner, one Emmett Watson, just kind of opened and closed the place according to the wishes of his regulars. That's a real nice Bar Bar touch, and may I add, I think a lot of employers could take a hint from it.

Elsewise, Emmett's was a bit of a mishmash, a kind of Irish beer bistro, if that's possible. I did like the admonition on the television set which read SMALL-SCREEN TV FOR SPORTING EVENTS ONLY.

EMMETT WATSON'S (1916 Pike Place)

What You Feel Like When You Get There: 3

Yuppity Doo Da: 5

Oh Say Can You See? 2

Crapola: 4 (Standard Irish fare, but *lots* of it.)

Holding Forth: 3

What You Feel Like After Three Drinks: 3

Just a Little Something To Wash My Drink Down With: 3

Old Fart Factor: 4

What You Feel Like When You Leave: 3

You Go Figure: 4 (Irish bistro?)

Nowhere Coefficient: 3.4

14

Bar Bar 601: More Advanced Theology (on Old Farts)

I'll guaran-god-damn-tee you one goddamn thing . . .

We have here some addenda on that most critical Bar Bar player, the Old Fart. I truly can't imagine a Bar Bar without an Old Fart. For that matter, I really can't imagine *life* without Old Farts. Old Farts, to my mind, are the hidden caulk of civilization, a fact which the Indians and the Orientals seem to recognize a little better than we. Respect my elders? Hell, I worship the old coots. Put it this way: If I go through a day without at least one conversation with an Old Fart, I feel empty, deprived, and somehow spiritually vacant. Maybe that's one reason I've never feared growing old: I truly look forward to being an Old Fart and only hope I can live up to the challenge.

The key to Old Fartdom is, of course, a particular world view which is at once serene and ornery. On the surface, Old Farts would appear to be pretty easy-going guys—"Who gives a shit?"—but advancing years and the freedom of retirement tend to haul forth all sorts of long-stewing nags and bitches about this and that. Hence, for every time you hear an Old Fart say "Who gives a shit?" you'll also hear him say, "I'll guaran-damn-tee-you-one-goddamn-thing." Among other things, Old Farts are society's conscience, and considering the moral vacuousness of the Yuppity Doo Da movement, they are now more valuable than ever.

157

Atkinson's Field Guide to Old Farts

SECTION I:
So That You May Know Them When You See Them

1. Nose that looks like independent organic growth.
2. No ass.
3. String tie, or something similar.
4. Liver spots.
5. Bad hair.
6. Bad coat.
7. Pants that droop at 45-degree angle off no ass.
8. Hands that look like garden implements.
9. Bad belt.

SECTION II:
So That You May Know Them When You Hear Them

The most prominent sound uttered by an Old Fart is not a word or a phrase. It is a deep and distinctive guttural utterance, a kind of mega-grunt, suggestive of creeping emphysema or maybe a bad carburetor. At any rate, this particular utterance is something on the order of a universal tongue, and a very interesting experience indeed is to find a Bar Bar filled with Old Farts, which will usually sound a little like a zoo at feeding time.

SECTION III:
How to Talk to an Old Fart

1. "Uh huh."
2. "Yep."
3. "No shit."

SECTION IV:
What You're Most Likely to Hear from an Old Fart

1. About how if you're a younger guy, you're probably not going to see a cent of all that Social Security money you paid in.
2. About how athletes today have forgotten how to be team players.

3. About how it isn't quite as easy to get it up any more, but who gives a shit, right?

4. About how if you just put Sevin dust on the roses in *February*, you won't have any of that nettlesome blackspot.

5. About how you can't barbecue anything worth a damn on a gas grill.

6. About how "I don't owe anybody *anything!*"

7. About taxes—*anything*.

8. About bridgework—*anything*.

9. About how Chevrolet still puts out the best damned car on four wheels anywhere.

10. About how to replace a blown 220 plug.

11. About how when Eisenhower died, they broke the mold.

15

The Transcontinental Drunk, part 8: The East Coast

Customer to other customer: *Reality is for those who don't drink.*

alk about ambitious: Boston to Providence to Philly to Washington to Baltimore to Atlanta. Only difference was I didn't take the wife along on this one. By the way, I forgot to tell you—I didn't want to talk about it—but guess who showed up? Let's hear it for *Dave!* I have to admit he was getting pretty good at this too. Actually had the gall to tell me he had business and relatives in Boston anyway, so would I mind if he joined me? I could literally feel that American Express card wince from within the confines of my wallet.

My theory on Boston is that it may be the strangest city in America that's trying very hard not to act like it. You got Yuppity Doo Da of the primordial type—*preppies*—on the surface; and yet how do you explain Celtic and Red Sox fans? It's known, mythologically at least, as your liberal cultural center, but I swear I saw fewer black faces here than I commonly see in Dallas—and that's saying something. This place is a big synergism of social frictions and collisions and non-sequiturs, and that makes barhopping here almost as strange an experience as it was in Miami.

Example? Okay, try my first Potluck, which just happened to be the bar at the Lenox Hotel, where I was staying. I was killing time, waiting for my local contact, journalist Renee Loth, so I decided to knock a couple back to get my Bar Bar Face on. Here's what

160

I mean about appearances and reality in Boston: This joint was a froufrou, High Bordello–style *piano* bar, filled with bad glitz and the definite sensation that it had been decorated by (a) Lady Astor or (b) some guy named Tracy. You get my drift.

But damned if it didn't turn out to be a helluva Bar Bar, largely by the sheer force of the collection of Old Fart regulars. This was as ferocious a series of Holding Forths as I heard anywhere, and that includes Montana. Example: "You ever feel like there's no luck but bad luck?" That from a Middle Fart who later instigated a rousing debate concerning the regional differences of crabs.

And on it rolled. The gang each introduced themselves to me, and a sweet old lady added, "We're all just like a fraternity here." That's some serious Bar Bar when you go bragging about yourself to a stranger. Now that we were all acquainted, the Middle Fart let loose with this gem: "Think about it," he mused. "There's no way to be insulted. Really." That's a class-A Mr. Knowsit there, and my only regret is that there wasn't a Mr. Hellyoudo present, and that before one could be summoned, I had to leave.

"Bye, Jim," they all said as I left.

PIANO BAR AT THE LENOX HOTEL (710 Boyle St.)

What You Feel Like When You Get There: 2

Yuppity Doo Da: 5

Oh Say Can You See? 4

Crapola: 1 (That High Bordello decor just can't be excused.)

Holding Forth: 5+

What You Feel Like After Three Drinks: 5

Just a Little Something to Wash My Drink Down With: 5 (A very nice and completely incongruous touch here: Chee-tos as a bar snack.)

Old Fart Factor: 5+

What You Feel Like When You Leave: 5

You Go Figure: 5 (The whole place.)

Nowhere Coefficient: 4.2

Renee and I met at the Eliot Lounge on Massachusetts Avenue, something of a local institution and probably a Bar Bar That Got Too Famous for Its Own Good. But two nice You Go Figures caught my eye: One was that this is a sports bar, festooned with banners and jock pix and numerous TV screens; but it's got to be a one-of-a-kind sports bar. In most large cities—notably New York—the Sports Bar Bar has become such a refined institution that you literally have football bars, hockey bars, baseball bars—presumably somewhere an Australian football bar. But this is the only marathoner's bar I've ever been in.

Yep, just a bunch of dedicated joggers, sitting around and knocking 'em back. Indeed, a good deal of the Legend 'n' Lore around here has to do with the intergalactically famous Boston Marathon. The bar is even on the course of the race. That's beyond You Go Figure into the rarefied realm of Whatever.

Another nice touch was the fact that the joint had just been remodeled and there was a bit of quiet grousing about it from some regulars. Bar Bars occasionally have to bite the bullet and undergo a little spiffing up—there are things like, oh, health codes to consider. But the key is whether or not it's met with a certain obstinance. That's *Atkinson's Fifty-sixth Rule of the Bar Bar:* If someone's complaining about change, you're in a Bar Bar.

THE ELIOT LOUNGE (on Massachusetts Ave. just off Boylston)

What You Feel Like When You Get There: 3

Yuppity Doo Da: 2 (A few too many alligators, guys.)

Oh Say Can You See? 5

Crapola: 3 (Serviceable sports stuff.)

Holding Forth: 3

What You Feel Like After Three Drinks: 3

Just a Little Something to Wash My Drink Down With: 3

Old Fart Factor: 3

What You Feel Like When You Leave: 3

You Go Figure: 5

Nowhere Coefficient: 3.3

We headed over to Foley's, which turned out to be a Bar Bar That Even If It Did Get Too Famous for Its Own Good It Wouldn't Matter. This is a basic Irish joint, a sometime journalists' hangout, which is nothing out of the ordinary. But this was: From what I was told, virtually every square foot of land surrounding Foley's was in some way a part of Boston's new subway line. This meant that to get to Foley's, you had to park like a *long way* away, and then traverse several blocks of not-so-ersatz post-Blitzkrieg rubble—I mean, impassable *rubble*—just to get to the parking area, which was also pretty much rubble.

Unless you stood at a certain angle, you really couldn't see Foley's—but then, over a certain mound of crap, you could see the bar, a beacon amongst the rubble—and it was *packed.*

This bar belonged to these folks, and I swear, the whole scene could have been from Kubrick. I had a picture of a small and motley band of regulars, dressed Rambo-style—sweating and caked with mortar—struggling up that last little hill, finally spotting Foley's, and then screaming in unison "Auugggggghhhhh!!!" and then just shooting the living fuck out of anything in sight.

Of course, once you got in there, you realized this Bar Bar had much more to it than the trouble it takes to get there. No women, absolutely. Much too light, but a certain sense of privacy prevailed nonetheless. Keys here were two things:

One: Renee and I had bellied up to the bar and then she decided to go to the ladies' room. In the meantime, some not-very-ambulatory-type fellow wandered in and lurched into her space and ordered a beer. Fine. But when the bartender spotted her coming back, he told the guy, "Hey, buddy, take a move. *Lady's* standin' here." Phew.

Second: Then I had to go to the men's room and just left about $45 in change on the bar. I thought of this about mid-piss—know what I mean? So on returning, I was not surprised—just heartened—to find all said change completely intact, even though the characters surrounding it had since changed.

FOLEY'S (E. Berkeley at Washington)

What You Feel Like When You Get There: 5

Yuppity Doo Da: 5

Oh Say Can You See? 2

Crapola: 3

Holding Forth: 3

What You Feel Like After Three Drinks: 4

Old Fart Factor: 4

Just a Little Something to Wash My Drink Down With: 3

What You Feel Like When You Leave: 5 (Actually, you know how it goes: It's always easier and somehow shorter returning? I did the Rambo "Auugghhhhhh!!!" like *real loud* going back over the bunker.)

You Go Figure: 5 (*You* just try and get in here.)

Nowhere Coefficient: 3.9

Renee had a nice scattershoot in mind for me: East Boston. Say you've never been there? Neither have most people who live in Boston. Other than Roxbury, this city's immense black neighborhood, this working-class, primarily Italian neighborhood is Boston's most invisible area. An exemplary joint here, Barney's and Santarpio's, and of special note is the Just a Little Something to Wash My Drink Down With each serves: mainline, very nasty Italian stuff—pizza, sausage sandwiches, that sort of thing.

Elsewise, they were just modest little shotgun-style affairs, made singular by the cultural collision of get-down Mediterranean values in a decidedly WASP city. They're the real thing, though, and the funky neighborhood alone is worth the visit.

BARNEY'S (299 Havre)

> **What You Feel Like When You Get There:** 4
>
> **Yuppity Doo Da:** 5 (Saying a heap in Boston.)
>
> **Oh Say Can You See?** 5
>
> **Crapola:** 4
>
> **Just a Little Something to Wash My Drink Down With:** 5
>
> **Holding Forth:** 3
>
> **What You Feel Like After Three Drinks:** 4
>
> **Old Fart Factor:** 4
>
> **What You Feel Like When You Leave:** 4
>
> **You Go Figure:** 4 (Neighborhood gets it there.)
>
> **Nowhere Coefficient:** 4.2

Did a quite remarkable scattershoot the next afternoon and evening that ran from a businessman's Yuppity Doo Da bar in the Paine Webber building downtown, through the Six Flags Over Bar Bar that the TV series *Cheers* was based on, to a South Boston low-funk Irish pub. You can find just about any kind of Bar Bar you want in Boston, if you can see beyond all the button-down shirts.

Started at a joint called Brandy Pete's, smack in the middle of the downtown financial district in the Paine Webber building. This bar had pretty much everything wrong with it, but since Bar Bar in Glass Highrise is an emergent breed, it's worthy of note. First things first: It's too light, there are way too many Yups here, and the brand of bar humor as displayed on the back bar is not even a You Go Figure: THE CUSTOMER IS ALWAYS WRONG says one sign. Heh, heh.

But I'll say this, there was a nice cadre of regulars at the bar and the bartender did pour a nasty-looking highball. Key here has to do with *Atkinson's Fifty-seventh Rule of the Bar Bar:* If a drink is being poured with the aid of technological intervention, you are not in a Bar Bar. And by technological intervention, I don't simply mean those insidious computerized booze guns that they use at Big Jed O'Fern's; I'm talking about something as seemingly innocuous as the shot glass. The free pour—what I call the Pour Pour—is not merely the preferred style of mixology in a Bar Bar, it is absolutely mandatory.

This cat was a more than adequate Pour Pourer, and that alone got this otherwise dreadful attempt at a Bar Bar a rating.

BRANDY PETE'S (267 Franklin St.)

What You Feel Like When You Get There: 1

Yuppity Doo Da: 2

Oh Say Can You See? 2

Crapola: 2

Holding Forth: 4 (Pretty fair financial-type stuff.)

Just a Little Something to Wash My Drink Down With: 2 (Specials on blackboard.)

What You Feel Like After Three Drinks: 3 (Credit to the bartender alone.)

Old Fart Factor: 3

What You Feel Like When You Leave: 3

You Go Figure: 1

Nowhere Coefficient: 2.2

If there is an epitome of the Bar That Got Too Famous for Its Own Good, it is the Bull and Finch, just off the Common. This is the joint that *Cheers* was based on, and as Bar Bars in the Movies go, it definitely ain't no Rick's Cafe Americain. But whaddaya expect? *Cheers* attempts to evoke the Bar Bar ethos, but I'm not so sure it's a Bar Bar—mainly because no Bar Barmaid I ever met looked like Shelley Long.

Yep, they got T-shirts too—big surprise. And probably any other kind of crapola you might want. Of some positive note, however, are two things: One, you walk *down* to the Bull and Finch, a very nice sign. The other is the presence of a sort of Bar Bar in Bar. If you head toward the men's room, check to your left and you'll see a small and intimate dining area with a bar that appears to be inhabited by the *real* regulars. Now that's a nice touch: Your Bar Bar get too famous for its own good? Just create another bar for yourselves.

THE BULL AND FINCH (84 Beacon)

What You Feel Like When You Get There: 2

Yuppity Doo Da: 2

Oh Say Can You See? 3

Crapola: 3

Holding Forth: 3

Just a Little Something to Wash My Drink Down With: 3

What You Feel Like After Three Drinks: 3

Old Fart Factor: 2

What You Feel Like When You Leave: 2

You Go Figure: 5 (The Bar Bar in Bar.)

Nowhere Coefficient: 2.8

We headed to the heart of Yuppity Doo Da, Beacon Hill, and while the joint in question, 7's, is just barely a Bar Bar, it does provide those few who still maintain some kind of interest in Yups—mine is morbid—a little more refined sociology on the breed. In the beginning, you had Yups Who Weren't Ashamed of It—nothing more, nothing less. Indeed, a central part of the Yuppity Doo Da ethos was flaunting. But as the culture shook down, it developed subcultures, one of which was on display at 7's: the Yuppie in Disguise. The key here has to do with a certain mode of protective coloration. These Yups doubtless wore their tartan plaids and polished cottons earlier in the day, when they were setting up those 401 K programs for some unsuspecting small-businessmen. But by night, they affect different plumage: You will see a lot of carefully tattered Reeboks, more carefully grunged-up blue jeans, lumberjack shirts and gimme caps, that sort of thing. It's a kind of attempt—largely failed—to re-create the particular stylish slovenliness of our college attire in the '60s.

Elsewise, 7's appeared to be a bar disguising itself as a Bar Bar: The basic elements—a long stand-up affair with creditable Irish-type crapola on the back bar—were all there. But something was wrong, and I think it might have been that everything appeared to have been put there for a reason. Call that *Atkinson's Fifty-eighth Rule of the Bar Bar:* If anything about the place appears to be planned or preconceived for some specific effect, you are not in a Bar Bar.

7'S ALE HOUSE (77 Charles St.)

What You Feel Like When You Get There: 2

Yuppity Doo Da: 1

Oh Say Can You See? 3

Crapola: 3

Holding Forth: 2

What You Feel Like After Three Drinks: 2

Just a Little Something to Wash My Drink Down With: 3

Old Fart Factor: 1

What You Feel Like When You Leave: 3

You Go Figure: 1

Nowhere Coefficient: 2.1

On up Beacon Hill, near—no, next to—the statehouse, is a little Grotto Bar Bar known as The Golden Dome. As you might expect, pols hang out here, and here's how much: When they have a roll-call vote, it's broadcast on the PA system in the bar. When somebody semi-famous is going to be on the tube, the office staff gathers here to cheer.

Physically, I can think of no bar I've been in outside of Istanbul that had quite this, uh, subterranean effect. *Man,* have you walked into the womb, the lair of the Bar Bar.

Also, there was a particularly arresting Bar Bar Fool hanging about, who looked like a cross between Moe of The Three Stooges and Larry Hagman—or do they look alike?

THE GOLDEN DOME (150 Bowden)

What You Feel Like When You Get There: 4

Yuppity Doo Da: 3

Oh Say Can You See? 5

Crapola: 3

Holding Forth: 4

What You Feel Like After Three Drinks: 3

Just a Little Something to Wash My Drink Down With: 4

Old Fart Factor: 5 (What would *you* call approximately 97 guys who look just like Tip O'Neill?)

What You Feel Like When You Leave: 4

You Go Figure: 3

Nowhere Coefficient: 4.0

We really expected to find the Eire Pub in South Boston just like that, but one problem was that we thought it was the "Erie Pub"; a second was that we called it that; a third was that along the way, we encountered *Atkinson's Fifty-ninth Rule of the Bar Bar:* Simply, this axiom says that if someone can give you minimally precise directions to the joint, it probably isn't a Bar Bar.

After three or four fairly shuddering passes through Roxbury, we finally found a pleasant bearded fellow on a street corner who knew *exactly* where it was.

"See, you go on up here, hook a left, go all the way through the rotary, then turn right on that first street . . . called . . . Well, the name's indifferent to you because at that point, the directions will be implicit to you."

"Got it."

"Okay, then you just follow on down the road, maybe a mile, no, *two* miles, and you'll pass through this Howdy Doody sort of section with a Burger King and a McDonald's, and then it'll be right on your right."

That was the edited version, of course, and the more amazing thing was that we found it after only one more pass through Roxbury. Worth it, too. There are doubtless eight jillion of these sorts of joints in South Boston, the city's sprawling hard-core Irish neighborhood. But the Eire is as good an exemplar of the "Southie" Bar Bar as one could find. Big ol' gymnasium of a place, filled with bright red faces. How serious was it? It's still called the Eire Pub, a *Men's Club*—that's how serious.

THE EIRE PUB (Adams at Gallavin, Dorchester)

> **What You Feel Like When You Get There:** 5 (Amazed, following those directions.)
>
> **Yuppity Doo Da:** 5
>
> **Oh Say Can You See?** 3
>
> **Crapola:** 4
>
> **Holding Forth:** 3

What You Feel Like After Three Drinks: 3

Old Fart Factor: 5

Just a Little Something to Wash My Drink Down With: 4

What You Feel Like When You Leave: 3

You Go Figure: 5 (It's near a "Howdy Doody section"?)

Nowhere Coefficient: 3.8

We headed for Cambridge to check on a couple of Harvard bars, which are not going to get a rating because, as quaint as college bars can be, they are never Bar Bars because there aren't any Old Farts. The Plough and Stars, however, does deserve some mention and an Atkinson Transcontinental Award for Strangest Ersatz I encountered. Here we are in the middle of Cambridge, with all these preppies, and this joint's a C&W music bar! Go Figure.

Before I headed off to Providence, Dave and I took a Potluck for lunch at a joint called Joe's, and here again there won't be a rating. But some observations are in order, if only to prove to you the extent to which I sacrificed my body in the process of all this.

Here's how cagey Jed O'Fern and company have gotten: They've actually learned how to give a fern bar the appearance of a Bar Bar. Like with this place: Nice name; you walked down to it; the bar seemed suitably dark and woody. I was riding high— thought I had another banger of a Potluck.

Oops. There went the Fern Meter, and rather than go into a lot of detail, lemme just quote directly from my notes:

We asked the bartender if there was really a guy named Joe, and he said, "No!"

They served a Bloody Mary with a big green bean in it.

Dave commented at one point, "Great burger," and the bartender said, "Oh, really?"

'Nough said.

I hopped the train on down to Providence, which turned out to be the best little hidden jewel of a Bar Bar town I've ever run across. This particular phenomenon was explained rather succinctly to me by a fellow writer who grew up there: "Look, it's got more Catholics, more Democrats, and more Italians per square foot than any other state in the nation. That adds up to more drinkers per square foot."

I wish I had had more time here, because I definitely got the feeling that this is a no-miss sort of Bar Bar town. But here's a nice up-the-scale-and-back-down barhop as provided by a couple of great Ruppies (everybody in Providence, I would soon learn, is kind of a Ruppie).

A good place to start is Murphy's, which amounts to a sizable You Go Figure if you consider the fact that it's owned by a Greek guy named Greg Karambales. Nice little saloon with a deli set up to one side and a nice display of that particular type of Bar Bar Crapola known as People Who Are Not Nearly as Famous as They Think Who've Been Here Crapola.

This genre is something of a dying breed, at least insofar as I could tell during my travels, but Murphy's had definitely kept the faith. Basically, this form of wall adornment involves dozens of framed glossies of a particular sort of celebrity who stumbled through the bar at some time. You are not going to find your Robert Redfords in any of these impromptu galleries. Rather, celebs on the order of, say, Herschel Bernardi. In Murphy's case there were several notables, but a personal favorite was Barbi Benton. And of course, each photo features the obligatory effusive and phony salutation and autograph, wherein the star generally misspells the owner's name.

MURPHY'S (55 Union)

> **What You Feel Like When You Get There:** 4
>
> **Yuppity Doo Da:** 5
>
> **Oh Say Can You See?** 5
>
> **Crapola:** 5+

Holding Forth: 3

What You Feel Like After Three Drinks: 4

Just a Little Something to Wash My Drink Down With: 3

Old Fart Factor: 5

What You Feel Like When You Leave: 4

You Go Figure: 5

Nowhere Coefficient: 4.3

Actually, I'm going to do a little quick editing here, because my Ruppies were a bit off on a couple of joints. You can skip Hemingway's and Panache, unless you want confirmation that Yuppity Doo Da can invade even a backslider's paradise like Providence. The former is a glitzy sort of oyster bar in a new bank building and a definite insult to the saloon tastes of its namesake; the latter is a wine bar and I don't think I need to go any further than that.

But back downtown, I was directed to a couple of class-A winners that restored my faith. One was a joint called the Safari Club. Remember Atkinson's rule that if the first thing you hear is a lie, you're probably in a Bar Bar? Check this: On the far wall behind this bullpen-type bar that strangely resembled a cock-fighting pit was this hand-printed advisory: ANYONE USING EXCESSIVE PROFANITY OR CONTRABAND WILL BE ASKED TO LEAVE!! Uh huh.

I participated in a dandy round of Holding Forth concerning a child molester who'd just been sent up the river. I engaged with the participants as a kind of sociological test. The question was, is it literally possible to Hold Forth without the aid of *any* knowledge about the subject at hand? Sure it is. I had no idea who the child molester was, what the facts of the case were—nothing. But I did just fine debating the relative merits of his guilty sentence. Indeed, I think I convinced one Old Fart that I actually knew more about the case than he did.

Of particular note here was the presence of a superb young lady bartender, who stood about 6'2" and didn't appear to take any shit off anyone. "Yeah," she mused, "people ask me all the time why I don't get in more fights." Beautiful.

THE SAFARI LOUNGE (103 Eddy St.)

What You Feel Like When You Get There: 5 (Presence of immediate lie.)

Yuppity Doo Da: 5

Oh Say Can You See? 4

Crapola: 4

Holding Forth: 5

What You Feel Like After Three Drinks: 4

Just a Little Something to Wash My Drink Down With: 5 (Not a potato skin in sight.)

Old Fart Factor: 4

What You Feel Like When You Leave: 4

You Go Figure: 4

Nowhere Coefficient: 4.4

Nearby was the long-ago-mentioned Mike's 17 Bar, which may have been the best Bar Bar I visited anywhere. It's a perfect 5 and fairly screamed into Atkinson's Top 10. How serious is this joint? Okay: For starters, Pete the bartender posts a sign behind the bar each day that advises regulars of when last call is going to be that night. Phew. It has a men's room *only,* and near the coin-operated bowling game (the single best Bar Bar game ever invented) was another great sign, which advised NO GAMBLING. Okay, sure.

Not enough for you? All right. Pete was overheard to say this: "Maybe I should just start drinking my mistakes." Class-A Bartender Holding Forth there. As for crapola, how 'bout old '50s-style cheesecake pinup posters? Perfecto. After a couple of pops, I was ready to ring up Big Jed O'Fern on the pay phone, haul his ass up to Providence, sit him down, and say, "See? *Here's* how you do it!"

MIKE'S 17 BAR (17 Snow St.)

What You Feel Like When You Get There: 5 (Perfect name.)

Yuppity Doo Da: 5

Oh Say Can You See? 5

Crapola: 5

Holding Forth: 5

What You Feel Like After Three Drinks: 5

Just a Little Something to Wash My Drink Down With: 5 (Hey, they only went to the trouble to put in one bathroom; you think they're going to countenance a kitchen?)

Old Fart Factor: 5

What You Feel Like When You Leave: 5

You Go Figure: 5

Nowhere Coefficient: 5

That evening I joined up with a couple of Providence Ruppies for what I call a Bar Bar Gang Bang, wherein the participant willingly submits himself to being raped by an indeterminate number of Bar Bars. In this case, we started with Leo's, the "in" joint for young pols and lawyers and whatever else passes for upwardly mobile in Providence. It's a plain and serviceable enough joint, though I did notice the presence of a swordfish steak special on a blackboard.

LEO'S (99 Chestnut)

What You Feel Like When You Get There: 3

Yuppity Doo Da: 4

Oh Say Can You See? 5

Crapola: 3

Holding Forth: 3

What You Feel Like After Three Drinks: 3

Just a Little Something to Wash My Drink Down With: 2

Old Fart Factor: 2

What You Feel Like When You Leave: 3

You Go Figure: 3

Nowhere Coefficient: 3.1

On to Lupo's, a get-down music bar, which immediately demanded a further revision of Atkinson's rule regarding live music. That would be this: The playing of live music is to be frowned upon in a Bar Bar, except when it's a biker bar and the band and the bikers seem to be friends. Got it?

Phew. I had previously countenanced the fact that, in the name of thoroughness, I would need to include at least one Biker Bar Bar in this. I'm just very glad that I had traveling companions when I did so. Actually, one feels a strange sense of security in a Biker Bar Bar. Hey, these guys are like anyone else: They don't mind tourists as long as you tip well and keep your mouth shut, and I'm up to that any day.

LUPO'S (377 Westminster)

What You Feel Like When You Get There: 2

Yuppity Doo Da: 5

Oh Say Can You See? 5

Crapola: 5

Holding Forth: 2 (Bikers don't talk much.)

What You Feel Like After Three Drinks: 3

Just a Little Something to Wash My Drink Down With: 5

Old Fart Factor: 5 (I saw an Old Fart Biker!)

What You Feel Like When You Leave: 3

You Go Figure: 3

Nowhere Coefficient: 3.8

We wound up the Gang Bang at a pleasant little grotto called the Custom House, which caught my attention real fast because you walk down into it. It's a tad on the restored and precious side, but that single architectural feature made up for it.

THE CUSTOM HOUSE (36 Weybst)

What You Feel Like When You Get There: 5

Yuppity Doo Da: 3

Oh Say Can You See? 5

Crapola: 2

Holding Forth: 3

What You Feel Like After Three Drinks: 3

Just a Little Something to Wash My Drink Down With: 3

Old Fart Factor: 3

What You Feel Like When You Leave: 3

You Go Figure: 2

Nowhere Coefficient: 3.2

Took the train to Philadelphia and encountered Bar Bar on Train—an extremely pleasant and fulfilling experience. By the way, Philly can get kind of strange on you. It's definitely Eastern seaboard, European, Catholic, get-down, and yet—remember the Quakers? Makes your bar work very strange.

Two finds of note. One: Paddy's. This is pretty basic Irish stuff here, but with a couple nice You Go Figures. One involved the principal wall adornment, which was mounted jackalope heads; the other was the fact that Paddy's had no sign—a real purist Bar Bar touch. Serviceable joint, though, and the regulars had concocted a nice variation of girl watching where you spot one early and actually take your beer out on the sidewalk and watch her all the way down the block.

PADDY'S (200 Race St.)

> **What You Feel Like When You Get There:** 5 (No sign is always a 5.)
>
> **Yuppity Doo Da:** 4
>
> **Oh Say Can You See?** 3
>
> **Crapola:** 5 (Jackalope heads.)
>
> **Holding Forth:** 5 (Girl watching counts.)
>
> **What You Feel Like After Three Drinks:** 4
>
> **Just a Little Something to Wash My Drink Down With:** 3
>
> **Old Fart Factor:** 4
>
> **What You Feel Like When You Leave:** 4
>
> **You Go Figure:** 5
>
> **Nowhere Coefficient:** 4.2

One other very nice stop would be Kelley's, the Oldest Bar in Philly and a Transcontinental Award winner for Bar Bar in strangest neighborhood in America. As described to me by the bartender—who, by the way, actually did look *exactly* like Moe in The Three Stooges—the surrounding area included blacks, Irish, and Yuppies, comprising a kind of a You Figure in itself.

Elsewise, Kelley's was right on target, including the fact that it was 6 P.M.—presumably mainline cocktail hour—and yet I was the only guy in the bar. Call that *Atkinson's Sixtieth Rule of the Bar Bar:* If there are more people in the bar at 3 P.M. than at 3 A.M., you're probably in a Bar Bar.

In this case, Moe was more than a little pissed about it and eventually decided just to close the place down. "Fuck 'em," he said. "Fuck all of 'em." Then he pulled a beaut of a You Go Figure by offering me a ride back to my hotel. He'll get a plaque too: Best Bartender Car.

Oops! You're going to have to swallow one more dose of etiology here, 'cause Bartender Car is a real important aspect of this whole deal. I'll be getting into this a bit more in Advanced Advanced Theology in just a bit, but suffice it to say that *Atkinson's Sixty-first Rule of the Bar Bar* states that bartenders, they are different from you and me. Maybe it's the nocturnal lifestyle, I don't know, but I've never met a bartender who was remotely normal. They're eccentrics; they're hermits; they're the best exemplar of that tiny and mysterious pocket of American culture known as the Working Bum. By the way, writers tend to find their way into that pocket as well.

Check out a bartender's wardrobe sometime: straight off the rack, all right—the rack at Goodwill. And cars? Yeah, I can give you an archetype: 1967 Caprice, no muffler, at least three-toned, a few scraps of vinyl roof left. Inside, something along the lines of a ten-year-old's closet. I'm not sure Moe's was a Caprice, but it didn't miss on any other count.

KELLEY'S (5346 Woodland)

What You Feel Like When You Get There: 5 (Neighborhood.)

Yuppity Doo Da: 5

Oh Say Can You See? 4

Crapola: 4

Holding Forth: 3

What You Feel Like After Three Drinks: 4 (I presume; Moe decided to split before I could really see.)

Just a Little Something to Wash My Drink Down With: 3

Old Fart Factor: 5 (Moe will do, though he was kind of a Middle Fart.)

What You Feel Like When You Leave: 5 (Hey, a ride from the bartender?)

You Go Figure: 5 (Neighborhood.)

Nowhere Coefficient: 4.2

It's been said that there's no heartier drinking town than Washington, D.C., and that would follow *Atkinson's Sixty-second Rule of the Bar Bar:* The extent to which one becomes a Bar Barfly is in direct proportion to the degree of guilt he feels about his line of work. Hence most coteries of Bar Bar regulars will include the following: lawyers, journalists, judges, real estate brokers, developers, other bar folks—and, of course, politicians. My DR (Designated Ruppy) here wasn't any of those: He was Bob Mann, an old newspaper buddy who was a few months away from resigning as Senator Edward Kennedy's press secretary. Almost the perfect Ruppy, I'd say.

We'll get to the heavy-duty political joints where everybody looks like Tip O'Neill in a second. The best barhopping in Washington, however, has to do with . . . strip joints. Yep, for some damn reason, the ever-so-funky downtown of Washington is just chock full of real low-down, '50s-style strip joints. Go figure.

A nice two-stop run here would be Camelot's and King Arthur's. They're fairly indentical old joints with the conspicuous exception that Camelot's doesn't serve booze—or didn't when I dropped by—because of some problem with their liquor license. (Hello, Tip? Listen, I got this problem . . .) Anyway, the experience of plopping down $4 for a Coke for the honor of watching some lady bare herself is not one I'll soon forget, try as I might. No rating here, but if you're in town to visit your senator, you might avail yourself of this peculiar Capital tradition.

The current general-purpose Power Bar Bar would seem to be Joe & Mo's, brought to you by those now very rich guys who started the Palm in New York. The decorative style would be Early Living Room—low ceiling, plush carpet, homey and intimate lighting. As per the present rage, the bar sits in the middle of the dining area, but that doesn't seem to harm the quality of the ambiance.

JOE AND MO'S (1211 Connecticut)

What You Feel Like When You Get There: 3

Yuppity Doo Da: 2 (This will be more or less standard in Washington, for obvious reasons.)

Oh Say Can You See? 3

Crapola: 1

Holding Forth: 4

What You Feel Like After Three Drinks: 3

Just a Little Something to Wash My Drink Down With: 2

Old Fart Factor: 3

What You Feel Like When You Leave: 3

You Go Figure: 1

Nowhere Coefficient: 2.5

Traversing the social scale, at least in one direction, I dropped by Millie and Al's, a Georgetown College Bar Bar. It's loud and bright and won't get a rating, but if you feel like watching a bunch of kids almost throw up, it's worth a visit.

Over on the Senate side of Capitol Hill, the most venerated Senate Bar Bar is The Monocle. How venerated is it? No less than Jack Kennedy used to knock a few back at the small table in the front window here, and of course Tip O'Neill is a frequenter. It's pretty upscale, but any bar that's rumbling with Holding Forth at 12 noon sharp is the real thing.

THE MONOCLE (107 D St.)

What You Feel Like When You Get There: 3

Yuppity Doo Da: 4

Oh Say Can You See? 4

Crapola: 4 (Pix of pols—nice stuff.)

Holding Forth: 4

What You Feel Like After Three Drinks: 3

Just a Little Something to Wash My Drink Down With: 1

Old Fart Factor: 4 (O'Neill is a grade-A O.F.)

What You Feel Like When You Leave: 3

You Go Figure: 3

Nowhere Coefficient: 3.3

Much funkier is the House-side Power Bar Bar, a joint called the Tune Inn. I knew this place was the real thing when I noted the back bar sign reading MANAGEMENT MAY REVOKE SQUATTER'S RIGHTS. Just a little shotgun tavern with mooseheads and other frontier crapola, which forms a nice You Go Figure in the middle of Washington.

Just a Little Something to Wash My Drink Down With? Uh huh: chili and burgers. Special Atkinson Transcontinental Award to Ginny for Best Bar Bar Waitress I ran across. Phew: Ginny allowed as how she'd been working at the Tune Inn for thirty years—yeah, that's *three zero*. "Yep, I missed two months when I got married, two months when my husband died, and three months when I almost lost my leg."

TUNE INN (331½ Pennsylvania Ave.)

What You Feel Like When You Get There: 4

Yuppity Doo Da: 4

Oh Say Can You See? 3

Crapola: 4

Holding Forth: 5 (Ginny's alone was superb.)

What You Feel Like After Three Drinks: 4

Just a Little Something to Wash My Drink Down With: 5

Old Fart Factor: 4

What You Feel Like When You Leave: 4

You Go Figure: 5 (30 years?)

Nowhere Coefficient: 4.2

Another nice Kennedy hangout was the Irish Times, which turned out to be just about the most genuine Saloon Saloon I've been in anywhere. Endless stand-up bar and terrific old scuffed-up wooden booths. Special Atkinson Transcontinental Award for Best Overall Crap on Floor, Walls, and Ceiling.

IRISH TIMES (14 F St., N.W.)

What You Feel Like When You Get There: 5

Yuppity Doo Da: 3

Oh Say Can You See? 4

Crapola: 5

Holding Forth: 3

What You Feel Like After Three Drinks: 5

Just a Little Something to Wash My Drink Down With: 4

Old Fart Factor: 5

What You Feel Like When You Leave: 4

You Go Figure: 3

Nowhere Coefficient: 4.1

Ah, but my favorite bar in Washington was a sort of Potluck. Little joint in Georgetown called Mr. Eagan's. What can you say about a bar that has a Bar Bar library? That is some serious worship of the faith, particularly when the entries are obscure sociology texts and the like.

Another nice touch was the presence of makeshift Bar Bar decor, in this case, the TV stand, which was a couple of beat-up beer boxes. Watched a little U.S. Open tennis here and overheard this bit of Holding Forth:

"I really have to say that I don't believe *anything* that guy said."

"Who?"

"The guy from Orkin."

Well, you had to be there.

The Amtrak to Baltimore costs $11, and it is the best $11 I ever spent. This is very serious Bar Bar country. Here is how serious: At Bertha's at Fells Point, they not only had Scotch eggs as bar food, they had this sign: ABUSE—99¢.

But I'm ahead of myself. We actually started the Baltimore run on "The Block," which is the damnedest, best downtown preservation project I've ever seen. Reason number one is that nobody went and got a federal grant to do it; reason number two is that the preservation involves strip joints.

Yeah, sorry, we're back to that again. But I swear . . . Well, remember the strip joint scene from possibly the best movie ever made, *Diner*? Yeah, well that one's here, right on the block. Name's Pam Gail's and it featured a brief glimpse of some fresh sociology. For years those people who get paid to do such things have wondered what a woman feels like when she takes her clothes off in front of a bunch of men who've paid for the privilege. But here's one for you: What does a woman feel like when she's taking her clothes off in front of . . . no one? Get back to me, will you? Just a memo will do. Or better yet, have my gal call your gal, we'll run it up the flagpole and have lunch on it, right?

Up and down this three-block section of downtown, it's just strip joint after strip joint, and the thing is, there's not much sense of sleaze. Hell, one barker out front actually stressed hygiene in his pitch. "Cleanest girls in Baltimore" is what he said, and if that's not a You Go Figure, I don't know what is.

Now, back to Fells Point, which is really going to give you all you need here. Start with Bertha's, and right away you have a Transcontinental Co-Award Winner: Best Crapola. Doll's head, miniature boats, nautical rope, and to finish it off just right, a few spare musical instruments. Okay: Then you have classical music on the stereo, Scotch eggs as appetizer, and between all the rope and saxophones, some large Rubenesque paintings. No, I can't explain it.

BERTHA'S (734 S. Broadway)

What You Feel Like When You Get There: 4

Yuppity Doo Da: 5

Oh Say Can You See? 3

Crapola: 5+

Holding Forth: 3

What You Feel Like After Three Drinks: 4

Just a Little Something to Wash My Drink Down With: 5 (Scotch egg: hard-boiled egg wrapped in sausage, then wrapped in pastry, deep-fried. Whew.)

Old Fart Factor: 3

What You Feel Like When You Leave: 4

You Go Figure: 5

Nowhere Coefficient: 4.1

On to John Stevens Ltd., established in 1854, and quite naturally
a claimant of Oldest Bar in Baltimore honors, and hey, who's going
to argue? Atkinson Transcontinental Award for Best Bar Bar bar
in America—an absolutely stunning old piece of oak, all gargoyles
and stuff like that. A bit of Six Flags Over Bar Bar here, but in a
different way. The two guys I stood next to and chatted with were
admiring the back bar as well:

"It's just that . . . I don't know . . . I feel that the sense of what
the craftsmen were *saying* with this, what they were *emoting,* is
somehow lost in this dive. You know?"

"Yeah. Want some more broccoli-in-sour-cream?"

JOHN STEVENS LTD. (1800 Thames and Ann Sts.)

What You Feel Like When You Get There: 3

Yuppity Doo Da: 3

Oh Say Can You See? 3

Crapola: 3

Holding Forth: 5

What You Feel Like After Three Drinks: 3

Just a Little Something to Wash My Drink Down With: 4

Old Fart Factor: 4

What You Feel Like When You Leave: 4

You Go Figure: 5

Nowhere Coefficient: 4.0

Atkinson's Sixty-third Rule of the Bar Bar says this: If you find
a Six Flags Over Bar Bar and you look hard enough, you're probably going to find the real thing just around the corner. The real

thing in question is The Wharf Rat, my favorite Bar Bar in Baltimore for several reasons.

One: It willingly and happily lived in the shadow of John Stevens Ltd. Two: It was presided over by the best pair of Bar Bar brothers I've seen in a while. The older one, of course, didn't have the job but knew all about how to do it; the younger one was tending bar and having a little trouble.

"Two martinis please," I said.

"I don't make those," said the younger one.

"Nah, go on, give it a shot," said the older one, sipping on his beer.

Understand when I say "younger" I'm talking about 67 or so. So for the next twenty minutes I instructed this Old Fart on how to make a martini—or should I say *we* did, because Big Brother was in there too.

Go ahead and give it a Transcontinental Award too, for Next-to-Best Bar Bar Game I ran across. Game in question was that deal where you put in a quarter, then you manipulate this little crane around and try to pick up some piece of crapola. I went for the teddy bear, but wound up with a beautiful matching set of earrings—retail price $15, or so the sign said.

THE WHARF RAT (801 S. Ann St.)

> **What You Feel Like When You Get There:** 4
>
> **Yuppity Doo Da:** 4
>
> **Oh Say Can You See?** 3
>
> **Crapola:** 5 (Just the shit in that machine was enough.)
>
> **Holding Forth:** 3
>
> **What You Feel Like After Three Drinks:** 4
>
> **Just a Little Something to Wash My Drink Down With:** 3
>
> **Old Fart Factor:** 5
>
> **What You Feel Like When You Leave:** 4

You Go Figure: 5 (I don't make martinis?)

Nowhere Coefficient: 4.0

Well, if you're on a roll in Baltimore, why not just stop off at a Black Bar Bar that serves Italian food? Perfect. Called Merendino's, and suffice it to say two things: The sausage and green bell pepper sandwich was an outstanding Just a Little Something to Wash My Drink Down With. Better yet was the old black lady Holding Forth from across the transom: "I believe they gave you more meatballs 'an me. Where'd you get them meatballs?"

MERENDINO'S (2000 Maryland)

What You Feel Like When You Get There: 4

Yuppity Doo Da: 5

Oh Say Can You See? 3

Crapola: 3

Holding Forth: 5 (See above.)

What You Feel Like After Three Drinks: 4

Just a Little Something to Wash My Drink Down With: 5

Old Fart Factor: 4

What You Feel Like When You Leave: 4

You Go Figure: 5 ("Say, you wan' fettucine or wha', man?")

Nowhere Coefficient: 4.1

Whatever went on at the Atlanta Airport goes without saying, so let's not say it, okay? We're going to need to drop back for some sociology here and just go ahead and call this Atkinson's Travel Tip #4.

We have this problem in America, and it has to do with the conjunction of teenagers in the dull-normal range and the everyday, ordinary computer. I have nothing against either one taken by itself. But when you put the two of them together in a situation that requires somewhat more techno-dexterity than, say, a game of Donkey Kong, all hell breaks loose.

Take the Marriott Marquis Hotel . . . please. First, Melinda or whatever the hell her name was couldn't find my reservation; then she could, but it was for the wrong kind of room; then—oops!—just like that, it disappeared again. Meanwhile, Fred and Martha from Topeka—all 11,000 of them—were having the same problems, so what you had was a scene on the order of what that main road out of Chernobyl must have looked like.

Finally she said, "Okay, you have a room, but it won't be ready until 4:30 or so."

"But the room's only guaranteed until 4."

"Yeah, that's a point."

No wonder they burned this fucking place down.

I can't say my Bar Barhopping did much to improve things. Atlanta is your basic Sunbelt Somewhere, which means pretty much every edifice in the place is little more than ten years old. Three discoveries of some off-the-wall note, however.

Manuel's Tavern is the venerated Bar Bar of choice here, and despite the fact that it's become a bit of a Six Flags Over Bar Bar, it's still a creditable saloon. Of particular note is that it's owned by a politician, always a good sign. And the Just a Little Something to Wash My Drink Down With—burgers and chili—was just fine.

MANUEL'S TAVERN (602 N. Highland)

What You Feel Like When You Get There: 3

Yuppity Doo Da: 2

Oh Say Can You See? 3

Crapola: 4

Holding Forth: 3

What You Feel Like After Three Drinks: 3

Just a Little Something to Wash My Drink Down With: 5

Old Fart Factor: 3

What You Feel Like When You Leave: 3

You Go Figure: 3

Nowhere Coefficient: 3.2

A pretty fair Potluck I ran across downtown is Fitzgerald's, which is located someplace in the labyrinthine tunnels underneath Peachtree Center. At first blush, it'll make your Yuppity Doo Da Meter fairly scream, but they did have the UCLA game on and the bartender did run off this guy who was just hanging out without having bought a drink.

FITZGERALD'S (Peachtree Center)

What You Feel Like When You Get There: 2

Yuppity Doo Da: 4

Oh Say Can You See? 4

Crapola: 3

Holding Forth: 4

What You Feel Like After Three Drinks: 3

Just a Little Something to Wash My Drink Down With: 2 (I think it was a fish joint.)

Old Fart Factor: 3

What You Feel Like When You Leave: 3

You Go Figure: 2

Nowhere Coefficient: 3.0

The *in* joint these days is something called the Creekside Cafe, and of course it's not by a creek and it's not a cafe. It's a big old meat market is what it is, and I think I sensed the presence of swordfish kabobs. This joint has apparently supplanted Harrison's as Atlanta's gathering spot for whatever passes for beautiful people here. I mean, the bartender told me that sometimes, if you're lucky, you can spot Ted Turner here, which just sent a chill up my spine.

I mention the Creekside even though it won't get a rating because it did give me reason to slightly revise one of Atkinson's rules. I have mentioned on several occasions that hustling women and that sort of business is strictly a contra-Bar Bar sort of activity. I did not mention, however, what particular rule should be invoked when a lady hustles *you*, which is pretty much what happened to me. Figure it out for yourself.

16

Bar Bar 701: Advanced Advanced Theology (on the Bar Bar Bartender)

Bartender to customer: *Some people think Tip is the name of a dog.*

Those immortal words were uttered by the previously mentioned Joe Miller (RIP), who even in spirit remains my favorite archetype for that peculiar breed known as the bartender. Joe was eccentric, temperamental, irascible, alternately dear and cruel, completely irresponsible, and totally beloved. But the key to Joe, as with all great saloon keeps, was that he had no discernible past or future.

Check with any Bar Barfly on this: You can drink at an establishment for ten, even twenty years and you're not going to know much more about your bartender than the day you first walked in. Take Joe: About all I ever knew was that he was from Canada originally, his dad had been a rum runner or some such, he liked to play golf, and no, there wasn't any particular reason he wound up in Dallas, Texas. That's it, and even the small coterie of Old Farts who'd followed him from previous bars didn't know much more.

This is the cornerstone of *Atkinson's Sixty-fourth Rule of the Bar Bar:* Deep as the friendships developed in a Bar Bar are, they generally do not exist outside the four walls of the cathedral. I have found this to be literally true, even to the extent that Bar Barflies work at avoiding contact outside the Bar Bar. Part of this is vanity: You don't want those guys to know what you really look like, like in normal everyday light. Jesus—the first time I saw Joe on the street it scared the hell out of me. But there is a spiritual side to this as well: You have the feeling you might bruise those precious relationships if you pushed them beyond their proper time and place.

Even if you wanted or needed to know more about your Bar Bartender, it isn't likely you'd be able to find out. This is because no bartender I've ever spoken with at any length has been even remotely coherent. Maybe it's years of sneaking one behind the bar, or maybe it's having heard one too many lies, but bartenders have their own thought patterns and their own argot. They're spacemen, is what they are, and pity the poor innocent who actually attempts to make sense out of something they say.

Example? Okay, here's an only slightly reconstructed Joe Miller-ism. "I don't know, you know? This guy comes in . . . and then boom and boom. So I went boom, and then damned if the guy doesn't pull a McGilly on me." Understand: Joe talked like that *all* the time. The nice thing was, of course, no one ever dared say something like "What in the *hell* are you talking about?" We all would just nod and say, "No kidding? That's great, Joe."

One other thing to know about bartenders is that they're not on your side. Oh, they're there to float a tab if you're a little light one week, and they'll listen to just about any problem you might have. But on the crucial front of remaining remotely sober, they're The Enemy, and a cunning one at that.

Atkinson's Field Guide to Bartender Sabotage

The Retrograder: This is by far the most universally employed form of bartender sabotage. Stated simply, The Retrograder is a perfectly timed drink on the house that zaps the poor victim just as he's summoned sufficient resolve to head home for dinner. I am not certain where bartenders pick up the knack, but they can spot something in your eyes, something in your gait maybe, that tells them you're just about to wimp out. *Blam!* Here comes the retrograder, and of course you have no choice but to consume said libation, which in turn can possibly move you into the Fuck Dinner chamber.

The Ice Trick: This is an interesting variation of The Retrograder developed by Joe's protégé, Louis Canalakes. Most highballs in a Bar Bar are considerably more than the basic ounce shot, so you're generally dealing with two or three drinks in one glass to begin with. What Lou would do is let you sip that thing, say, halfway down, and then when you turned your back, he'd just plop a handful of fresh ice in there and presto, you had a *whole new drink.* Maybe there is such a thing as *one* drink after all: My recollection is that Lou got me wasted on one a couple of times.

The Depth Charge: This is the current rage in bartender sabotage and it involves a new and increasingly popular form of consumption known as the shooter. There have always been your classic shooters, of course: shot of whiskey with a beer chaser; tequila. But shooters have really taken off in recent years with the proliferation of gimmick shots like the kamikaze (shot of vodka with Rose's lime juice) and all manner of froufrou schnapps (peach, cinnamon, blueberry, root beer).

Sensing this shift in the marketplace, bartenders have begun to get heavily into their own shooterology. You have bartenders busily mixing up all kinds of alchemies: Bailey's Irish Cream with a shot of Stoly in it; equal parts Tia Maria, Grand Marnier, and Kahlua (appropriately dubbed a "strapper"). You even have this little number, doubtless developed in New Orleans: a raw oyster doused with cocktail sauce, covered with a shot of vodka. Talk about your Just a Little Something.

All of this was just fine until bartenders began giving these things away. A shooter paid for is bad enough, but if the guy is just slinging them across the bar at you, you can be in real trouble, real fast. Unlike other libations, the shooter has a particularly vicious time-release effect, and while you might feel great at the moment, it's only a matter of time before The Fade sneaks up and jumps on the back of your neck.

I'll tell you: This shooterology business has gotten serious enough to provide me cause to amend Dan Jenkins' ten chambers of inebriation, which as you'll recall wound up with a state known as Bulletproof. This is done with deepest respect, Dan, but a Wham Bam, for example, can take you well beyond Bulletproof. *Wham Bam?* Uh huh. Here 'tis, with full credit to Steve Harris at Hamby's in downtown Dallas, who's done a pretty fair job of getting me Bulletproof over the years: one half ounce each of Tia Maria, Kahlua, Grand Marnier, peppermint schnapps, and vodka. You sling down a couple of those, and you're talking not merely bulletproof or invisible; you're talking *transmogrified.*

Where could all this end up? I don't know, but it is not a good sign to see that distillers have gotten into shooterology as well: A cute little number that eased onto the shelves recently is something called Rumple Minze. It's just your basic schnapps, except that the bastards went and made it 100 proof. If you'd like to try some, just ask your bartender for a pop of Thunderfuck, which is the nickname it now goes by.

Fun Facts

The most loyal whiskey drinkers in the United States are in Mississippi, where two thirds of the drinking populace knocks back bourbon, scotch, or rye on a regular basis. The stoutest whiskey haters are in Wisconsin, where only one in four drinkers like the amber stuff.

17

Bar Bar 801: Postgraduate Level Theology (on Spousal Relations)

I was just on my way out the door and guess what, hon? I ran into Mike, and he was so wasted, there was just no way I was going to let him drive. So I'm feedin' him some coffee and then I'm gonna drive him home. I should be there in, oh . . . give me a coupla hours.

Well, we were bound to encounter some unpleasantness sooner or later. This Bar Bar business isn't all fun and games, and one reason for that has to do with the congenitally strained relationship between Bar Bars and that competing institution known as marriage.

I'm not even going to try to kid you with any false hope here: We're talking a terminal problem, and the only question is which institution is going to land the final blow. Wives hate Bar Bars—always have, always will—and the psychology here is pretty damned interesting.

For some time, I had assumed the reason for this was simply a matter of jealousy. But years of juggling what amounts to two marriages have taught me that it's not the fact that you're *there* that pisses 'em off; it's that you're *not there,* as in "He's not here." Wives care less that you're at the Bar Bar knocking a few back than that you lie to them about it before, during, and after. One place that husbands are not supposed to be is Nowhere.

What's that, you say? Why not just tell 'em the truth? Because you can't. I've tried and it's impossible. Ordinarily, one has to

196

psych up to tell a fib; but in the case of bars and wives, the opposite is true. You gotta try to get the Truth Face on, and unless you're a better man than I, no matter how hard you try, that same damned lie is going to come out.

Facing this state of affairs squarely, I have arrived at a strategy. As long as you're going to be lying anyway, why not just lie *better?*

● *Atkinson's Bar Bar Field Guide* ●
to Spousal Relations

PART 1:
The Lie Before the Fact

Face it, guys. The time-honored classic fib here—"I'm goin by Joe's for *one*"—has seen its better days. I sure hate to see the old pardner go, but there isn't a woman outside of maybe someplace like Chattanooga who's going to buy *that* anymore.

No, a slightly more intricate strategy is necessary here, and if you've got a better idea, please let me know. Here's mine: Tell 'em you *may* go by Joe's for a pop or two and then *don't*. They'll be so damned shocked to see you, they won't know what to do. In effect, you've lied your way into a free pass a couple of nights later. Continue the same strategy for a week, a month; mix it up. The key here is confusion—sorta like when the defense shows blitz and then doesn't—and nothing could be more confusing to a wife than for her husband to hint he might drop by the Bar Bar and then show up for dinner right on time.

PART 2:
The Lie in the Midst of the Fact

Face facts here too, guys: The old standard—"I was on my way out the door and Fred bought me one"—is also a dog that just won't hunt anymore.

The key here, as illustrated at the beginning of this chapter, is to get right into the flow of the present societal concern about drinking and driving and use it to your advantage. You can lay it off on a friend, or—I swear this is laboratory tested—on *yourself.* "I'm on my way, dear, but I was feeling a bit groggy, so I'm gonna have a cup of coffee or two before I get on the road." What's she gonna say?

PART 3:
The Lie After the Fact

Nope, apologies aren't going to work, and that old saw about "I just lost track of time" isn't either. Look, it's as plain as the nose on your face: You feel like shit, you look like shit, so once again, use it to your advantage. Look, a hangover is an *illness,* and no woman I know can resist mothering a sick person, period. I wouldn't go so far as to feign retching, but selected low moans from behind the newspaper will not be ignored. Of course, if you don't have to *feign* retching, go ahead and play that porcelain tuba.

PART 4:
The *All-Purpose* Lie.

Here *is* a case where what's getting older—"He's not here"—*is* getting better; but you have to be careful. If you're in the first, say, five years of your marriage, never mind. He's Not Here is going to work. After five years, however, they catch on, and while He's Not Here will work occasionally, you need to mix it up. Take that call every now and then and 'fess up, and at that point invoke any of the Lies in the Midst of the Fact. Then she's never going to know whether you're there or not, which is pretty much your Nirvana state of Nowhere.

PART 5:
Assorted Tips

1. If you're doing the calling, do not under any circumstances proceed beyond two lies. I have known only one fellow who made the third call, and he's not only not married anymore, he's not drinking at the Bar Bar either.

2. Contrary to popular belief, it is okay to bring your wife by the Bar Bar, but only with, say, the same frequency that you write your grandmother, which would be once a year when you thank her for the Izod shirt you're not going to wear. Exposing the wife to the Bar Bar will engender a bit of confidence in her and keep

her imagination from running wild, particularly if you can some-how make certain that the night you take her by, every other lady in the house is coyote ugly.

3. Contrary to popular belief—and you can make this *Atkinson's Sixty-fifth Rule of the Bar Bar*—it is *not* acceptable at all for your wife to start hanging out at the Bar Bar *on her own.* You see this heresy very seldom, but it is considered strictly bush league and may get you sent to the untouchable caste by fellow regulars. I've seen bartenders subtly take care of this problem, but in general it will be considered your responsibility, so keep your eyes open.

4. Whatever else happens, always keep in mind *Atkinson's Sixty-sixth Rule of the Bar Bar:* You can probably find another wife. But can you find another Bar Bar?

18

The Transcontinental Drunk, part 9: Denver/Montana

Customer: *What happened last night?*
Other customer: *It got drunk out.*

There was a point at which I got Irished out, hit critical mass as far as your Blarney Stones and all that jazz. I hankered for a rawer, less urban Bar Bar ethos and that meant one thing and one thing only: I went to Montana.

I first dropped off in Denver, perhaps the most legendary drinking town in the Old West. Too bad: Denver, like Atlanta, has had most of its rich history Sunbelted out of it. Unless you know just where to look, it's just another reflecting glass and concrete jungle, distinguishable from a Dallas or a Phoenix only by the presence of the Rockies.

I quickly found out just how hard it is to avoid your Irish theme these days. Hadn't been in town more than twenty minutes and there I was, bellied up to the impossibly long bar at Duffy's Irish Tavern downtown. That's okay, though, 'cause everything else about this joint more than made up for it. You know you're in a Bar Bar when you hear this sort of thing right off:

"You guys heard the one about how the Polacks got the hostages out of Iran?"

"No, but why do I think I'm just about to hear it?"

"Know how the Polacks got the hostages out of Iran?"

"No."

200

"Same way the Americans did!"

This turned out to be a dandy place to watch the baseball playoffs, particularly since they only charged a buck fifty a pop. An additional feature was that Duffy's was open for breakfast, a kind of interesting Just a Little Something to Wash My Drink Down With twist if there ever was one.

DUFFY'S (1635 Court Place)

>**What You Feel Like When You Get There:** 4

>**Yuppity Doo Da:** 3

>**Oh Say Can You See?** 4

>**Crapola:** 4

>**What You Feel Like After Three Drinks:** 4

>**Holding Forth:** 5 (Bad joke qualifies.)

>**Old Fart Factor:** 4

>**Just a Little Something to Wash My Drink Down With:** 5

>**What You Feel Like When You Leave:** 4

>**You Go Figure:** 5 (Breakfast.)

>**Nowhere Coefficient:** 4.1

Slipped past Denver's most famous bar, the Ship Tavern at the Brown Hotel, on my way back to the room. Name's a Go Figure, if you consider that Denver is just about as landlocked as you can get. Cozy little businessmen's joint, with an outstanding Just a Little Something to Wash My Drink Down With: prime rib sandwiches and potato salad off a buffet line. That'll do. So will the Old Fart next to me, who performed what I like to call an Old Fart Mugging. That's where no sooner have you sat down than the guy's all over you with some Weather Holding Forth. Boy, did he wanna *rap*. Swear it's true, he actually said, "Yeah, colder 'an a witch's tit out there."

THE SHIP TAVERN (321 17th St.)

> **What You Feel Like When You Get There:** 3
>
> **Yuppity Doo Da:** 3
>
> **Oh Say Can You See?** 4
>
> **Crapola:** 2
>
> **Holding Forth:** 5 (Old Fart Muggings are always a 5.)
>
> **What You Feel Like After Three Drinks:** 4
>
> **Just a Little Something to Wash My Drink Down With:** 5
>
> **Old Fart Factor:** 5
>
> **What You Feel Like When You Leave:** 4
>
> **You Go Figure:** 5 (Name.)
>
> **Nowhere Coefficient:** 4.0

Did a very nice scattershoot that night that started uptown and wound up down on Skid Row, where that legend in his own mind, Jack Kerouac, used to hang out. Uptown found me at My Brother's Bar, which is just about the best Bar Bar name I've heard in a while. A tad Yupped up, but the Oh Say Can You See? factor made up for a lot. It'll get an Atkinson Transcontinental Award for Best Music If You're Going to Have It: just long tapes of classical shit, which as a backdrop to Holding Forth can be extremely funky.

MY BROTHER'S BAR (2376 15th)

> **What You Feel Like When You Get There:** 4
>
> **Yuppity Doo Da:** 3
>
> **Oh Say Can You See?** 5
>
> **Crapola:** 3
>
> **Holding Forth:** 3

What You Feel Like After Three Drinks: 4

Just a Little Something to Wash My Drink Down With: 3

Old Fart Factor: 3

What You Feel Like When You Leave: 4

You Go Figure: 5 (Bach over scotch?)

Nowhere Coefficient: 3.7

Off to Eddie Bohn's Pig 'n' Whistle, and if you don't think that's a 5 for name, just take the book back and I'll be glad to refund your money. Nice Legend 'n' Lore here: Eddie's a former boxer and boxing commissioner or some such, and if you give him half a chance, he'll be plenty surly to you.

An honorable mention here for crapola: big murals of pigs and signs like BE 21, BEHAVE, OR BE GONE. Centerpiece of the back bar was a bunch of stuffed ducks and fish and a mounted rabadeer. Rather than get into a lengthy explanation, lemme just quote what the sign under it said: THIS RABADEER WAS CAPTURED AT NIGHT BY USING LIGHTS TO BLIND THE LITTLE BUCK, ELIMINATING ANY POSSIBILITY OF A SLIGHT PRICK FROM HIS VICIOUS HORNS, WHICH ARE MORE POISONOUS THAN RATTLESNAKE VENOM. Oh, now I understand.

Eddie's will also get an award for Best Back Bar Survival Kit: aspirin, Tums, and Chiclets. (Yes, presence of Chiclets is a You Go Figure.) If all that isn't enough, check this sign: ALL OUR VISITORS ARE WELCOME—SOME COMING AND SOME GOING . . .

EDDIE BOHN'S PIG 'N' WHISTLE (4801 W. Colfax)

What You Feel Like When You Get There: 5

Yuppity Doo Da: 5

Oh Say Can You See? 4

Crapola: 5+

Holding Forth: 4

What You Feel Like After Three Drinks: 5

Just a Little Something to Wash My Drink Down With: 5

Old Fart Factor: 5

What You Feel Like When You Leave: 5

You Go Figure: 5

Nowhere Coefficient: 4.7

On to Skid Row. Take your choice here. My personal favorite was Herb's Hideout—yes, yes, that's a 5 for name alone. And an Extra Special Transcontinental Award for Best Bar Bar Third World Clientele. Jeepers: These guys looked like they'd gotten turned away at the soup kitchen. This was a nice touch as well: I actually saw a guy get *thrown out* for being too drunk and acting up. Eighty-sixed at Herb's Hideout? Yep, saw it with my own eyes, and if that's not a You Go Figure, I don't know what is.

HERB'S HIDEOUT (2057 Larimer)

What You Feel Like When You Get There: 5

Yuppity Doo Da: 5

Oh Say Can You See? 5+

Crapola: 4

Holding Forth: 2 (Funny thing about Skid Row bars—there's *no* sound.)

What You Feel Like After Three Drinks: 5

Old Fart Factor: 5

Just a Little Something to Wash My Drink Down With: 5

What You Feel Like When You Leave: 5

You Go Figure: 5

Nowhere Coefficient: 4.6

If you want to upscale your Skid Row visit, drop by the Chapultepec Lounge, which is just about the funkiest music joint I've been in this side of Tobacco Road in Miami. How funky? Legend 'n' Lore has it that Sting dropped by and played here. That won't get it a Bar Bar rating, but it does place it a cut above.

Ah, but no Denver Skid Row scattershoot would be complete without dropping by the El Bronco Bar, arguably the oldest Bar Bar in Denver and a great place to observe this city's decidedly Latin underbelly. *Atkinson's Sixty-seventh Rule of the Bar Bar* says this: If the first thing you hear when you walk in a joint is a loud argument in a foreign language, you're in a Bar Bar.

EL BRONCO BAR (next door on Larimer)

What You Feel Like When You Get There: 4

Yuppity Doo Da: 5

Oh Say Can You See? 5

Crapola: 5

Holding Forth: 5

What You Feel Like After Three Drinks: 4

Just a Little Something to Wash My Drink Down With: 4

Old Fart Factor: 5

What You Feel Like When You Leave: 5

You Go Figure: 5

Nowhere Coefficient: 4.7

Okay, let me explain some of the methodology on this Montana run. One way to look at this project, I realized, was as a sort of *Heart of Darkness* foray. Milwaukee had been plenty deep into the jungle all right. But Montana . . . Montana was where I would find Kurtz. The *horror,* indeed.

I could have gone to Billings or Butte, but I didn't know any

Ruppies there, and damned if I was going to go out and get drunk in Montana alone. But in the small western Montana town of Missoula I did indeed have a Ruppy. Name's Jim Crumley, and like me, he's the author of several highly underrated literary works for which he was also highly underpaid, which is just about as Ruppy as you can get. He also knows his Bar Bars like the back of his hand.

An important thing to remember about Montana Bar Bars is that in most cases, they were the first monument to civilization attempted in the town. Most of your cultures will usually start with a church, or with your more Teutonic types maybe an army or a government building. But you get the feeling Lewis and Clark and the rest of those guys took a quick vote and decided, heck, let's get some place where we can have a pop or two, and then we'll discuss stuff like schools and hospitals.

This makes Montana barhopping pretty much a no-miss proposition, and not surprisingly it was in Missoula that I found the most perfect Bar Bar I have ever been in before or since. More on that later. Let me tell you how I got there.

We started out at Missoula's one and only alleged fern bar, the Eastgate Liquor Store and Lounge. Atkinson Transcontinental Award for Best Fern: A solitary and woeful thing that had never had any better days to see. Elsewhere, just a bunch of video keno games and this especially stunning bit of wall crapola: Seems the big social event upcoming that weekend was something called a "Testicle Festival," and I'm afraid that's exactly what you think it is. Yep, all the Rocky Mountain Oysters you could eat and free beer to boot. Like the tag line said, "Have a Ball!"

EASTGATE LIQUOR STORE AND LOUNGE (900 E. Broadway)

What You Feel Like When You Get There: 5 (That "fern" is an outstanding contra-icon.)

Yuppity Doo Da: 5

Oh Say Can You See? 4

Crapola: 5 ("Testicle Festival" sign.)

Holding Forth: 4

What You Feel Like After Three Drinks: 5

Just a Little Something to Wash My Drink Down With: 5

Old Fart Factor: 5

What You Feel Like When You Leave: 5

You Go Figure: 5 (Fern again.)

Nowhere Coefficient: 4.8

On to Luke's, which can be described real quick:
(1) get-down biker bar, including chicks with serious tattos;
(2) music by the Loudest Band in America (the plaque's in the mail);
(3) crapola included black and white glossies of *dead* regulars and one other priceless touch, a large autograph from that Near-Celebrity I'd Most Like to Get Drunk With, Hunter Thompson. No rating, though, because that band could cause severe tympanic-type problems if you hung around long enough, and so could, for that matter, the bikers.

No such problem at the Trail's Inn, which also had an adjacent Trail's Inn West, which would be right next door, presumably to the west. At this point, my Ruppy guide Jim suggested, "Time for a *real* drink?" and I of course said, "Yeah." The bartendress, a somewhat wholesome and definitely buxom young lady, simply replied, "Tequila?"

We said yeah, but here was the main thing: She said, "You want that with fruit salad?" Ordinarily this phrase is used with regard to the Bloody Mary, said "fruit" involving the celery, olives, or whatever other kind of green and fresh crapola you want to put in there. But here she had invoked the phrase simply to designate a slice of *lime*. Are people serious about drinking in Montana? Well, they *ask* if you want lime with tequila. That is serious enough for me.

Elsewise, we observed an Almost But Not Quite Fight at the

pool table, and in the meantime I got some Montana Bar Bar education. I'm a sucker for Bar Bar euphemisms, particularly of the colloquial kind, and Montana has a real beauty: Ordinarily you order a bourbon and water, or a scotch and water, or whatever. But in Montana, I learned, you simply say "scotch-ditch" or "bourbon-ditch." Etiology? Uh oh, I know I promised, but I can't resist. Yep, it is because the drinks used to taste *so bad* in Montana that people blamed it on the water and, of course, bitched that it must have come from a ditch. Just didn't want you to go off confused or something.

TRAIL'S INN (1112 W. Broadway)

> **What You Feel Like When You Get There:** 4
>
> **Yuppity Doo Da:** 5
>
> **Oh Say Can You See?** 5
>
> **Crapola:** 4
>
> **Holding Forth:** 5
>
> **What You Feel Like After Three Drinks:** 5
>
> **Just a Little Something to Wash My Drink Down With:** 5
>
> **Old Fart Factor:** 5
>
> **What You Feel Like When You Leave:** 5
>
> **You Go Figure:** 5 (Trail's Inn . . . *West?*)
>
> **Nowhere Coefficient:** 4.7

Well, if you're in western Montana, why not do a rural scatter-shoot and start with what used to be called Harold's Place and Laundromat in Milltown? The laundromat is long gone, but the fact that it ever existed gets this joint a nice You Go Figure right off. So does the Bar Dog, an ancient Peekapoo. Extra points, too, for presence of that most revered of Just A Little Somethings—pickled hard-boiled eggs.

Legend 'n' Lore? Yeah: There used to be a stuffed elk head mounted here that was *soooo* big *that* . . . it tore the wall down.

HAROLD'S CLUB (downtown Milltown)

> **What You Feel Like When You Get There:** 5 (Name alone.)
>
> **Yuppity Doo Da:** 5
>
> **Oh Say Can You See?** 3
>
> **Crapola:** 4
>
> **Holding Forth:** 4
>
> **What You Feel Like After Three Drinks:** 4
>
> **Just a Little Something to Wash My Drink Down With:** 5
>
> **Old Fart Factor:** 5
>
> **What You Feel Like When You Leave:** 5
>
> **You Go Figure:** 5
>
> **Nowhere Coefficient:** 4.6

On up the valley to Potomac and the Potomac Bar, which had just about the best Bar Bar porch I've ever seen. Ordinarily outdoor seating is to be viewed with the same jaundice that one might view fried potato skins. But this rickety little affair stared straight at the Rockies, and that'll give it an exemption. Tell you what, too: Any place that serves something called the "Awful Burger" can't be all bad.

THE POTOMAC BAR (Hwy. 200)

> **What You Feel Like When You Get There:** 4
>
> **Yuppity Doo Da:** 5
>
> **Oh Say Can You See?** 5
>
> **Crapola:** 4

Holding Forth: 4

What You Feel Like After Three Drinks: 5

Just a Little Something to Wash My Drink Down With: 5

Old Fart Factor: 5

What You Feel Like When You Leave: 4

You Go Figure: 4

Nowhere Coefficient: 4.6

We headed back toward Missoula and dropped off at Reno's in East Missoula, which is sort of like Missoula's ghetto, if you can get into that. Reno's, true to its namesake, is pretty much wall-to-wall video gambling games and the like. But the true character of the place may be found outside, at the front entrance. The steps up to the joint are framed by wrought iron banisters, which had been not merely dinged by automobile bumpers, but pretty much bent and gnarled beyond recognition. It's its own form of advertising, if you know what I mean. Reno's will also get an Atkinson Transcontinental Award for Best Rest Room Euphemisms: TARZANS and JANES.

RENO'S (on main highway in E. Missoula)

What You Feel Like When You Get There: 4

Yuppity Doo Da: 5

Oh Say Can You See? 4

Crapola: 5

Holding Forth: 4

What You Feel Like After Three Drinks: 5

Just a Little Something to Wash My Drink Down With: 5

Old Fart Factor: 5

What You Feel Like When You Leave: 5

You Go Figure: 5 (Tarzans and Janes?)

Nowhere Coefficient: 4.7

As I mentioned, Missoula is pretty much a no-miss Bar Bar kind of place, but there are gradations of greatness, levels of Nowhereness. What I mean to say is that the next afternoon and evening, I found the most perfect Bar Bar I have ever been in. It's called the Oxford Bar and Grill and you know you're in for something special right off when you are informed that the joint has been here since 1883.

This is the primordial frontier saloon I had been seeking, virtually intact: a long stand-up affair with an adjoining grill that serves nothing but pure grease. A few tables and chairs and . . . the poker table. Yep, they do that here too and the only law they have is that the pot can't exceed $100. Damned civilized, I'd say.

You wanna talk about Old Farts? Case the guys at the front poker table at the Oxford. These guys looked like they showed up sometime in '29 and just hadn't moved since. Not much Holding Forth there, but at the bar there was a pretty serious round concerning some poor tourist who'd gotten the worse end of an encounter with a grizzly bear at Yellowstone the weekend before.

Graffiti? Sure. Try this: "Kill 'em all. Let God sort 'em out." All of this and they only charge $1.50 for highballs. My Uncle John, RIP, used to say that whenever he had a twinge of agnosticism, he'd go to the mountains to remind himself that there just had to be a Big Guy in the Sky. In Montana, you can be respiritualized another way as well: by heading to the Oxford Bar and Grill.

THE OXFORD BAR AND GRILL (Higgins & Pine)

What You Feel Like When You Get There: 5

Yuppity Doo Da: 5

Oh Say Can You See? 5

Crapola: 5

Holding Forth: 5

What You Feel Like After Three Drinks: 5

Just a Little Something to Wash My Drink Down With: 5

Old Fart Factor: 5

What You Feel Like When You Leave: 5

You Go Figure: 5

Nowhere Coefficient: 5

Fun Facts*

Per-capita consumption of beer in America is roughly 20 gallons per year.

---

*Erdoes (see Acknowledgments).

19

Bar Bar 901: So Advanced You May Not Still Be Reading This Theology (on the Nut o' the Day)

Customer to other customer: *I like this place. How did I get here?*

Like any good church, Bar Bars frequently serve as impromptu sanctuaries for the wayward, shiftless, lost, strung out, or just plain nuts. Hence my current moniker for yet another frequently sighted Bar Bar character that I have reserved for special theological discussion: the Nut o' the Day.

As the label implies, the Nut o' the Day is not a regular at the Bar Bar. He's a walk-on, a stranger who drifts into the bar for no apparent reason one day—and usually one day only—and then disappears, never to be seen again. Nuts o' the Day vary, but generally speaking, they are drunk when they arrive, a bit uncertain of how or why they arrived, and usually a little, shall we say, out of your mainstream ebb and flow of life. This tends to make them obnoxious, and an awful lot of Nuts o' the Day I've seen have set records for least amount of time it takes to get barred. But no Bar Bar would be complete without them, for like the Bar Fool, Bar Nuts provide what every Bar Bar needs every now and then: something different to talk about at the time, and something different to lie about the next day.

You tend to get more of your Bar Nuts in your downtown spots and in depressed economies, where yesterday's perfectly respectable employed-type guy becomes, overnight, a potential Bar Nut. I have been able to personally observe this species in, of all places, my hometown of Dallas which in the post-oil recession began to spawn Bar Nuts. You had your run-of-the-mill bums, of course; but you also had out-of-work geologists, bankers, you name it—guys who weren't exactly drifting about the streets with a Safeway bag full of dirty laundry and a toothbrush, but who definitely had a lot on their minds and not much of anyone to tell it to.

A prime spot to observe this emergent species became my favorite downtown Dallas haunt, Hamby's, a plain old hamburger joint made a Bar Bar by bartender Steve Harris and a coterie of about a dozen mostly daytime regulars whom I've been sipping with now for seven years or so. Hamby's was almost perfectly situated and designed for Nut o' the Day traffic: It sat right at a major downtown intersection; it had a large front window, very suitable for peering in; it was near a couple of bus stops. Indeed, it was a fairly remarkable scientific exercise to watch the Nut Meter rise almost in direct proportion to the plummet in the price of crude oil during the summer and fall of 1986.

In fact, I started keeping a flowchart, kind of like naturalists do when they go out and count whooping cranes or whatever, and I swear this is true: For the month of August 1986, there was at least one nut per day at the bar. That is some serious social history.

Subspecies? Of course, and here is an Atkinson Field Guide that is truly ahead of its time.

Atkinson Field Guide to Nuts o' the Day

The Bum: Your garden-variety geezer, and you know the ensemble: old double-knit slacks, Nik-Nik shirt, sport coat, and shoes three sizes too big. Tie. By the way, ever notice how all Bums, regardless of age, race, or creed, walk exactly alike? Steve and I figured out that is because they all wear someone else's discarded shoes. Just a little FYI stuff here.

Anyway, the Bum's been shooting some Ripple since 8 A.M. and is liable to say something like, "Jus' one lil' beer, and then I gotta go to the house." Yeah, sure, buddy. What house? One thing we did notice was that the Bums of today are a good deal more aggressive than they used to be, which means there may have been a Bum Liberation Movement out there that we didn't know about. This is true: This guy walked in one day and I said something like, "How's it goin'?" He said, "It'd be goin' a lot better if you'd buy me a beer."

Young 'n' Ornery: This emergent breed of Bar Nut has really come on lately. A good shorthand way to understand him is that he's a New Collar Ruppy, which means he's not only ornery but potentially dangerous. Kind of guy who wears a lot of keys on his belt and asks the price of every different bottled beer. We had one at Hamby's who eased up to the bar, ordered a beer, and then inside of five minutes allowed that he was (a) a bounty hunter, (b) a drug-abuse therapist, and (c) mighty pissed off at this decadent society. When I asked him how he, uh, managed to juggle his varied interests, he gave me this cold schizophrenic stare and said, "What's the name of this place?"

You Already Have Enough Friends but He Doesn't: You've doubtless met this fellow at, say, the airport. He's the sort who doesn't understand that certain life functions—going to the grocery store, standing in line at the movies—necessitate the proximity of strangers, and that when involved in those circumstances, it's okay—no, preferred—to continue to act like strangers. What he thinks is that by the happenstance of physical proximity, you have become a friend.

This is no shit. Call Steve and ask him about it, if you doubt me. This guy came in one day, kind of an ersatz Richard Gere Nut o' the Day, sidled up to the bar, ordered a cocktail, and inside of five minutes asked me this: "Where'd you and your wife meet?" I gave Steve the Regular in Distress look, and of course he just smiled and said he had to do inventory. (You got it—that's another form of bartender sabotage, and hence *Atkinson's Sixty-eighth Rule of the Bar Bar:* If you happen to get stuck with the Nut o' the Day, don't expect any help.

Sometimes Nuts o' the Day defy categorization. As Exhibit A, let me present one Mr. Butler, who strolled in one day and immediately caught our attention by jacking down twelve Jack Daniels on the rocks inside of an hour and a half. He was a respectable-enough looking fellow, suited and tied and toting a briefcase, so someone chanced asking him what he did for a living.

"*CPA*. In town for a convention. Got a room at the hotel up the way." This might have flown, had it not been for the fact that when he was asked where he was from, he said Plano, which happens to be a suburb ten miles north of Dallas. Considering his consumption, I guess you'd have to call that CPA-like planning in advance.

Well, it should come as no surprise that Mr. Butler forgot his briefcase, and even less of one that we proceeded to rummage through it in some kind of sick archeological frenzy. Boy, if that briefcase could talk: Inside were several legal files, each concerning some form of action against Mr. Butler; another file contained an estimate on the damage to his car from a presumably recent wreck. And the pièce de résistance: five reasonably expensive neckties, tags and prices still attached. Hmmmm. "See ya, dear. I'm goin on down to the CPA convention, but first I'm gonna go lift some ties and get trashed at the first joint I can find." Go figure indeed.

I dropped in a couple of weeks later and asked Steve if Butler had been in to retrieve his briefcase. Steve said, "What briefcase?"

Bar Bar 102: So Advanced You May Not Care Anymore Theology (on Bar Bar Cocktails)

Customer to bartender: *My bartender used to make my martinis by pourin' some gin in a glass, dropping in a little ice, and then just thinking about vermouth.*

It's time to 'fess up, get down, make some enemies out there. Here's Atkinson's Field Guide to the Best Cocktails in America, and yes, it is arbitrary, capricious, whimsical, and a tad tainted by bouts with frontal-lobe memory loss. But what the heck: I've discovered that people don't necessarily care if they're getting correct decisions anymore, just so long as someone makes a damned decision. That's why those Gallup polls always show judges to be much more popular than state representatives, though a careful perusal of what each type of decision-maker has done for us lately would doubtless reveal that they've each effected an equal amount of social retrogression. This is especially true of folks who hang out in bars, who are quite used to discussing half- and non-truths with utter seriousness for hours, even days—and don't kid me, if you've read this far, *you* hang out in bars.

THE BEST COCKTAILS IN AMERICA

1. The martini at the Aub Zam Zam Room in San Francisco. Smooth, dry, only a specter of vermouth. Costs a buck seventy-five. Need to know any more?
2. Any whiskey highball at the Oak Bar at the Plaza Hotel in

New York. I never thought I'd live to say this, but this depth-charged little beauty is stiffer than any I've ever had—and that includes the nitroglycerin they serve at my beloved Joe Miller's in Dallas.

3. The Tequila Sunrise at the Kentucky Club in Juarez, Mexico. Made with real stuff and the right color—*purple*, not sickly yellow.

4. Beer and a shot at Koz's Mini-Bowl and Beer in Milwaukee. It's a quarter for the beer, 75 cents for the shot of schnapps. You can get swacked for a fiver. 'Nough said.

5. The scratch Bloody Mary at the Oxford Bar and Grill in Missoula, Montana. Heavy on the Tabasco and with olives—beautiful. Guy even asked if it was right when I ordered a second. A buck and fifty doesn't hurt.

6. The scratch Bloody Mary at the Part Two Burger Bar in Queens. Heavy on the horseradish, and this guy too asked if I wanted an extra jolt of hot stuff.

7. Coffee and cognac at Huber's in Portland, Oregon. Sorry, Buena Vista in San Francisco. This was extra heavy on the cognac, and they don't serve it in a commemorative mug.

8. Vodka rickey at the Plough and Stars in Cambridge, Massachusetts. A jerk-off college music joint, yes. But they served my favorite cocktail in what had to be a 16-ounce tumbler and my recollection is, when I gave the lady a five, she gave me back three.

9. Wine spritzer at Dick's Place in Mendocino, California. Bet you didn't think you'd find that paragon of Yuppity Doo Da libations listed here. Well, it's done somewhat begrudgingly, but Dick's half-blind old bartender mixed it just right, wine and soda, and just served it in a plain glass. Besides, with the Pacific Ocean to look at, everything goes down great.

10. Cherry Ale at Barney's Beanery in Los Angeles. I ordinarily loathe eccentric beer, but this stuff was just so *weird*, it deserves mention.

11. Any second drink at Louie's in Dallas: Lou doesn't take any chance with waiting until your fourth or fifth; he depth-

charges numero 2, which usually ensures there is a fourth
or fifth.
12. The Wham-Bam at Hamby's Dallas. Bartender Steve Harris'
idea of humor, but this evil concoction of four liquers will
generally catapult you well beyond laughing drunk.

21

The Transcontinental Drunk, part 10: The Southwest

Customer to other customer: *Why don't you just sober up and go home?*
Other customer: *I did that earlier.*

lbuquerque, Santa Fe, Tucson. Nothing ersatz about these shitkickers and chiefs, and if you don't believe me, you try bringing up the AIDS epidemic at Johnny Ringo's in Tombstone, Arizona. In Tombstone, they still call 'em homos and they're usually pretty generous with their modifying adjectives.

Not to worry, though: Every good bar run needs a dose of ersatz something, so after several days of listening to Marty Robbins and staring into the darkness along with guys wearing blankets from Sears (I don't know why, but the Indians who make those nifty patterned blankets in these parts never use 'em; they seem to prefer to just yank the old baby-blue flannel job off the bed and toss it around their shoulders), I tacked on a little weekend run to the Cosmos of Ersatz—Vegas.

More on that later—and yes, there will be a brief discussion of how the advance money was holding up. I started the run in Albuquerque, which may best be described as kind of a poor man's Dallas. The Sunbelters, that secret fraternity of developers and architects who have presided over much of the Glassing of America, have done their number here too, but somehow you can't see a show called *Albuquerque!* popping up in prime time.

But as with Atlanta, the Sunbelting process has taken its toll on Bar Bars. I didn't go to any of the 8 billion fern bars here, but I have little doubt they're the same as that single example I found in Milwaukee, with maybe some kind of disgusting colloquial touch, like a cactus salad munchie. Anyway, the pickings are slim, but hey, that's what I'm here for, I guess, so here's what I dug up with the help of a Ruppy or two.

A very pleasant Bar Bar experience may be had at Al Monte's, said experience being trashing the afternoon away watching *The Dating Game* and sipping Corona with lime. Ostensibly this is a restaurant, and it's a You Go Figure restaurant at that: serves Mexican food by day, Italian at night. Huh. But the bar is a cozy sliver of a room, dominated by an immense fireplace and an adequately taciturn young bartender. A particularly interesting touch in many southwestern Bar Bars is the deployment of chairs instead of stools at the bar itself. I'm a backslider and a purist when it comes to messing with the basic canons of the church, but pulling up a captain's chair to a long, low-slung bar is kind of a nifty way to get drunk. Cuts down the premium on the joint's liability insurance too, I suspect.

AL MONTE'S (1306 Rio Grande)

What You Feel Like When You Get There: 3

Yuppity Doo Da: 4

Oh Say Can You See? 5

Crapola: 2

Holding Forth: 5 (Daytime TV watching is always a 5.)

What You Feel Like After Three Drinks: 4

Just a Little Something to Wash My Drink Down With: 2

Old Fart Factor: 3

What You Feel Like When You Leave: 4

You Go Figure: 5 (If you didn't like the enchiladas verdes for lunch, you can always come back have have the linguini with clam sauce for dinner.)

Nowhere Coefficient: 3.7

Ah, but it was time to face the music, and they've got a shitload of that at the Caravan East, which, by the way, has one of the most abstruse You Go Figure dress codes I ran across. In fact, go ahead and expect a Transcontinental Award and I've even got a suggestion for where they can put the plaque.

This is mainline, shitkicker, two-step dance hall territory, and everybody knows that cowboys can be very strange when it comes to people who don't look like them. Here's what happened: I was wearing my preferred drinking garb, what I like to call the New Everyman Suit, which consists of suitably faded Calvin Klein jeans, sweatshirt, Adidas jacket, tennis shoes. I'm not sure why, but aside from sheer comfort and durability, this particular combination seems to zoom past every conceivable kind of dress code and has a peculiar chameleonic quality that allows one to go from the local dive to the bus station to suburban Bennigan's without being noticed in any locus. Not so at the Caravan East, however.

I was just strolling along, ready for another bit of Holding Forth concerning the "homo" problem, when this guy at the door says, "Wait a minute." I reached for my wallet, thinking there might be in force that most disgusting bar practice, the cover charge, but the guy shook his head and pointed at the hood of my sweatshirt.

"You wanna go in, you're gonna have to take off that shirt."

I was real glad I'd fortified myself with some juevos rancheros. I was rational. "Uh, yeah, but I don't have another shirt, see. This is my shirt. I only wore one tonight for some reason." He didn't get it.

"Well, then tuck that hood in under the jacket. We don't like those hoods out. 'Course, you'll probably have it back out by the time you get to the bar." He actually laughed, at something. Go figure—please—and in this case, I'd appreciate *any* possible explanation you come up with.

But then there was the Caravan East itself. Let me say this: I have tried, I really have, with this cowboy stuff. Hell, I'm from Texas, occasionally wear cowboy boots, remain an ardent fan of quality westerns like *Gunsmoke* and Eastwood's early stuff. *But,* enough is enough. Even an hour spent at the bar at a joint like the Caravan East can make you wonder if, in fact, these shitkickers are the real thing—if, in fact, *any* shitkickers are the real thing. Maybe all cowboys are ersatz these days. What I do know is that they can be real jerks and, yeah, if there's a Cowboy Liberation Movement out there, don't hesitate to write a nasty letter or to try to pipe-bomb my car. I mean it.

Oh well, despite all the *"Yeeeee . . . haaaaaw!"* and stuff, the bar here was a serviceable representation of the real thing, starting and ending with the Oh Say Can You See? factor. Just remember to get about half in the bag before you go, to wear earplugs (the only thing worse than the Loudest Rock Band in the World is the Loudest C & W Band in the World), and, oh yeah, make that a hoodless sweatshirt, if you're so inclined.

THE CARAVAN EAST (7605 Central Ave.)

What You Feel Like When You Get There: 1

Yuppity Doo Da: 5

Oh Say Can You See? 5

Crapola: 3

Holding Forth: 3

What You Feel Like After Three Drinks: 3

Just a Little Something to Wash My Drink Down With: 3

Old Fart Factor: 5

What You Feel Like When You Leave: 3

You Go Figure: 5

Nowhere Coefficient: 3.6

I truly enjoyed Charlie's Backdoor, however, and yes, that is a
5 for name. In fact, make it a 5+, because it actually has a back
door, like around *back* in the alley. The *front* door leads to the
restaurant *only*. If you want a drink, you have to go outside and
around *back*. Nice touch.

Elsewise, solid on all fronts, including Monday Night Football
watching, with sound up—a must. I doubt I'll ever live in Albuquerque, can't imagine wanting to. But it's nice to know even
this Sunbelt ghetto has the real thing.

CHARLIE'S BACKDOOR (8224 Menaul)

What You Feel Like When You Get There: 4

Yuppity Doo Da: 5

Oh Say Can You See? 5

Crapola: 5

Holding Forth: 4

What You Feel Like After Three Drinks: 4

Just a Little Something to Wash My Drink Down With: 4

Old Fart Factor: 4

What You Feel Like When You Leave: 4

You Go Figure: 3

Nowhere Coefficient: 4.2

Boy, had I forgotten what a nice place Santa Fe is. Unlike Carmel, it still works as a decent place to be, even if you're not a
tourist. There are plenty of Old Farts standing around with their
hands in their pockets looking at ripoff Indian jewelry and asking
the wife every five minutes if it's lunchtime yet. But somehow
they don't overwhelm, as in Carmel.

Bar Bars? Well, yes and no. The La Fiesta at the La Fonda Hotel
is just a hotel bar, nothing more, nothing less; and the Dragon

Room at the Pink Adobe restaurant had a few too many yups for my taste. But the little bar at El Farol was the real thing, so real that I got into the real southwestern swing and did something no grown man with SAT scores over 1,000 should do: I started drinking tequila.

You know how it goes with tequila: Memory loss is just about 100 percent, so I can't really tell you how many I had, but this will give you an indication: Afterward, I went on down to the plaza and bought the wife a piece of ripoff Indian jewelry. You've got your laughing drunk, your crying drunk, your kissing drunk. But *shopping* drunk—now that's some serious. In fact, let's call that *Atkinson's Seventieth Rule of the Bar Bar:* You can use your breathalyzers and your walk-the-line tests if you wish. But I say the easiest way to determine if a guy's had enough is if he just suddenly up and decides he wants to go buy some shit.

EL FAROL (802 Canyon)

What You Feel Like When You Get There: 4

Yuppity Doo Da: 3

Oh Say Can You See? 5

Crapola: 3

Holding Forth: 3

What You Feel Like After Three Drinks: 4

Just a Little Something to Wash My Drink Down With: 3

Old Fart Factor: 3

What You Feel Like When You Leave: 4

You Go Figure: 3

Nowhere Coefficient: 3.5

My favorite joint in Santa Fe turned out to be The Bullring, primarily because of the ferocious bit of Holding Forth I was made an audience to by this housepainter who used to teach English. You get a lot of that in these parts: your Ersatz Blue Collar guy who has about six college degrees but never could figure out what to do with them and so decided he'd just start acting like he was dumb and uneducated and be a housepainter.

"I tell you, though. I don't rip people off. I only do quality work. Only quality. If some customer doesn't like what I've done, I won't take a cent from him."

I'm not sure I believe that, but it does say something about the state of things when people actually start bragging about doing a competent job.

THE BULLRING (4140 Old Santa Fe Trail)

What You Feel Like When You Get There: 5

Yuppity Doo Da: 4

Oh Say Can You See? 5

Crapola: 4

Holding Forth: 5

What You Feel Like After Three Drinks: 5

Just a Little Something to Wash My Drink Down With: 4

Old Fart Factor: 5

What You Feel Like When You Leave: 5

You Go Figure: 3

Nowhere Coefficient: 4.5

About once on every other run, I have found, I just up and stumble across a Bar Bar Nirvana—like Providence or Kansas City. I'm not at all sure what else Tucson is, but these folks here do have terrific taste in bars.

Of course, it helped to have an excellent Ruppy in tow, which Carole Ann Bassett, who strings for the *New York Times* in these parts, definitely was. Indeed, it may be said that Carole Ann made a spirited bid for a Transcontinental Award as Best Ruppy, but alas, I'm afraid poor Dave would commit suicide if I didn't give it to him. So take your plaque, Dave; Carole Ann is still prettier.

We began at the Buffet Club, whose What You Feel Like When You Get There factor was significantly enhanced by the presence of the Empire Laundromat next door. The Empire turned out to be plenty special because it was a Bum Laundry: yeah, Old Farts and a couple of Indians just off the train washing their stuff. A couple of them even came next door and had a few pops while they were waiting for their shorts to dry. What a life.

The Buffet scored well on all counts: Presence of best Bar Bar game of all—shuffleboard—and some fairly interesting crapola, like this big stuffed buffalo head with a gimme cap on. Also, an award is probably in order here for Best Old Lady Fart I ran across: one of those types who had become the self-appointed unofficial greeter for the joint. I'm not sure, but I think I met her more than once.

THE BUFFET CLUB (538 E. 9th)

What You Feel Like When You Get There: 5

Yuppity Doo Da: 5

Oh Say Can You See? 4

Crapola: 5

Holding Forth: 4

What You Feel Like After Three Drinks: 5

Just a Little Something to Wash My Drink Down With: 5

Old Fart Factor: 5

What You Feel Like When You Leave: 5

You Go Figure: 5 (Laundromat.)

Nowhere Coefficient: 4.8

My theory about downtowns is that there are bums and then there are bums. But only a few cities, like Tucson, have a true Urban Third World, a full-blown subculture consisting of every conceivable sort of outcast, ne'er-do-well, and weirdo. A most interesting place to observe this is The Esquire, which I was told used to be an Indian hangout, but presently appeared to be the turf of street blacks.

You want to talk about Oh Say Can You See factors? Goodness sakes. You've got mineshaft dark. Tunnel dark. This was more on the order of skin-flick movie-house dark, and don't say you don't know what I mean.

Elsewise, a $1.50 beer-and-a-shot special, which showed management knew its clientele, and some fine graffiti in the ladies' room, discovered by Carole Ann: most of a wall covered with ladies' lip prints and the inscription "Smitty gives great face." And yes, I'll be glad to send The Esquire a plaque for Best Untrue Bar Bar Rule I ran across: On the wall behind the pool table, a sign instructing "No Loitering."

THE ESQUIRE (225 E. Congress)

What You Feel Like When You Get There: 4

Yuppity Doo Da: 5

Oh Say Can You See? 5

Crapola: 5

Holding Forth: 4

What You Feel Like After Three Drinks: 5

Just a Little Something to Wash My Drink Down With: 5

Old Fart Factor: 5

What You Feel Like When You Leave: 5

You Go Figure: 4

Nowhere Coefficient: 4.6

You may continue your sojourn into the Urban Third World directly across the street, at the Manhattan, which earned an award right off for Best Oh Say Can You See? factor anywhere. This joint was beyond skin-flick movie-house dark; it was *sooooo* dark that it seemed to be closed. You want to talk about your relative degrees of Nowhere: When a joint doesn't even seem to be open, that's some Nowhere.

Clientele? Glad you asked. Lemme just make a quick run around the bar for you, said bar being a kind of bullpen arrangement roughly the size of a soccer stadium. Proceeding clockwise you had: an Old Lady Fart with three apparent teeth; two Injun-type guys; then a black guy doing his best to look like Doctor Detroit; a couple more Injuns; and then, of course, the gay bartender. Phew. I'll tell you what this joint was—it was a bar full of Nuts o' the Day. Under the circumstances, the fact that the rafters were still bedecked with Christmas decorations made perfect sense.

Why, this is precisely the sort of place where you would expect to, say, meet a Navajo named Larry, which is just what happened, I'd say, oh, seventy-eight times. You know the routine with Bums: eye contact; the waveringly extended hand; three-minute handshake. Every five minutes, repeat the process. Larry's story? Well, first off, it should come as no surprise that he wanted a cigarette. Yeah, and a drink. Then he wanted to know how to get home. Now, I have spent a helluva lot of time hanging out in bars, but that is a real new one on me. Tell me about Nowhere: Larry was so far Nowhere he didn't know how to get home. Oh yes: He did ask for another cigarette.

THE MANHATTAN (46 N. 6th)

>**What You Feel Like When You Get There:** 5
>
>**Yuppity Doo Da:** 5
>
>**Oh Say Can You See?** 5
>
>**Crapola:** 5 (Leftover Christmas decor is always a 5.)

Holding Forth: 5

What You Feel Like After Three Drinks: 5

Just a Little Something to Wash My Drink Down With: 5

Old Fart Factor: 5

What You Feel Like When You Leave: 5

You Go Figure: 5

Nowhere Coefficient: 5

The way things were going, it made perfect sense to visit a Hispanic bar called the Shamrock next. Oh yeah, there's an explanation all right: See, the original owner was Jewish. But he got shot or something, and so now it's owned by an Italian. Just didn't want you to get confused or anything.

Basic cantina motif and a marvelous Mexican Old Fart who tried to hit on Carole Ann. I know I've handed out several crapola plaques already, but that whiskey bottle fashioned as a bust of John Wayne on the back bar deserves something. So does that burned-out Viet vet who seemed to think he was my friend. I think his name was Larry, too.

THE SHAMROCK TAVERN (1428 S. 6th)

What You Feel Like When You Get There: 4

Yuppity Doo Da: 5

Oh Say Can You See? 3

Crapola: 5

Holding Forth: 4

What You Feel Like After Three Drinks: 5

Just a Little Something to Wash My Drink Down With: 4

Old Fart Factor: 5

What You Feel Like When You Leave: 5

You Go Figure: 5 (Name.)

Nowhere Coefficient: 4.5

The Roundup, as the name would seem to indicate, is a big, brawling shitkicker joint, which has been around since 1957 according to the owner, Cowboy Dave, who has asthma. Same old cowboy shit, but a nice You Go Figure was the dance band's rousing rendition of "Gloria." Yep, and it was a sing-along too.

THE ROUNDUP SALOON (1527 E. Benson Highway)

What You Feel Like When You Get There: 3

Yuppity Doo Da: 5

Oh Say Can You See? 4

Crapola: 5

Holding Forth: 3

What You Feel Like After Three Drinks: 3

Just a Little Something to Wash My Drink Down With: 3

Old Fart Factor: 5

What You Feel Like When You Leave: 3

You Go Figure: 3

Nowhere Coefficient: 3.7

Well, after roughly sixty-three Corona-and-tequilas why not have a nightcap at a biker bar called The Bashful Bandit? Tell you what, too: When do these guys have last call? *Whenever they want.*

Actually, as in Providence, with sufficient prefueling, a biker bar can be a most enjoyable experience. At least you don't have to worry about having to buy anybody a drink.

Some nice Holding Forth here too, of the Parking Lot Holding Forth genre. Guy and his moll, sitting on a speed bump, discussing the fact that, the way they saw it, we were all brothers and sisters. Yeah, yeah, that's it!

THE BASHFUL BANDIT (1686 E. Speedway)

What You Feel Like When You Get There: 4

Yuppity Doo Da: 5

Oh Say Can You See? 5

Crapola: 4

Holding Forth: 5

What You Feel Like After Three Drinks: 4

Just a Little Something to Wash My Drink Down With: 5

What You Feel Like When You Leave: 4

Old Fart Factor: 4

You Go Figure: 3

Nowhere Coefficient: 4.3

While in the area, I decided to take a drive south and visit a few Completely Not Ersatz cowboy bars in small towns like Tombstone and Bisbee. These places can get a little heavy-handed with the Wyatt Earp crapola, but if you know where to look, there are still plenty of real Bar Bars in these parts.

For example, in Tombstone, skip the Crystal Palace, which is just a tourist trap, and slip on down to Johnny Ringo's. Among other things, Johnny's has the best collection of barflies I've ever seen—the six-legged kind, I mean. Indeed, a favored pastime seemed to be fly swatting, which is just fine with me.

Elsewise, heavy-duty Marty Robbins on the juke, bar dice, and this quite quaint bit of crapola: gimme cap with a little clock on it and the inscription TIME FOR A DRINK. Heh heh. Also, an award here for Best Men's Room Rubber Machines: "DixieLite" and "Treasure Chest."

JOHNNY RINGO'S (on Allen, the main drag, Tombstone)

What You Feel Like When You Get There: 4

Yuppity Doo Da: 5

Oh Say Can You See? 4

Crapola: 5

Holding Forth: 5

What You Feel Like After Three Drinks: 5

Just a Little Something to Wash My Drink Down With: 5

Old Fart Factor: 5

What You Feel Like When You Leave: 5

You Go Figure: 3

Nowhere Coefficient: 4.7

I headed on over to The Lucky Cuss, which gets an extra-special 5 for name for sheer poetry. It's been around since the 1880s, and if you let one of the many exemplary Old Farts manning the bar here get away with it, you're likely to hear a whole shitpot full of what it was like back then.

An outstanding piece of back-bar crapola was a stuffed *fawn*— yeah, right, that's a baby deer—surrounded by several stuffed fish. I like stuffed crapola because there's a real statement in there. Also, the Cuss is likely to get a Transcontinental Award for Best Old Lady Fart Bartender.

THE LUCKY CUSS (on Allen)

What You Feel Like When You Get There: 4

Yuppity Doo Da: 5

Oh Say Can You See? 4

Crapola: 5

Holding Forth: 4

What You Feel Like After Three Drinks: 4

Just a Little Something to Wash My Drink Down With: 4

Old Fart Factor: 5

What You Feel Like When You Leave: 4

You Go Figure: 4

Nowhere Coefficient: 4.3

Down the road a piece is a little place called Bisbee, which used to be a mining town but presently has turned into the damnedest haven for urban outcasts—worn-out hippies, strung-out dopers— I've ever seen. There's probably some pretty important sociology in all this, but thinking about sociology too much usually gives me a headache. Suffice it to say you've probably got a lot of this dynamic going on, particularly in your warmer climes: Older generation dies off; principal industry leaves; younger generation leaves to find jobs; ghost town. Then one day this burned-out hippie with just enough of the self-awareness left in him shows up and goes, "Hey, I can be here and nobody will know or give a shit. Great." And don't kid me: The urban underculture has a grapevine. Bingo: Inside of a year, you've got a semi-thriving little commune.

Oh well, as for Bar Bars, Bisbee has one: the bar at the Copper Queen Hotel. A tiny little saloon, up on the mezzanine level, which is kind of nifty, because if you want to be inspired, you can look at the mountains; if you want to be entertained, you can look down at the dopers and make fun of 'em.

THE COPPER QUEEN (at the Copper Queen Hotel)

What You Feel Like When You Get There: 4

Yuppity Doo Da: 4

Oh Say Can You See? 4

Crapola: 3

Holding Forth: 5

What You Feel Like After Three Drinks: 4

Just a Little Something to Wash My Drink Down With: 4

Old Fart Factor: 3

What You Feel Like When You Leave: 4

You Go Figure: 3

Nowhere Coefficient: 3.8

A confession: I fear for the first time I have transgressed Atkinson's Oath, which was to trudge through snow and sleet, wind and hail, Yuppies and munchies and video Donkey Kong games in search of the truth—for you, my loyal readers. But I copped out on this lesbian biker bar I'd heard about in Bisbee. Whew. I'll just let you use your imagination, because that's what I did. Too bad in a way: I'm sure the Holding Forth would have been quite inspired.

Somehow it made a certain sort of free-associative sense to have had a nightcap in Bisbee and then to find myself ensconced at the casino bar at the Desert Inn less than twelve hours later. From the Ultimate Nowhere to the Ultimate Somewhere, or something like that.

The noted social historian Hunter S. Thompson has already done so good a number on this Six Flags Over tacky that I hesitate to attempt to add anything. But a couple quick notes before I get on to the arduous task of trying to find something remotely resembling a Bar Bar in this place.

Vegas has been called the capital of a lot of things: glitz, greed, senselessness, broken dreams, you name it. But for my money, all of those tags have missed the mark. In truth, Vegas is the capital of one thing and one thing only: It is the capital of Big Butts.

No, really. Next time you're there, walk the strip up one side and down the other and see if you don't come away with a single image, a single icon ringing in your mind: a big fat butt, swathed in fuschia double-knit, just quivering and bouncing its way along, almost as if carried by its own life force. Everywhere you look in this place, on street corners, in the casinos and restaurants, it's butts, butts, butts. Late at night, at prime time on the strip, the wide-angle view can be downright surreal: an ocean of Big Butts, each bobbing to its own rhythm, like whitecaps illuminated by the moon's glow. Why, you *see* so many Big Butts here, you'd almost swear it makes people start acting like them, but then again, I could be wrong about that.

Ah well, on to business. At the suggestion of a friend who's been to Vegas several times, I did a kind of Potluck scattershoot of both strips—Las Vegas Boulevard and the older joints downtown. The attempt here was to try to find traces of Bar Bardom in the various casino bars. My findings aren't going to set the world on fire, but I did come up with a little something. Of the newer, larger hotel-casinos, my favorite casino bar was the little circular job at the Desert Inn. One reason was that they had a couple of cocktail waitresses who'll knock your socks off. The other was the bartender, Doug, who did just about as good a job of creating Nowhere in the middle of Somewhere as humanly possible.

Of the downtown joints—and really, I prefer them to the larger casinos—the bar at the California Hotel casino was just fine. Neither is going to get a rating, but a casino scattershoot is definitely in order, particularly if you manage to push yourself away from the blackjack table while still $80 up, which is what I did.

But breathes there a real Bar Bar amidst all the neon? Yes, I found two, and if you don't think I paid the price just to excavate those, then you haven't been to something called The Elephant Bar. This had been described to me as possibly the real thing, and by Vegas standards, maybe it is. But I'm not even going to consider listing a bar that had a twenty-five-year-old bartender named Tony. Sixty-five, maybe. Twenty-five, no.

But if you really want Nowhere here in the Nexus of Somewhere, try P.J.'s, an after-shift hangout for dealers and bartenders and waitresses. It's got an outstanding Oh Say Can You See? factor, and the Holding Forth is suitably cynical. Put it this way: I tried out my Capital of Big Butts theory and pretty much everyone caught on, except, of course, for that guy with the big butt across the bar, playing electronic keno.

P.J.'S (2300 S. Maryland Parkway)

What You Feel Like When You Get There: 4

Yuppity Doo Da: 4

Oh Say Can You See? 5

Crapola: 4

Holding Forth: 4

What You Feel Like After Three Drinks: 4

Just a Little Something to Wash My Drink Down With: 4

Old Fart Factor: 4

What You Feel Like When You Leave: 4

You Go Figure: 5 (A real bar in Vegas?)

Nowhere Coefficient: 4.2

Something approaching Bar Bar Nirvana may be found at a little joint called State Street, which you might call a Bar Bar Formal. I don't get into the tuxedoed help bit too much, but here in Vegas it actually works nicely, as does the presence of a dance floor where Old Fart couples can dance that funny slow-slow-quick-quick step they used to teach in junior high school gym class.

There's a tony restaurant attached, but the bar is suitably off to itself and the big, brassy lady bartender was just fine. Pretty decent Legend 'n' Lore here involving Big Frank and various shit he's done here after hours, too. Excellent self-promotional crapola on walls as well, featuring important people like Shecky Greene.

Anyway, it all works, and that includes the Hungarian guitarist, who couldn't play worth a shit but who could Hold Forth.

STATE STREET (2570 State St.)

What You Feel Like When You Get There: 3

Yuppity Doo Da: 4

Oh Say Can You See? 4

Crapola: 2

Holding Forth: 4

What You Feel Like After Three Drinks: 4

Just a Little Something to Wash My Drink Down With: 3

Old Fart Factor: 3

What You Feel Like When You Leave: 4

You Go Figure: 3

Nowhere Coefficient: 3.4

22

Bar Bar 202: So Advanced It's Probably Irrelevant but Who Cares—I Need to Fill A Couple Pages Theology (on Hangovers)

Customer to other customer: *Let you be in my hangover if I can be in yours.*

Well, here we are. I tried to keep this 'til late, and I'm going to keep it short. But considering the subject, I didn't feel I could leave out the particular state of being known as the morning after. Be a little like writing a book about smoking and not mentioning the Large C.

Actually that right there is part of the problem with The Hangover. Whatever else can be said about it, it is an overrated, overly feared, downright mythologized malady. You know: "God, I feel like Sherman marched into Georgia last night—right over my tongue." All right, I'll grant that hangovers aren't any picnic; but they aren't as bad as all that. It's an illness, to be sure, but a good start in combating the little rascal is to stop putting it in the realm of melanoma or, say, paranoid schizophrenia.

The key to the hangover is Atkinson's Theory of Relativity: It *seems* like a bad dose of lung cancer relative to how you felt during the process of acquiring it. You know, like that overindulger who winds up with a coronary arrest at fifty-seven: It hurts all the worse because all he can think about is how much he enjoyed all that cholesterol, caffeine, and whatnot he ingested in the process of screwing up his heart. The psychological overlay is the problem, and as with a coronary arrest, the only way to successfully battle the sucker is to pull out the heavy artillery. Yes, *Atkinson's Sev-enty-first Rule of the Bar Bar:* When it comes to hangovers, the only way to feel better is to feel worse first.

Take it from medical science: Guy has a cardiac arrest and those docs don't just stroke him on the head, give him a couple aspirin and tell him to ride out the storm. They pull out the bazookas—those big shocker dealies or their own fists. And if it's bad enough, they'll rip open your whole chest and fiddle around in there awhile. If that's not a case of making you feel worse to feel better, I don't know what is. What's still the most common "mainte-nance" chemical for heart patients? *Nitroglycerin,* and I think you know what else they use that for.

The hangover should be attacked with similar Visigothic over-kill. Don't patty-cake around with stuff like a peanut butter sand-wich and milk, a couple aspirin, or that most futile of antidotes: more sleep. You and I both know that stuff doesn't work, and the only reason we keep trying it is that like all sick people, we're afraid to face the truth: The only good cure is a cure that's worse than the illness.

With these precepts in mind, I perused my notes in search of the best and worst hangover cures I heard about—or tried—during my travels.

ATKINSON'S FIELD GUIDE TO SURVIVING THE MORNING AFTER

What Doesn't Work	What Works
Aspirin	Percodan
Coffee	Hot water spiked with mustard seed.
Cold shower	Sauna 'til you can't breathe, then cold shower
Glass of cold milk	Glass of warm milk
More sleep	No sleep
Drinking only beer or wine the night before	Drinking only tequila the night before
Ham and eggs	Greasy Tex-Mex

A raw egg (some people swear by this, but for my taste, it doesn't make you feel bad enough)

A whole jalapeño, sliced and consumed in one gulp, followed by a bite from a raw onion, a shot of schnapps, and a strip of fried bacon (getting my point now?)

Talking to other people with hangovers

Talking to regular old everyday people

Calling in sick

Going in to work

Just one drink to take the edge off

Several drinks to take the edge off

Of course, let's face it, even feeling-worse-to-feel-better has its limits, and as a matter of self-protection—yeah, and public safety too—I would not advise you to try the following tasks for the duration:

Driving someplace where you have to get directions
Yard work, particularly tree pruning
Jump-starting your car
Reworking your Form B, Itemized Deductions
Wearing any combination of shirt, tie, suit, and shoes you haven't tried before.
Shopping
Writing a memo
Trying to use the conference-call option on your business phone for the first time
Flossing your teeth
Taping a favorite record on cassette
Darts
Trying to tell a joke
Self-serve at the gas station
Reading the editorial page
Remembering who you might have insulted the night before
Accepting a call from your insurance agent or stockbroker
Needlepoint
The Phil Donahue Show

Taking care of those overdue traffic tickets
Trying to look like anything other than a soggy piece of newsprint

---

Ask Dr. Bar Bar

Dear Dr. Bar Bar:
Would you please tell me your top-ten favorite all-time bars in mov-
ies? My favorite was the disco in Saturday Night Fever.
COULDN'T THINK OF ANYTHING ELSE TO ASK

Dear COULDN'T THINK OF ANYTHING ELSE TO ASK:
Wish you had. The answer is no. What the hell do you think this is,
the goddam downtown library? And as for your personal favorite, I'm
so disgusted I'm going to refund the money you spent on this book
myself. On the other hand, no, I won't, because then I'd have your
address on my Rolodex and that could only be extremely bad karma.
What I will do, though, is tell you my all-time single favorite Bar Bar
as portrayed in the movies. No, it's not Rick's in Casablanca, *and no,*
it's not the gin joint in The Verdict. *It's the bar in* Star Wars. *Yep, that*
had real Bar Bar ambiance, the whole deal, and damned if I'm not so
sure I didn't see some of those same fellows along the way.

23

The Transcontinental Drunk, part 11: Cincinnati/Cleveland/Pittsburgh

---

Customer to other customer: *I guess you could say alcohol has pretty much ruined every part of my life, but heck, if I had to do it all over again, I wouldn't change a thing. Buy you a drink?*

The first conversation I had of any length on this run was with a guy in Cleveland whose pension was about to be eighty-sixed by LTV and oh yeah, he was waiting on a donor for a heart transplant. Phew. Talk about your Heart of Nowhere, your cosmic-level Big E (Existentialism). This barhop through the blue-collar Northeast made Missoula seem like Palm Springs.

But more on that later. Ostensibly I put together this run for statistical reasons: As I could best reckon, these three cities probably had more neighborhood bars per square mile than any other run I'd been on. I knew for a fact—fact as in one of those book of mosts—that Pittsburgh had more than any other single city, which is possibly why it was recently named the nation's most livable city. Anyway, I figured it was the most logical place to wind up my bar hop: I'd sensed the presence of Kurtz in Missoula; I was pretty sure I could find him at the Flat Iron Cafe in Cleveland or Chiodo's in Pittsburgh.

I started the run in Cincinnati because I love the place, and though it's suffered a good deal more Yupping up than the other two cities, if you can pick through all the Lauren and conversations about linguini, it has an exemplary handful of the real thing left.

Exhibit A would be Arnold's, which is one of the few saloons claiming to have been around since 1861 that truly looks as if it hasn't changed a thing. Example? Okay, the first door you pass says LADIES' ENTRANCE. Good enough? There's more.

The MEN'S ENTRANCE leads to a stand-up-only bar, peopled by a variety of non-ersatz types: New Collars, The Perpetual Student, Hangers-Out. Italian food only, and, surprising for an Oldest Bar in the City, no self-promotional crapola like T-shirts.

ARNOLD'S (210 E. 8th)

What You Feel Like When You Get There: 5 (That "Ladies' Entrance" sign will do.)

Yuppity Doo Da: 5

Oh Say Can You See? 4

Crapola: 4

Holding Forth: 4

What You Feel Like After Three Drinks: 5

Just a Little Something to Wash My Drink Down With: 3

Old Fart Factor: 4

What You Feel Like When You Leave: 5

You Go Figure: 4

Nowhere Coefficient: 4.3

It's just a quick jaunt through the winter slime to The Phoenix Cafe, and it's definitely worth the trip. This is an old newspaper pressmen's bar and a lot of these guys look like they finished replating page one back when the Japs eighty-sixed Pearl Harbor, came on over to have a couple of pops, and just never went back. Of special note here was the marvelous verbal parrying between a couple of Old Farts to my left over who was going to buy whom the next drink.

"You gonna buy me that double like you promised?" said the one with the nose that looked like a red bell pepper.

"I never promised you nuthin', but I'll buy you a single just so you'll shut up."

And on it went. Finally the second guy said, "Okay, have your fucking double." Then he leaned over to me and whispered, "Yeah, and I don't even like the son of a bitch." That's an Atkinson Transcontinental Award for Best I Couldn't Have Said It Better Myself I overheard anywhere.

Of course, that little exchange wasn't nearly as scintillating as the soliloquy presented by my buddy to the right, who went on for at least twenty-seven minutes about how his wife didn't know how to make liver and onions worth a shit and so tonight he was going to show her his secret formula. Hey, give the guy a break: beats trying to talk about the Bengals' chances for the playoffs.

THE PHOENIX CAFE (64 Walnut)

What You Feel Like When You Get There: 4

Yuppity Doo Da: 5

Oh Say Can You See? 4

Crapola: 4

Holding Forth: 5

What You Feel Like After Three Drinks: 5

Just a Little Something to Wash My Drink Down With: 5

Old Fart Factor: 5

What You Feel Like When You Leave: 5

You Go Figure: 3

Nowhere Coefficient: 4.5

That'll give you some idea of the gems that are left downtown. But out in the city's scores of neighborhoods, there are tons more little down-the-corner Bar Bars, of which The King's Lounge in Hyde Park is a mighty nice exemplar. One of my Ruppy tipsters had described the place this way: "You'll see. Food is incidental."

Yeah, and so is just about everything else with the exception of drinking and lying. With the exception of the Aub Zam Zam Room in San Francisco, I have not seen a better example of the Minimalist School of Bar Bar interior decor. One square room, very dark; two tables, a jukebox on one wall; one long bar on the other. TV set. Bartender. Old Farts. What else do you need?

Geraldo Rivera's "American Vice: The Doping of a Nation" was on the tube, and somehow that seemed fitting, though I can't quite explain why. At any rate, Geraldo, here's your Transcontinental Award for Most Obnoxious Single Individual to Watch on TV in a Bar Bar, and yeah, that includes Merv Griffin, Soupy Sales, Sam Donaldson, and Gary Bender.

Not that I had much time to be grossed out by Geraldo. I was quickly and irretrievably in the throes of being raped by the Old Fart to my left. Here's where this non-stop bit of Holding Forth went: Started with the aforementioned "alcohol has ruined my life" lament; on to how, so what, Richard Burton was a drunk too; to how when he lived in Chicago, he knew a good buddy of Al Capone's; to how Mexico was about to invade just any minute.

This was presented pretty much as non-stop stream-of-consciousness, though he would occasionally punctuate it with that time-honored Old Fart utterance: "You see what I'm tryin' to say?"

Tell you what, though. I'll say this for fifty years of boozing it a bit too hard: It does enforce a certain crystalline cynicism that can't be found elsewhere. While the rest of the patrons gasped and gee-whizzed at Geraldo's histrionics, my Old Fart buddy would have none of it. "This is all like a fuckin' movie, that's all," he said, and I don't think Tom Shales could have summed up Rivera's particular brand of journalism any better.

THE KING'S LOUNGE (3505 Michigan Ave.)

What You Feel Like When You Get There: 5

Yuppity Doo Da: 5

Oh Say Can You See? 5

Crapola: 4

Holding Forth: 5

What You Feel Like After Three Drinks: 5

Just a Little Something to Wash My Drink Down With: 5

Old Fart Factor: 5

What You Feel Like When You Leave: 5

You Go Figure: 4

Nowhere Coefficient: 4.8

A must run if you're in this area, though it has nothing to do with Bar Bars, is Newport, Kentucky, just across the Ohio River. Newport is one of those little ticky-tacky Sinbelts that sprouted up back in less—or more, as the case might be—civilized times, when guys thought it was a big deal to pay money to go watch some lady take off her clothes. Come to think of it, guys still think that's a big deal, but seldom will they have an opportunity to hit a joint like The Brass Ass.

It's straight out of the '50s, and if you don't believe me, get this: I got *B-girled*. Yep. Just standing there having a pop or two, espying the scenery, and this girl comes up and says hi and the next thing you know, I'm buying her a drink. What the hell? It was only eight bucks, and she seemed to like me so much she even wanted me to buy her another one.

I could describe in great detail the particular sensation of flying into Cleveland in a snowstorm in a prop plane with a rapidly incubating case of the flu, but I'm coming down the home stretch here and I really don't want to lose those few of you I still have left with me.

Speaking of the flu, however, I'm here to report a significant immunological breakthrough. It's simply this: If you feel the on-slaught of that yearly virus, go with your penicillin, your Actifed, your super-strength Bufferin if you wish. But I'm here to tell you the best and most certain way to kick that little peckerwood's ass is to go to Cleveland. Yep. You might think that walking five blocks through downtown Cleveland in subzero wind chill would bring on the Big P (pneumonia), and in any other venue that most certainly would be true. But we're talking Cleveland here, and it may not be Nobel-prize-worthy, but the plain fact is, *no* virus can survive Cleveland. No kidding: Felt like a million bucks the next day. Who says there isn't anything nice to say about Cleveland?

You can start with Moriarty's here, and for that matter, end with it too. It's a perfect 5 Nowhere Coefficient, starting with the splendid Oh Say Can You See? factor, proceeding through the burly barkeep with a whiskey voice that sounded something like cement being made, and on to the Holding Forth, which when I arrived centered on the extermination of household pests.

But the true Holding Forth here was the aforementioned Big E rap by that guy who was waiting on a new heart and suddenly, thanks to Big Business, probably didn't have any way to pay for it, when and if it arrived. Oh yeah, one more bit of Big E: Under doctor's orders, the guy was only allowed to have one drink per week, proving, I suppose, that there actually is such a thing as one drink.

As for Just a Little Something to Wash My Drink Down With, there was the perfectly respectable chili dog, and on the back bar by far the best bar sign I saw anywhere: THIS BAR IS DEDICATED TO THOSE LOVING SOULS OF OTHER DAYS—WHO AGAIN WILL MAKE DRINKING A PLEASURE—WHO ACHIEVE CONTENTMENT BE-FORE CAPACITY—AND WHO, WHATEVER THEY MAY DRINK—PROVE ABLE TO CARRY IT—ENJOY IT—AND TO ACT LIKE GENTLE-MEN." Another award there for Best Couldn't Have Said It Better Myself.

MORIARTY'S (1912 E. 6th)

What You Feel Like When You Get There: 5

Yuppity Doo Da: 5

Oh Say Can You See? 5

Crapola: 5

Holding Forth: 5

What You Feel Like After Three Drinks: 5

Just a Little Something to Wash My Drink Down With: 5

Old Fart Factor: 5

What You Feel Like When You Leave: 5

You Go Figure: 5

Nowhere Coefficient: 5

Just up the way is a little joint called Herb's Guard House, which is a 5 for name but elsewise is only a modest attempt at the real thing. A bit on the light side, and I sensed the bartender might be a gentleman of the other persuasion. I did, however, observe several regulars in residence at the magic hour of 4 P.M., and by the way, I also almost got picked up by a fifty-year-old woman wearing sensible shoes. In case you haven't already guessed, among other things Cleveland is the Sensible Shoes Capital of the universe.

HERB'S GUARD HOUSE (1925 E. 6th)

What You Feel Like When You Get There: 3

Yuppity Doo Da: 5

Oh Say Can You See? 4

Crapola: 2

Holding Forth: 3

What You Feel Like After Three Drinks: 4

Just a Little Something to Wash My Drink Down With: 3

Old Fart Factor: 4

What You Feel Like When You Leave: 4

You Go Figure: 3

Nowhere Coefficient: 3.5

For a heavy dose of the not-even-attempting-to-be-ersatz Cleveland, a must stop is the Flat Iron Cafe, way down in the Flats. The book on this joint is this: It's a time-honored blue-collar/businessmen's bar most of the time, but occasionally, according to my cabbie, it becomes a biker bar. Go figure.

Anyway, it's got a fine Old Fart bartender, alpaca sweater and all, and the finest back-bar survival kit I've ever seen: Hershey's, Reese's Peanut Butter Cups, gum, Alka-Seltzer, Ronson lighter flints, beer nuts, Certs, and cigars.

My drinking companion was this ersatz Springsteen guy named Ritchie, who was knocking a few back while his rig was getting unloaded down the way. Wanna know about Big E? Ritchie had come *to* Cleveland and later that night, he was *going back to* New Jersey. Phew. I may not feel too comfortable around you New Collar types, but I gotta tip my hat. You guys really got the shaft and I'm just damned surprised you haven't up and taken it to the streets. Jersey to Cleveland to Jersey? And we wonder why there's a child-abuse problem in this country.

About the Flat Iron, two other things of theological note: One was the fact that when Ritchie played some music on the jukebox, a couple of Old Farts told me if they were my age, they'd beat the crap out of him, which seemed about right. The other was that along about 9, the Old Fart bartender just up and said, "Drink up. We're closing." I like close-when-you-want, though I can't say it was the wisest move in the world to proceed from the Flat Iron on down the way to Reflections—a biker strip joint.

Egads. After bolting a beer and a shot of schnapps, I got on the blower to Yellow Cab *real quick.* Cabbie must have figured out my straits too, 'cause when he arrived, he charged into the room, grabbed me, and rushed me out to his cab with the urgency of an EMS paramedic.

THE FLAT IRON CAFE (1114 Center)

What You Feel Like When You Get There: 4

Yuppity Doo Da: 5

Oh Say Can You See? 4

Crapola: 5 (Survival kit.)

Holding Forth: 5

What You Feel Like After Three Drinks: 5

Just a Little Something to Wash My Drink Down With: 4

Old Fart Factor: 5

What You Feel Like When You Leave: 5

You Go Figure: 5 (Businessmen and bikers?)

Nowhere Coefficient: 4.7

Flash! Bulletin! Extra! Pittsburgh takes itself seriously! No shit! Got named nation's most livable city a year or so ago and bought it! Got all kinds of slogans and billboards about ballet and opera and stuff! Thinks it's the San Francisco of the East! Even has some Yuppies!

Oh well, it is only through disillusionment that we find the pure truth, and despite this city's hell-bent desire to be something it really has no business wanting to be, it's still got a whole bunch of fine Bar Bars. It's also got the best cabdrivers this side of Tokyo, and this one in particular is gonna get a plaque, which I figure is the least I can do, since he gave me a joint.

It started this way: I caught a cab out to a joint called the Squirrel Hill Cafe, and me and this cabbie started talking about bars and one thing led to another and pretty soon he was giving me more tips and by the time I got there, he was saying he'd come back and get me and then we'd really do some barhopping.

Okay, so I cooled my heels awhile at the Squirrel Hill, talking some pretty heavy sociology with a New Collar named Garry. Garry was coming off a rough night—rough as in he was wearing an ill-fitting sweat suit bequeathed to him by the young lady he'd wound up with—and recovering the best way he knew how, which was to get shitfaced all over again.

"Yeah," he said, "you know my mother never cussed, but for some reason she still calls me an asshole. Never could figure that out." Excellent stuff—go on.

"Well, I guess my real problem is that I just wish somebody would give me something to do. I work kinda part-time at this auto shop—here, here's a business card—but I still wish somebody would give me something to do." Bingo, Garry: You just coined the New Collar lament, and no, I couldn't have said it better myself.

The Squirrel Hill will also earn an Atkinson Transcontinental Award for Best Graffiti. Get this: "A complacent chuckle, a place in the history books."

THE SQUIRREL HILL CAFE (5802 Forbes)

What You Feel Like When You Get There: 4

Yuppity Doo Da: 5

Oh Say Can You See? 5

Crapola: 5

Holding Forth: 5

What You Feel Like After Three Drinks: 5

Just a Little Something to Wash My Drink Down With: 4

Old Fart Factor: 5

What You Feel Like When You Leave: 5

You Go Figure: 5

Nowhere Coefficient: 4.7

Well, my ride was right on time, and sans the meter, we headed out barhopping. Well, actually, we only made one other joint because we had to drop by my cabbie's apartment to play with his cat.

Fine by me. I was cruising by the time we reached Primanti Brothers, a late-night Bar Bar that doesn't open until 11. He hurried me out of the car and said, "You go ahead. I'm gonna go make some fuckin' money."

Primanti Brothers is a serviceable Bar Bar in all ways, but of special note is the Just a Little Something to Wash My Drink Down With, which earned a plaque. You may already know this, but there are sandwiches and then there are sandwiches. Then there are Primanti sandwiches: You order salami and cheese, melted. You want the large loaf of course. Here's what you get: cole slaw; Italian dressing; salami; cheese; mayo; chopped onion. But then here's what else you get: french fries. On the side, eh? Forget it: In Pittsburgh, they put those suckers right on the sandwich. Yes, that's right, *on* the mother.

PRIMANTI BROTHERS (46 18th St.)

What You Feel Like When You Get There: 4

Yuppity Doo Da: 5

Oh Say Can You See? 4

Crapola: 4

Holding Forth: 3

What You Feel Like After Three Drinks: 4

Just a Little Something to Wash My Drink Down With: 5

Old Fart Factor: 3

What You Feel Like When You Leave: 5

You Go Figure: 4

Nowhere Coefficient: 4.1

Next day, I went to the true Heart of Nowhere, the oldest, most famous steel-mill-worker bar in Pittsburgh, joint called Chiodo's. Here's the book: beer and a shot for $1.25; "Mystery Sandwich" (Go Figure); more Old Farts than you could find at a car show.

·Just a Little Something to Wash My Drink Down With? Yeah, on special, fried fish and macaroni and cheese: $3.00. Okay? And of course, we had this particular kind of Holding Forth: "Yeah, I had to take a urine test and I was clean. Wanna see?"

"Said your piss was red . . ."

"I'll show you. It was blue. Come on, asshole, let's go see."

Also, an extra-special Transcontinental Award here for Best Ever Crap on Ceiling, Floor, Walls. Gracious, you had beach balls, footballs, old strings of bullets of various calibers, lamps, ax handles, and of course a model airplane or two. Never had really crystallized the thought before, but the true de rigueur Bar Bar decor is pretty much exactly along the lines of a nine-year-old's bedroom.

CHIODO'S (107 W. 8th, Homestead)

What You Feel Like When You Get There: 5

Yuppity Doo Da: 5

Oh Say Can You See? 5

Crapola: 5

Holding Forth: 5

What You Feel Like After Three Drinks: 5

Just a Little Something to Wash My Drink Down With: 5

Old Fart Factor: 5

What You Feel Like When You Leave: 5

You Go Figure: 5

Nowhere Coefficient: 5

24

The Transcontinental Drunk, part 12: Texas

I know I'm a drunk, but I'm an honest person.

What was it old T.S. Eliot said about how you will end where you began and know the place for the first time? That's sort of what I tried here. I guess I could have started my stagger for the truth in my home state, but it just always made more sense to me to wind up here. Save the best for last and all that.

I say best because, while I can't honestly say bars in Texas are any better than they are anyplace else, they are *my* bars, and *Atkinson's Seventy-fourth Rule of the Bar Bar* says this: When it comes to judging the relative merits of a Bar Bar, the crucial operative factor is whether the joint is *yours* or not.

My nose first led me to Houston, and the reasoning was very simple: As earlier noted, Bar Bars are about nothing if not about existentialism, and these days, if you want a major existential hit— what I call the Big E—you head straight for post-oil-boom Houston. Phew. For those of you unfamiliar with the particulars of the present malaise down that way, let me put it this way: Let's say you have a house, two cars, four kids, and make $50,000 a year, and that's *just* enough. Then let's say one day some guy who looks like George Shultz walks in and informs you that henceforth that $50,000 is only going to be valued as $20,000, but your monthly nut is going to remain the same. No explanation, no mitigation:

You're suddenly, inexplicably, irretrievably broke.

That's more or less what happened to this once sassy and robust city when whoever it is who decides such things decided one day that henceforth a barrel of crude oil, the city's primary money-producing commodity, would be worth not $35 but, oh, let's make it $17 or so. Ka . . . *blewy!* One day everything's just tripping along fine and then just like that, guys are starting to jump out of bank buildings and "foreclosure" and "Chapter 11" are part of the new lexicon. I've seen economic fortunes flow and recede, but I'll be damned if I've ever seen a boom go bust with more ferocity and suddenness. I'll tell you how bad it is: Houston's freeways, once a terribly unfunny joke just about any time of day, are all of a sudden eerily uncongested and passable.

All of which is to say the Big E you sense in the Bar Bars here is mighty funky. Of note, though, is that with a few exceptions, most of the city's great Bar Bars have survived the holocaust swimmingly, suggesting that it really may be true that when the Big Guy in the Sky gets fed up this next time around, the only things left standing will be cathedrals, Bar Bars, and a couple of Sears stores.

Houston doesn't have much of what most civilized people would call a neighborhood, but Grif's is still a model neighborhood pub. The regulars at this unassuming little tavern have gotten a tad pushy with the Grif's crapola—T-shirts, etc.—but any joint that's got a handful of Old Lady Fart regulars will pass muster.

The evening I dropped by, you had this kind of Holding Forth: "They can take the car; they can take the wife if they want. But as long as they can't take my dick, I'll be standing." Tell me about the Big E.

GRIF'S (3416 Roseland)

What You Feel Like When You Get There: 4

Yuppity Doo Da: 3

Oh Say Can You See? 4

Crapola: 3 (Too much of it's self-serving Grif's crapola.)

Holding Forth: 5

What You Feel Like After Three Drinks: 4

Just a Little Something to Wash My Drink Down With: 4

Old Fart Factor: 5

What You Feel Like When You Leave: 4

You Go Figure: 3

Nowhere Coefficient: 3.9

My favorite beer Bar Bar anywhere has to be Kay's, a little dive that serves as home to a mixed clientele of Rice University students and sundry Old Farts. It could pass as a Deco Crapola Museum, and any place where you're more confused *after* the bartender gives you directions than before is the real thing.

I'm not a big fan of beer bars because I'm not a big fan of beer. But Kay's will do because they don't make a Six Flags Over megaproduction out of how many weird brands they have—an increasingly distressing trend in this genre. Just the basics—Bud, Lite, etc.—and that's that.

KAY'S (2324 Bissonet)

What You Feel Like When You Get There: 4

Yuppity Doo Da: 5

Oh Say Can You See? 5

Crapola: 5

Holding Forth: 4

What You Feel Like After Three Drinks: 4

Just a Little Something to Wash My Drink Down With: 5

Old Fart Factor: 5

What You Feel Like When You Leave: 4

You Go Figure: 3

Nowhere Coefficient: 4.4

A real strange Bar Bar experience may be had at Marfreless, a dungeon-like joint that in the best tradition of the Mother Church eschews a sign announcing its presence. It also has the best Bar Bar door in the United States. Yep, it's one of those metal jobs, like to a utility room or some such.

Interiorly, this place has it down as well. You can drink in the bar; you can drink upstairs in this cosmically dark loft. Or if you choose, you can drink in this little room off the loft and get incredibly paranoid. Why not? Everyone else is.

MARFRELESS (2006 Peden)

What You Feel Like When You Get There: 4

Yuppity Doo Da: 3

Oh Say Can You See? 5

Crapola: 4

Holding Forth: 4

What You Feel Like After Three Drinks: 4

Just a Little Something to Wash My Drink Down With: 5

Old Fart Factor: 4

What You Feel Like When You Leave: 4

You Go Figure: 4

Nowhere Coefficient: 4.1

I hesitate to include the following establishment as a Bar Bar, but the glitzy joint at the Remington Hotel in Houston has emerged as a totally unexpected Atkinson Transcontinental Award winner: Best Bar Bar That Would Appear to Be Anything But That. As for appearances, the only thing Bar Bar-ish about it is that the Oh Say Can You See? factor is well in place; elsewise, it's a big expensive Somewhere.

But appearances can be deceiving—even with Bar Bars—and what appears to have happened here is that the sheer force of the ongoing recession has turned this ostensibly upscale pick-up joint into something akin to the real thing. Yes, everybody's overdressed, and yes, the Atkinson Lip Gloss Meter nearly went off the scale. But a certain Bar Bar camaraderie has developed, expressed best by an older fellow I sat next to: "I don't know what I'd do without this joint," he said reverently. "Sometimes I wish I could take it home with me." Can a Somewhere become a Nowhere? Sure, if the Big E is strong enough.

THE REMINGTON BAR (at the Remington Hotel)

What You Feel Like When You Get There: 2

Yuppity Doo Da: 2

Oh Say Can You See? 5

Crapola: 1

Holding Forth: 4

What You Feel Like After Three Drinks: 3

Just a Little Something to Wash My Drink Down With: 3

Old Fart Factor: 3

What You Feel Like When You Leave: 4

You Go Figure: 5 (Any Somewhere that becomes a Nowhere is a 5.)

Nowhere Coefficient: 2.9

A completely different sort of You Go Figure is my favorite downtown Houston spot, Leo's Broadway Bar. Yes, there is a Leo, and no, there isn't a Broadway in sight, so yes, that is a 5 for name alone. Appearances are deceiving here as well: Leo's rests on the bottom floor of one of those ubiquitous reflecting-glass high-rises and from outward appearances would seem to be a kind of double-knit deli. But in fact, it's a more than creditable Bar Bar peopled by some retired guys, a few businessmen, and a bunch of out-of-work oil types.

LEO'S (711 Fannin)

> **What You Feel Like When You Get There:** 4
>
> **Yuppity Doo Da:** 5
>
> **Oh Say Can You See?** 5
>
> **Crapola:** 5
>
> **Holding Forth:** 4
>
> **What You Feel Like After Three Drinks:** 4
>
> **Just a Little Something to Wash My Drink Down With:** 4
>
> **Old Fart Factor:** 5
>
> **What You Feel Like When You Leave:** 5
>
> **You Go Figure:** 4
>
> **Nowhere Coefficient:** 4.5

Some of my favorite Bar Bars in my home state are down the Gulf Coast, in Corpus Christi and adjacent old fishing hamlets like Port Aransas. In Corpus, one need go no farther than the exquisitely named Elizabeth's Cocktails, an old sailors' joint right downtown by the water. The several times I've been here I have witnessed that most remarkable of Bar Bar events: a few sailors getting a bit rowdy and being absolutely shushed and humbled by the little old lady bartender.

Elsewhere, there's a fine lie in the men's room which says FRENCH TICKLERS SOLD AS NOVELTY ITEMS ONLY. And I swear this is true: Each and every time I've been here, I've overheard

Holding Forth about somebody having to get somebody else out of jail.

ELIZABETH'S COCKTAILS (902 N. Chaparral)

What You Feel Like When You Get There: 4

Yuppity Doo Da: 5

Oh Say Can You See? 5

Crapola: 4

Holding Forth: 5

What You Feel Like After Three Drinks: 5

Just a Little Something to Wash My Drink Down With: 5

Old Fart Factor: 5

What You Feel Like When You Leave: 5

You Go Figure: 4

Nowhere Coefficient: 4.6

Across the water, you could do much worse than a two-part scattershoot involving the Rod and Gun Club and the contiguous Shorty's, the latter being the subject of more Legend 'n' Lore involving fisticuffs than just about any Bar Bar in Texas, which is saying something. Put it this way: The last time I dropped by, I just kind of poked my head in the opened door first to check out the crowd and this regular glanced up at me and then just reached over and slammed the door in my face. That's some serious Bar Bar, and the thing is, I wasn't in the least bit chapped.

SHORTY'S ROD AND GUN CLUB (821 Tarpon)

What You Feel Like When You Get There: 4

Yuppity Doo Da: 5

Oh Say Can You See? 5

Crapola: 5 (The Rod and Gun has one of those great old sea-motif wall murals.)

Holding Forth: 4

What You Feel Like After Three Drinks: 5

Just a Little Something to Wash My Drink Down With: 5

Old Fart Factor: 5

What You Feel Like When You Leave: 5

You Go Figure: 4

Nowhere Coefficient: 4.7

Some of the best barhopping around may be accomplished in the Texas hill country, the still mostly rural regions of central Texas surrounding San Antonio and Austin. There is a ferocious collision of drinking cultures here, some Czech-German running head-on at about 60 into your Latino. The result is a uniquely Texan sort of Bar Bar, what we call the icehouse.

The Texas icehouse is a monument to unfettered capitalism. In its purest form, it is a combination grocery-store-bar-hardware-outlet-gas-station-you-name-it that just kind of acquired functions as time went by. Regrettably, most icehouses are now gone, and my favorite, Bill's in Fredericksburg, is so gone as to be practically forgotten. But in its heyday, Bill's was the mold when it came to this particular breed: It sold, among other things, beer, live ammo, block ice, and bait. So here's to you, Bill, a solid 5 in memoriam.

Here's a pretty good Texas hill county scattershoot, based on

---

Fun Facts

The heaviest drinkers of hard liquor in the world are the Poles, who consume somewhere in the range of 1.5 million gallons of booze per year.

---

years of experience which started with my college days. Why not start with Ray's Place in Bastrop? It's got beer, it's got rubber machines that dispense "Funnie Fanny's Dirty Dozen." Also bait, if you wish to fish, and some of this kind of Holding Forth: "Now she's complainin' that I'm giving it to her too much—you know?" Yeah, sure, buddy.

RAY'S PLACE (1308 Chestnut)

    What You Feel Like When You Get There: 4

    Yuppity Doo Da: 4

    Oh Say Can You See? 5

    Crapola: 5

    Holding Forth: 5

    What You Feel Like After Three Drinks: 4

    Just a Little Something to Wash My Drink Down With: 4

    Old Fart Factor: 5

    What You Feel Like When You Leave: 5

    You Go Figure: 3

    Nowhere Coefficient: 4.4

Proceed to Pflugerville and drop by Knebel's Tavern, where you'll be greeted by Burwell "Tuff" Knebel, who will pretty quickly explain that folks call him Tuff because they can't remember Burwell. No, that's not a You Go Figure, though it could be.

There's a very nice Just a Little Something to Wash My Drink Down With at this little beer joint: German sausage and potato salad on a piece of butcher paper. No muss, no fuss.

KNEBEL'S TAVERN (102 Pecan)

    What You Feel Like When You Get There: 4

    Yuppity Doo Da: 5

Oh Say Can You See? 4

Crapola: 4

Holding Forth: 4

What You Feel Like After Three Drinks: 4

Just a Little Something to Wash My Drink Down With: 5

Old Fart Factor: 5

What You Feel Like When You Leave: 4

You Go Figure: 4

Nowhere Coefficient: 4.3

Texas is a state defined in great part by its highways and so you have a whole genre of Freeway Bar Bar, of which the best exemplar I've ever found is the Speedway Inn, several miles north of Austin on I35. It's just a shotgun shack, perennially peopled by domino-playing Old Farts and decorated with posters promoting things like four-wheel-drive mud runs.

Last time I was by, the Holding Forth concerned lung cancer, and when you hear that being tossed around, you're generally in a Bar Bar.

THE SPEEDWAY INN (I35, Jarrell)

What You Feel Like When You Get There: 4

Yuppity Doo Da: 5

Oh Say Can You See? 4

Crapola: 5

Holding Forth: 4

What You Feel Like After Three Drinks: 4

Just a Little Something to Wash My Drink Down With: 5

Old Fart Factor: 5

What You Feel Like When You Leave: 4

You Go Figure: 3

Nowhere Coefficient: 4.3

For such a quaint old place, San Antonio is surprisingly bereft of Bar Bars, but two joints should be noted, if only because they are two of the best *looking* Bar Bars I've seen anywhere.

Smack in the middle of the business district sits the Esquire Steakhouse, and if you can find a more legitimate saloon, I'll be good for the drinks. It's this impossibly long stand-up-only job, cluttered with terrific Hispanic Old Farts knocking back beer and tequila, and like a cathedral, even when full it is eerily quiet.

THE ESQUIRE STEAK HOUSE (153 E. Commerce)

What You Feel Like When You Get There: 4

Yuppity Doo Da: 4

Oh Say Can You See? 5

Crapola: 4

Holding Forth: 4

What You Feel Like After Three Drinks: 4

Just a Little Something to Wash My Drink Down With: 5

Old Fart Factor: 5

What You Feel Like When You Leave: 4

You Go Figure: 3

Nowhere Coefficient: 4.2

Little Hipps is ostensibly just a cruddy little beer bar, but it is worthy of a Transcontinental Award when it comes to crapola.

Ceiling: beach balls in fishnet. Walls: those wonderful old four-color displays of food. Floor: peanut shells and cigarette butts. Oh yeah, there's also the live Amazon turtle, in case you're interested.

LITTLE HIPPS (1423 McCullough)

What You Feel Like When You Get There: 3

Yuppity Doo Da: 4

Oh Say Can You See? 4

Crapola: 5

Holding Forth: 3

What You Feel Like After Three Drinks: 3

Just a Little Something to Wash My Drink Down With: 4

Old Fart Factor: 3

What You Feel Like When You Leave: 3

You Go Figure: 5 (Turtle.)

Nowhere Coefficient: 3.7

Austin's a university town, which makes it a little light on the Bar Bar side. But I can't resist mentioning what really was my very first Bar Bar: the Scholtz Beer Garten. Ordinarily, *Atkinson's Seventy-fifth Rule of the Bar Bar* states that liquor was not intended to be consumed out of doors, but I'll make an exception for this rowdy backyard of a Bar Bar, which also serves estimable Just a Little Something to Wash My Drink Down Withs of the German variety. Of special note here are the perennial battles over whether to eighty-six this joint. But last I heard, someone had bought it and was going to spruce it up and reopen. Anytime people are trying to shut a joint down and it just won't go away, you're probably talking about a Bar Bar.

SCHOLTZ BEER GARTEN (1607 San Jacinto)

What You Feel Like When You Get There: 3

Yuppity Doo Da: 2

Oh Say Can You See? 4

Crapola: 3

Holding Forth: 3

What You Feel Like After Three Drinks: 4

Just a Little Something to Wash My Drink Down With: 4

Old Fart Factor: 3

What You Feel Like When You Leave: 4

You Go Figure: 3

Nowhere Coefficient: 3.3

As well, I gotta mention the Cedar Door because these regulars recently one-upped Fox's in Miami by not merely rebuilding their Bar Bar faithfully but by having the whole damned thing moved to another venue when some developer named Billy Bob decided he wanted to build a big glass high-rise on its original site. That's some serious religion there, and you'd also be hard pressed to find a darker bar anywhere.

THE CEDAR DOOR (20 E. 1st St.)

What You Feel Like When You Get There: 4

Yuppity Doo Da: 4

Oh Say Can You See? 5

Crapola: 3

Holding Forth: 4

What You Feel Like After Three Drinks: $

Just a Little Something to Wash My Drink Down With: 5

Old Fart Factor: 4

What You Feel Like When You Leave: 4

You Go Figure: 4

Nowhere Coefficient: 4.1

For political talk of the Texas genre—meaning, generally speaking, sexist and brutish—a nice stopoff is Nick's, which replaced the legendary Quorum recently as *the* spot for Austin pols. It's a tad on the new side, but sixty-eight megatons of cigar smoke a day will take care of that soon enough, and under the tutelage of owner Nick Krajl (former proprietor of the aforementioned Quorum) this new joint's going to be just fine.

NICK'S (300 W. 15th St.)

What You Feel Like When You Get There: 4

Yuppity Doo Da: 3

Oh Say Can You See? 4

Crapola: 3

Holding Forth: 5

What You Feel Like After Three Drinks: 5

Just a Little Something to Wash My Drink Down With: 3

Old Fart Factor: 5

What You Feel Like When You Leave: 5

You Go Figure: 4

Nowhere Coefficient: 4.1

Actually, my favorite bars in Texas—outside of the beloved Joe Miller's, which we'll be getting to in due course—are way out west

Ask Dr. Bar Bar

Dear Dr. Bar Bar:
   In Semi-Tough, *Dan Jenkins listed his ten stages of drunkenness. These okay by you? Anything to add?*
HOPE YOU WON'T GIVE THIS A PUERILE, SMART-ASS ANSWER LIKE THE REST OF THEM

Dear HOPE YOU WON'T GIVE THIS A SMART-ASS ANSWER LIKE THE REST OF THEM*:*
   Guess what? You're in luck. I'm not feeling in the least bit puerile, and thinking on it, I do have a bit to add to Mr. Jenkins' almost seminal work on the subject. Dan's scheme was just fine, particularly those last two stages: invisible and bulletproof. But I don't think it went quite far enough. Beyond bulletproof you have, as earlier noted, transmogrified. *Then you have:*

Autistic drunk
Sociopathic drunk
Transcontinental drunk
Intergalactic drunk
Took Back Shit I Didn't Steal drunk
Polio drunk
Meltdown

in places like El Paso and Midland. There's not a better border bar to be found than the Kentucky Club in Juarez, just across the Rio Grande from El Paso. Yes, class, that name is a Go Figure, and if you don't feel uncomfortable knocking a few back with a bunch of guys in fairly scary-looking uniforms, this musty little place will do just fine.

THE KENTUCKY CLUB (Avenida Juarez, 629 Norte)

What You Feel Like When You Get There: 4

Yuppity Doo Da: 5

Oh Say Can You See? 4

Crapola: 4

Holding Forth: 4

What You Feel Like After Three Drinks: 4

Just a Little Something to Wash My Drink Down With: 4

Old Fart Factor: 5

What You Feel Like When You Leave: 4

You Go Figure: 5

Nowhere Coefficient: 4.3

Ah, but is there life after $13-a-barrel oil? Yeah, and you can even find it in Midland, right there at the bar at the 007 Lounge, which is just about the best bar name this side of Big Jim's Nowhere Tap Room. Tell me about Big E: This little bar is about the only thing that hasn't gone belly-up in the oil patch, which pretty much tells you that at least these people still have their priorities straight.

Nice crapola here, including this combination of wall signs on the back bar: THIS IS A REPUTABLE ESTABLISHMENT. TRY TO ACT LIKE IT. And then next to it: FUCK COMMUNISM. Go figure, and while you're at it, explain that big scallop shell type thing that serves as a phone stand.

I have never failed to find a lusty group of regulars at the bewitching hour of 3 P.M., and if all Texans took these guys' attitude—which is, fuck it—I think we might survive the oil bust a lot better. Put it this way: One time I was by, fellow next to me was so far into orbit he at one point just kind of reached over and kissed me on top of the head and said, "You're a good sumbitch, you know that?"

I'll say this too: The bartender here knows how to get you there. After a recent visit, I lurched back up the road to my hotel and on the way encountered a panhandler, which has become a pretty common occurrence in these parts lately. Wanna know why they call booze an attitude adjuster? I'm not sure, but here's a thought: Instead of stiffing the guy or just dropping a little change on him, I reached in my pocket and peeled off a $20. Tell you what: Scared the shit out of the guy too. Just kind of peered up at me like, "Je*sus.* If this fucker's crazy enough to give me twenty bucks, next thing he might just shoot me."

THE 007 LOUNGE (110 N. Big Spring)

What You Feel Like When You Get There: 5

Yuppity Doo Da: 5

Oh Say Can You See? 5

Crapola: 5

Holding Forth: 5

What You Feel Like After Three Drinks: 5

Fun Facts

Bourbon is no longer produced in Bourbon County, Kentucky.

Old Fart Factor: 5

Just a Little Something to Wash My Drink Down With: 5

What You Feel Like When You Leave: 5

You Go Figure: 5

Nowhere Coefficient: 5

The Den at the Stoneleigh Hotel has been a stalwart Bar Bar for a couple of decades now. Unfortunately it recently underwent some fairly serious Yuppity Doo Da type remodeling, meaning the stained carpeting is gone and so is that wonderful old peeling red-flocked wallpaper.

But you can't get a good Bar Bar down, and after a couple of weeks of grousing, the same old suspects settled in. The key was that management kept the considerable Oh Say Can You See? factor intact, so you don't really have to pay attention to whatever it is they did to spruce the joint up.

A nice feature of the Den, as with all hotel lounges, is the presence of the hotel itself. Not only does this provide some occasionally entertaining Nut o' the Day trade, but if you get a bit crapped out, you can always just get a single, sleep it off, and belly up all over again without having to explain a damn thing to the wife.

Indeed, my old friend John, who has since taken an extended leave on the wagon, had pretty much incorporated the Hotel Nap into his daily drinking regimen. Well, he had until that evening me and a couple other fellows decided he'd had enough sleep already, and besides, we needed a sixth for liar's poker, and so we bamboozled a key to his room out of the clerk, filled the men's room trash can with ice, and just went up and dumped it on his head. It's pretty entertaining to watch people wake up anyway, but when you get that parasympathetic nervous system kicking into gear all at once, kind of like with a circuit-breaker, it's a real scene.

THE DEN (2927 Maple)

What You Feel Like When You Get There: 5

Yuppity Doo Da: 5

Oh Say Can You See? 5

Crapola: 4

Holding Forth: 5

What You Feel Like After Three Drinks: 5

Just a Little Something to Wash My Drink Down With: 5

Old Fart Factor: 5

What You Feel Like When You Leave: 5

You Go Figure: 4

Nowhere Coefficient: 4.8

Well, with deepest apologies to some of the best drinking buddies a guy ever had, let me tell you about Hamby's in downtown Dallas, because it's about the most unlikely Bar Bar you're ever going to run across.

Actually, the etiology here is fairly instructive. For a good number of years, a loosely knit group of us used to hang out at the Bullington Point, which is just across the street. But it fell to new management and that management happened to be Iranian and so one thing led to another and soon enough, the joint's primary draw, bartender Steve Harris, left because of what he later termed "irreconcilable cultural differences."

"Yeah," said Steve, "like when we got to deep-fried goat kabob on the menu, I thought maybe it was time to go."

Being a certified downtownophile, Steve didn't want to leave the inner city, and neither did any of us. Unfortunately the best opportunity available was at a little hamburger joint across the street, place called Hamby's, which, while enjoying a good reputation as a fast-food hamburger restaurant, looked and felt about as much like a Bar Bar as the average Long John Silver's does.

Everything was wrong: The Just a Little Something to Wash My Drink Down With was served cafeteria style, which is a cut worse than off a blackboard; the Oh Say Can You See? was double the acceptable Atkinson Candlepower Scale; there were hanging plants; and what was supposed to be the "bar" was little more than a twelve-seat bullpen, presided over by a phosphorescent Tiffany-type light. Phewy Bob. As I told Steve, "Nothing personal, but I'd just as soon knock a few down back at the Trailways bus station."

Steve took all this stoically and suffered through a week or so of $5 tip days until the strangest—or maybe not so strange—thing happened: One by one, the group of a dozen or so who'd always drunk with him began to straggle back. We soon realized that, if anything, our hostile new environs made us closer knit, that much more rigid about the Theology. Besides, a running joke that involves drinking in a place that looks anything like a Bar Bar can be pretty entertaining daily stuff, and as earlier noted, the new location did drastically improve the Nut o' the Day traffic.

Inside of a month, we were, if anything, more ferocious regulars there than we had been at the other joint. Goes to show you *Atkinson's Seventy-sixth Rule of the Bar Bar:* You can take away the cathedral, but you can't take away the Church.

HAMBY'S (Akard at Pacific)

> **What You Feel Like When You Get There:** 1

> **Yuppity Doo Da:** 2

> **Oh Say Can You See?** 3

> **Crapola:** 2

> **Holding Forth:** 5

> **What You Feel Like After Three Drinks:** 5

> **Just a Little Something to Wash My Drink Down With:** 2

> **Old Fart Factor:** 5

> **What You Feel Like When You Leave:** 5

> **You Go Figure:** 5 (*This,* a Bar Bar?)

Nowhere Coefficient: 5 (The intangibles make up the difference, and since this is not only my book but my Bar Bar we're talking about, if you don't like the math, sorry.)

If you want to upscale considerably—even as the economy here is downscaling—there is one bar and one bar only: the elegant-to-a-fault bar at the Mansion Hotel, where what's left of Dallas's rich and wish-they-were-more-famous still gather to Hold Forth about whatever rich people talk about when only other rich people are around.

The demographics can be oppressive, but the bar is a magnificent physical specimen and the bartender is the real thing. The basics of the Church have been observed, and that's a lot more than you can say for most things that are predominated by rich people.

THE BAR AT THE MANSION (2821 Turtle Creek Blvd.)

What You Feel Like When You Get There: 3

Yuppity Doo Da: 3

Oh Say Can You See? 5

Crapola: 1

Holding Forth: 4 (Depends on your feelings about oil futures.)

What You Feel Like After Three Drinks: 3

Just a Little Something to Wash My Drink Down With: 2

Old Fart Factor: 3

What You Feel Like When You Leave: 4

You Go Figure: 2

Nowhere Coefficient: 3.0 (But hey, that ain't bad at all for a hotel bar, especially at a hotel where Larry Hagman stays all the time.)

If you want to downscale, and you're into Old Farts, there's also just one place and one place only: Stan's Blue Note, where you can still hear the clatter of dominoes, a rousing chorus of emphysematic coughing, and occasionally, Holding Forth of this genre: "Yeah, my back's so bad these days I even had to give up fucking."

STAN'S BLUE NOTE (2908 Greenville)

What You Feel Like When You Get There: 5

Yuppity Doo Da: 5

Oh Say Can You See? 4

Crapola: 5

Holding Forth: 4

What You Feel Like After Three Drinks: 5

Just a Little Something to Wash My Drink Down With: 4

Old Fart Factor: 5

What You Feel Like When You Leave: 5

You Go Figure: 4

Nowhere Coefficient: 4.6

And yes, even Dallas, the self-professed Buckle on the Sunbelt, has a tried and true sports bar, place called the Point After, which has ruined as many marriages as it has livers. It's just one big room, so dark you always feel like taking a shower afterward, and serves

---

Fun Facts

A popular gin in eighteenth-century America was something called Strip and Go Naked.

---

a meltdown-level highball. This joint's a Bar Bar in a lot of ways, but this ought to give you the best idea: It's where we all gathered to wake and raise one last drink to Joe Miller the day we buried him.

THE POINT AFTER (Greenville at Lovers Lane)

> **What You Feel Like When You Get There:** 5
>
> **Yuppity Doo Da:** 5
>
> **Oh Say Can You See?** 5
>
> **Crapola:** 4
>
> **Holding Forth:** 5
>
> **What You Feel Like After Three Drinks:** 5
>
> **Just a Little Something to Wash My Drink Down With:** 4
>
> **Old Fart Factor:** 5
>
> **What You Feel Like When You Leave:** 5
>
> **You Go Figure:** 5 (It's in a strip shopping center, near a male strip joint.)
>
> **Nowhere Coefficient:** 4.8

Epilogue

I was sober the day they told me Joe had the Large C, like terminal Large C. I hadn't planned it that way, but it was just as well. Heck, you can always get drunk, but when it comes to stuff like the Large C and dear friends, probably just as well that you take it on straight. Perspective on life, and all that.

None of us was particularly surprised, and to tell you the truth, at a time we worried as much about the Bar Bar's plight as Joe's. I'd had bars die on me—as in the wrecking ball—but I soon learned you can always build another church. But how do you replace a priest?

I *was* in the bag the day Joe passed on, or I proceeded to get that way extremely fast after learning of his death. That too seemed appropriate: Everybody says hey, when I pay the big tab, don't mourn, just lift one in my memory. But Joe really meant it. So we all gathered at Miller's, knocked a few back and kind of stared at one another, wordlessly asking "What the hell do we do now?"

Louis Canelakes, Joe's protégé behind the bar, his eerily identical incarnation, finally answered the question for me one night, long after we'd buried Joe and sent money and flowers and exhausted the sentimental value of the good old days. "You show up,

279

you have a drink, you pay your tab," he said. "This is a church. It's bigger than one guy. The only way it goes away is if you don't show up."

In the ensuing months, it was Louis' presence behind the bar that was most reassuring to those of us who had trouble understanding how a place like Joe Miller's could go on without the presence of a guy named Joe Miller. But a funny thing happened: Louis discovered that ultimately he couldn't be Joe Miller, he could only be Louis. "It's like, you know, I was second fiddle, straight man, and that's the way it worked. "I could be second fiddle to Joe, but not anyone else." So in time, Louis was off to start a place called Louis', and while none of us could particularly blame him, we really began to wonder about our Bar Bar.

Under the management of Joe's wife, Linda, there were changes, and most of them were minor. Some approved, some bitched. Some people hung out less; some who used to hang out less hung out more. A few stopped going.

But I still felt myself drawn to the place, to the people, and on December 17, the anniversary of Joe's funeral, I dropped by to knock a few back and to try to at last answer the question: Had the Church survived the death of the priest? Two drinks deep I realized, well yes, it sure had: I was still being lied to by assorted drinking buddies, being told the same old tired Polack jokes. Regulars were still buying each other rounds in that odd ritual of the Bar Bar. The bar was stocked with the usual suspects, and at a time it wasn't very hard to imagine that Joe was still there.

JOE MILLER'S (3531 McKinney)

What You Feel Like When You Get There: 5

Yuppity Doo Da: 5

Oh Say Can You See? 5

Crapola: 5

Holding Forth: 5

What You Feel Like After Three Drinks: 5

Just a Little Something to Wash My Drink Down With: 5

Old Fart Factor: 5

What You Feel Like When You Leave: 5

You Go Figure: 5 (Yep, the aquarium is still there.)

Nowhere Coefficient: 5

Then several months later, I dropped on by the opening of Louis' new joint and I realized something else. This little lower East Dallas haunt was designed and accessorized in perfect Bar Bar style: Hell, Louis was even upset that the blinds for his windows hadn't yet arrived and that the resulting presence of light might pollute the drinks and interfere with his avowed purpose to "create a Chicago ambiance right here in Dallas." Joe's death hadn't killed off a Bar Bar; it had actually spawned a new one. We Bar Barflies weren't suddenly without a Bar Bar; we suddenly had *two,* and any ecologist will tell you that's got to bode well for a species. *Atkinson's Seventy-seventh Rule of the Bar Bar:* There will always be Bar Bars, because there will always be Bar Barflies.

LOUIE'S (1839 Henderson)

What You Feel Like When You Get There: 5

Yuppity Doo Da: 5

Oh Say Can You See? 5

Crapola: 5

Holding Forth: 5

What You Feel Like After Three Drinks: 5

Just a Little Something to Wash My Drink Down With: 5

Old Fart Factor: 5

What You Feel Like When You Leave: 5

You Go Figure: 5

Nowhere Coefficient: 5

Postscript

A downside to living in a city committed to perpetual growth like Dallas is that every ten years or so, you have to reacquire your bearings. Like, landmarks you've trusted the presence of for years can be just up and bulldozed and gone one day, leaving you feeling like a visitor to your own city.

But among the very few edifices that still stand in downtown Dallas is the shabby little building that houses my original haunt, The Green Glass Tavern—the original Bar Bar. It stands virtually alone now, surrounded by parking lots and a whole bunch of reflecting glass highrises.

I dropped by recently and had a couple of pops for old times sake. The clientele has changed a bit: The newspaper pressmen who used to constitute the bar's foundation aren't nearly as much in evidence—maybe because there aren't nearly as many newspaper pressmen as there used to be. How 'bout that? The Bar Bar has outlived cold type.

These days, the Bar Bar is peopled by a strange collection of urban underculture types, but its essence remains the same: It's just as dark and cozy and absolutely, gloriously Nowhere as it always was. I sipped my beer and engaged in a little smalltalk with an Old Fart regular.

"Boy, it's damned amazing this bar survived all the construction and stuff down here. How 'bout ten years from now? You figure you'll still be here?"

"Yeah," he said. "Otherwise, where would we all be?"

Index of Bars